Little America

Little America

Australia, the 51st State

ERIK PAUL

PLUTO PRESS

First published 2006 by Pluto Press
345 Archway Road, London N6 5AA
and 839 Greene Street, Ann Arbor, MI 48106

www.plutobooks.com

British Library Cataloguing in Publication Data
A catalogue record for this book is available from the British Library

ISBN-10   0 7453 2540 8 hardback
ISBN-13   978 0 7453 2540 8 hardback
ISBN-10   0 7453 2539 4 paperback
ISBN-13   978 0 7453 2539 2 paperback

Library of Congress Cataloging in Publication Data applied for

10   9   8   7   6   5   4   3   2   1

Designed and produced for Pluto Press by
Chase Publishing Services Ltd, Fortescue, Sidmouth, EX10 9QG, England
Typeset from disk by Stanford DTP Services, Northampton, England

To Keiko

Contents

List of Tables

1
The New Imperialism

Current theories of international morality have been designed to perpetuate the supremacy of English-speaking peoples.

E. H. Carr

AUSTRALIA IN THE EMPIRE

Australia and the US have much in common. Both were born out of British invasions of the new world and the brutal dispossession of indigenous land and culture to form new nation-states. While their histories diverged for many generations, there has been a marked convergence in recent decades with Australia increasingly an adjunct to US foreign policy and more like the US in shaping its politics and civil society. Binding the similarities in economic and political culture is a shared messianic crusade to save the world from chaos and evil and a vision of a new world order promising prosperity and peace.

The Americanisation of Australia is an important phenomenon which is changing what Australia is about in ways the country relates to the world and transforms its economy and society. Why is Australia so close and so much like the United States? At the core of this issue is Australia's modern imperial history and the construction of a colonial mentality of dependency on protection from a powerful patron. Australia's nation-state is a modern creation of the British Empire and the expansion of Anglo-Saxon capitalism. From the beginning, Australia's nation-building has been sustained by a series of confrontations with Asia moving from colonial consolidation and Cold War to a new world of globalisation and war against terrorism.*

Australia's modern history as a nation-state has been shaped and constructed by its relations with non-Europeans. Captain Cook's landing on the shore of what is today Sydney marked the beginning of

---

* The geography of the Asia-Pacific includes all the countries listed under Asia in the Australian Bureau of Statistics, appendix 2 of the Balance of Payment Regional Series, 5338.0, 2001–02. Countries which are part of Asia can also be found under regional headings of West Asia, South Asia, Central Asia, Northeast Asia and Southeast Asia, in addition to a number of Pacific Island states important to Australia and discussed in this book.

more than 200 years of 'aggression, injustice and inhumanity towards the Aboriginal people of this land' (Coombs 1980). The dispossession of their land and culture began with the raising of the British flag and by 1830 the entire continent and the islands of Norfolk and Tasmania had been taken in the name of Britain. Aboriginal armed resistance in the interior of the continent continued into the 1920s. Torres Strait islands were taken by Queensland's colonial government in the 1870s, and in 1883 Queensland annexed what is today the southern half of New Guinea.

Invasion raised the question of proprietorship and the legitimacy of taking a continent from its inhabitants, which in turn engendered fear that people in the region, particularly Chinese, would take the land from British settlers. Asian migrants came in large numbers and their success in working the land and business enterprise brought them into conflict with Anglo-Irish settlers. In the 1880s non-Europeans were in a majority in tropical Australia. 'Asians made up half of the settler population in the Northern Territory and Western Australia and more than half in Darwin, Broome and Thursday Island' (Reynolds 2003:xv). Competition for resources formed the basis for the intense level of racism against Asians during that period. Architects of the white-Australia policy such as Isaac Isaacs manipulated the crowds with his call to free Australia 'for all time from the contaminating and degrading influence of inferior races' (Reynolds 2003:160).

Fear of invasion by Asia's 'yellow hordes' was legislated for in the 1896 New South Wales Coloured Races Restriction Bill, the first of many colonial laws, which barred entry to 'all persons belonging to any coloured race inhabiting the Continent of Asia, or the Continent of Africa, of any island adjacent thereto, or any island in the Pacific or Indian oceans' (Yarwood 1964:11). Alfred Deakin, who played a leading role in the creation of the continent's federation, tabled the commonwealth's first piece of legislation, the Immigration Restriction Bill of 1901, which he said was to uphold the purity of the 'British race' and to 'exclude alien Asiatics as well as the people of Japan' (Meaney 1999:18).

The act of federation led to new waves of dispossession and deportation. Asian settlers were encouraged to leave and thousands of islanders were deported after 1904 under the Pacific Island Labourers Act. Racism had become the foundation of Australia's identity. An anti-Asian mentality justified the taking of the continent and aggression against its Aboriginal population. Race supremacy legitimised the conquest. It brought to a quick end the existence of a vibrant multicultural society in northern Australia. As a result tropical Australia 'stagnated. It became a backwater – increasingly mono-cultural, socially conservative, provincial – which is the way it was seen by outsiders during much of the twentieth century. It also became more racist than it had ever been in the past' Reynolds 2003:187).

Australia's important military role in the British Empire was to expand and protect its territorial and commercial integrity. Australia sent troops to New Zealand to fight the Maoris' attempt to keep the British out of their islands. Then came military expeditions to the Sudan and South Africa, and to China to put down a native rebellion against European presence and the British policy of creating an addiction to opium amongst the Chinese. Later during the West's major civil war (World War I), Australia intervened in Turkey and Egypt, and added German northeast New Guinea to its growing empire. These were all preliminaries to the coming Pacific battles and mass killing of World War II.

Japan was modernising and rising to the challenge of Western imperialism. New ideologies about liberty and class struggle in the region were contesting Western presence and exploitation. Japan's territorial aggrandisement and commercial and military expansion challenged Anglo-American hegemony in a series of power plays among imperial players. The treaties between Japan and Britain in 1902 and Japan and the US in the Taft-Katsura agreement of 1905, were attempts to negotiate an understanding about the division of spoils in the Asia-Pacific region. Japan could keep Korea and Taiwan as long as it did not interfere with Anglo-American colonies and regional commercial interests. Imperial geopolitics put the contestants on a collision course and Australia was irremediably drawn into preparations for war. Prime Minister Alfred Deakin invited the US Great White Fleet to visit Sydney in 1908 as a sign that 'England, America and Australia will be united to withstand yellow aggression' (Macintyre 1999:142).

During WWI Prime Minister Billy Hughes warned Australians that should Germany win the war 'this lonely outpost of the white man's civilisation will be deprived of its scanty garrison and left open to cheap Asiatics, reduced to the social and economic level of Paraguay or some other barbarian country' (Victoria 2002:3). After the war, Hughes voted against Japan's motion for 'racial' equality in the League of Nations and made sure that trade in the newly acquired German New Guinea would be monopolised by Australia and free of Japanese and Chinese traders or migrants. In the 1930s Australia's restrictions on non-British imports brought retaliation against its wool export to Japan. Australia's discrimination against Japanese migrants became a source of anger and anti-Western sentiment in Japan which was manipulated to advantage by nationalistic and militaristic domestic forces (Walker 1999; Meaney 1996).

Preparation for war against Japan unfolded in the 1930s with the inclusion of Australia in the defence of the British Empire. Britain withdrew from the Anglo-Japanese alliance and reconfigured Singapore island as a naval fortress, partly to protect Australia's north, and the US built up its forces in colonial Philippines against Japan's southern expansion. Imperial confrontation gained momentum with the rise of nationalism and demands for independence in the region. Communism was a growing political force in many parts of Asia and a threat to colonialism and to Japan's militarist culture. In Australia, fascism was mobilising larger sections of society. Japan went to war on the slogan of 'Asia for the Asians' while the West called for an end of fascism in the name of liberty and freedom. With the fall of British Singapore and the surrender of some 16,000 troops, Australia was at war with Japan. The arrival in 1942 of General MacArthur in Darwin, to take command of all Australian forces, marked the beginning of Australia's role as an adjunct to the US empire.

Australia's confrontation with Asia after WWII was an integral part of the Anglo-American alliance against communism. The Cold War was another hegemonic war between the US and Russia which expanded throughout the world largely because it became entangled with anti-imperialist movements and wars in many territories occupied by Western forces. In Asia the rise of nationalism and demands for independence destabilised the entire region, and Mao Tse Tung's Communist Party victory in 1949 raised anew Australia's fears of an Asiatic invasion. Communism was the new enemy, another disease which, like the plague, had to be fought off throughout the Asia-Pacific region to save white Australia from destruction. Australia's new axis of evil went from China to the whole of Southeast Asia.

From the late 1940s, Australian military units intervened in Malaya, Singapore, Borneo, Korea, New Guinea and in Malta to defend British power in Egypt. In 1954 Australia joined the US, NZ, Britain and France in the Southeast East Asian Treaty Organisation (SEATO) to secure Western colonial interest in Indochina, Thailand and Pakistan. Other treaties signed in the 1950s such as ANZUS (Australia–New Zealand–US) further incorporated Australia in the Anglo-American alliance to regain control of the Asia-Pacific region. A watershed was the Vietnam war. Australia started by sending advisers in 1962 followed by a full-scale military intervention in 1965. At the time, Australia was collaborating with the US push for a regime change in Indonesia. Covert operations by intelligence agencies enabled General Suharto's military takeover and contributed to the massacre of large numbers of Sukarno supporters and other outcasts. Under Suharto's rule, close to 100,000 political prisoners were detained without trial for many years in Indonesia's gulag.

After the fall of the Berlin wall in 1989 and the disintegration of the Soviet Union Australia became a sheriff of the US new world order. Australia was the first country to join the alliance in the 1991 Gulf war against Iraq, and this was followed by sending troops to Cambodia to effect a regime change in 1993. In the late 1990s Australia became a major enforcer in controlling the 'arc of instability' to its north with operations in Papua New Guinea's (PNG) war against Bougainville, and, after Suharto's resignation in 1998, in the 'liberation' of East Timor from Indonesia. In 2002 Australia sent troops to Afghanistan and the following year took part in the US invasion of Iraq. In 2003 Australia's military went to the Solomon Islands to take over the administration of the country, and the following year began operations to resume control of the country's budget, courts and police force.

With the election of John Howard's conservative coalition in 1996, Australia became an integral part of the US–UK global geostrategy, and more assertive in its relations with the world and its region. A major regional task for Australia has been to advance the causes of market fundamentalism particularly in island states where Australia has a dominant economic position. Elsewhere in Asia, Australia has been engaged in strategies to weaken economic regionalism and promote an Anglo-American model of capitalism, particularly in the context of the Association of Southeast Asian States (ASEAN). One ploy has been the formation of the Asia-Pacific Economic Cooperation (APEC) to counteract the economic power of the European Union and weaken proposals for an East Asian economic bloc dominated by China which would exclude Australia and the US.

Australia's policy to secure the 'arc of instability' – the crescent of islands to the north of the continent – has been a fixture of foreign policy since federation. In 1943, H.V. Evatt, the minister for external affairs, declared that Australia's security 'depended upon it controlling an arc of territory from northern Australia stretching some 2,400 km to encompass Singapore, the Netherlands East Indies, New Guinea and the adjacent islands' (Day 2001:230). In more recent times, control of Australia's problematic north led to the 'liberation' of East Timor in 1999, followed by military intervention in PNG and the Solomon Islands. Moreover, Australia put neighbouring countries on notice about the right to preemptive strikes to safeguard its national interests when in December 2002 John Howard stated on public and commercial TV that he was prepared to order attacks against terrorists in Asia (Barker 2002). Of particular concern to Australia is the growing strength of Islam in Indonesian politics and attacks against Christian minorities in the region.

Beyond the Pacific islands states and Indonesia, Australia is shaping the formation of an East Asian version of Europe's North Atlantic Treaty Organisation (NATO) with Japan, South Korea and Singapore. The construction of a regional security architecture aims to maintain political regimes friendly to the Anglo-American alliance and destroy movements which might constitute a threat to its economic and political security. However, the main game is to manage a regional balance of power and encourage unfriendly relations between China and Japan, and to confront China's emergence as a potential challenger to US hegemony. Australia has an important role to play in this global power competition with the militarisation of the continent functioning as part of the US global nuclear and missile defence strategy (Bush 2002).

Australia's symbiotic relationship with the US is part of the global expansion of capitalism and the transformation of society by the unremitting pressure of a market economy. Capitalism has been an important factor in the history of modern Australia – from the early years of primitive accumulation through dispossession of indigenous land and resources to the eager adoption of an American model of capitalism in more recent years. Australia needs a substantial share of Asia's growing wealth to sustain its living standards and liberal democracy but the security of this enterprise is based on US hegemony to safeguard Australia's markets and capital investments in the region. US power is the country's insurance policy for the security of some 20 million people on one of the richest and largest pieces of real estate in the world.

The expansion of capitalist activities in Australia has led to a shift of power from citizens to corporations and a neo-right political elite. In recent years there has been a marked decline in Australia's democracy and a rise in the suppressive powers of the state. To a large extent the process has been dictated by the adoption of a US model of economic and political culture. This is clearly exemplified with the dominance in the country's universities of US business and management values and practices, and the political weight of neoconservative think-tanks in Australia's political life. Another major factor in the Americanisation of Australia are the restrictions imposed over the years on the rights of employees. Government policy to control labour practices and relations has disempowered the union movement. Legislation passed in late 2005 will further control labour relations and shift more workers to the minimum wage. The University of Sydney's Professor Russell Lansbury, a leading academic in industrial relations, commented that the new legislation will further undermine employees' right to work and will promote greater social inequity (Lansbury 2005).

Civil society is changing dramatically because of the widespread privatisation of public assets and the expansion of market forces in education, government services and infrastructure. At the same time the role and power of corporations has altered the nature of Australia's politics and civil society. There are many aspects to this change seen in the pressure of advertising and consumerism encroaching in everyday life and that of corporate excision of urban space. Corporations are gaining control of shopping areas, gated communities, parklands, schools, museums and libraries, roads and airports, as well as large tracts of rural Australia. Australia's market democracy is fuelled by postmodern greed and the accumulation of more wealth. An obsession on making money, buying bigger cars and houses, and the production of waste has become a dominant character in social and economic life. The politics of economic growth and mass consumption has become national policy and advertised as the solution to rising problems of unemployment, poverty and environmental degradation. While rich Australians benefit from generous tax cuts there has been a marked decline in the quality of public education, transport and health.

There are substantial social costs to Australia's neoliberal regime such as a high rate of incarceration and white-collar crime and political corruption. Social pathologies are a dominant feature of economic rationalism and a high percentage of the population suffers from mental-health problems. Australia shares with other affluent overdeveloped societies the more complex social problems of mass gambling and drug addiction. Another outcome is the looming environmental crisis signalled by many disturbing phenomena such as the unhealthy state of the country's major river systems, the extent of salinity and land degradation, and the loss of biodiversity (Lowe 2005). Despite a scientific consensus that Australia's climate is warming up, the government has made no significant effort to reduce Australia's ranking as the highest greenhouse-gas emitter per capita among industrialised countries.

Australia and the United States have a sense of exceptionalism in their foreign policy and manifest destiny to shape the world order. Their elite share a view that their civilisation is under threat from dark forces in Asia and in the Islamic heartland, and are suspicious of continental Europe's commitment to democracy. Both countries are partners in an Anglo-American Christian mission to protect and advance what is good and moral for the world. Australia's political and economic elite enthusiastically support the US-led agenda to reform and internationalise national economies and incorporate nation-states into a 'free trade' global economy. Anglo-American capitalism's recipe for success is popularised in Australia by works such as Thomas Friedman's *The Lexus and the Olive Tree* which claims that prosperity comes from wearing the 'Golden Straitjacket'. But Friedman reminds us that the pathway to a free world for market capitalism needs a firm hand and the 'hidden hand of the market will never work without [the] hidden fist' of the US military (Friedman 1999:373).

NEW IMPERIALISM

Since the end of the Cold War the US new world order has failed to deliver on the American dream of prosperity and liberty for all of humanity. The new world order is turning out to be another form of imperialism based on the politics of mass deceit. World poverty and inequality are increasing and the institutions of global governance are largely means by which rich countries maintain their affluence and set up rules which deprive others of the opportunities to join their ranks. The International Monetary Fund (IMF), the World Bank (WB), and the World Trade Organization (WTO) have generated economic stagnation and crisis and increased the suffering of the poor. The US-designed system of global governance has proven incapable of meeting the needs of humanity in times of crisis and unwilling to prevent human disaster as in the case of the 1994 Rwanda genocide (Dallaire 2004). Instead, the US-led coalition has chosen to respond to the problems of poverty and exclusion by military means and preemptive strikes against those who rebel against an unjust world system.

Since the end of the Cold War the G7 neoliberal and free trade policies have caused widespread human suffering and environmental degradation among poorer countries. Joseph Stiglitz blames the IMF for increasing poverty and inequality in many parts of the world (Stiglitz 2002). US finance capitalism has been a key instrument to gain control and bribe governments. Debt and the addiction to money and promises of more loans have been used to cajole and further bribe governments to reform their economies (Perkins 2004; Pettifor 2003; US 2003). Jadgish Bhagwati has denounced the 'Wall Street-Treasury complex' for engineering major financial crises and setting back the agenda on human development and democratisation (Bhagwati 2004). Chalmers Johnson describes the IMF as 'an instrument of American power, one that allows the United States to collect money from its allies and to spend the amassed funds on various international economic operations that serve American national interests' (Johnson 1998:659). Andrew Bacevich and others argue that globalisation is above all a coherent strategy to expand the American imperium (Bacevich 2001; Gowan 1999; Smith 2004).

A world capitalist economy entrenches poverty and makes it impossible for developing regions and countries to catch up with the richer parts of the world. Trade rules implemented by the WTO advance the interest of corporations and rich countries. Cambridge economist Ha-Joon Chang focuses on the nature of exploitation in the new world order in his findings that rules introduced by the WTO and other institutions of global governance are not meant to help poorer countries but to preserve the interests of the G7. He accuses rich countries of 'kicking away the ladder' from underneath poorer countries and preventing the have-nots from becoming 'Americans' (Chang 2003a). Wallerstein's world-system analysis describes the neoliberal offensive as 'one gigantic attempt to slow down the increasing costs of production – primarily by lowering the cost of wages and taxation and secondarily by lowering the cost of inputs via technological advance' (2003a:226). John Gray claims that global capitalism is 'endangering liberal civilization' and that the global free market is an Anglo-American project which 'engenders new varieties of nationalism and fundamentalism … imposing massive instability on developing countries' (Gray 1999:210).

Susan George has attacked globalisation's construct as directly opposed to human rights because its goal has little to do with the construction of 'an ethical, rights-based society in which each person is guaranteed a decent and dignified material livelihood and opportunities for personal attainment, but is also guaranteed freedom of expression, of political association, or worship and the like' (George 2003:18) Arundhati Roy claims that 'violating human rights is an inherent and necessary part of the process of implementing a coercive and unjust political and economic structure on the world. Without the violation of human rights on an enormous scale, the neo-liberal project would remain in the dreamy realm of policy' (Roy 2004). George makes the point that globalisation 'has inexorably transferred wealth from the poor to the rich. It has increased inequalities both within and between nations. It has remunerated capital to the detriment of labour. It has created far more losers than winners' (George 2003:18).

The situation could be remedied if rich countries shifted to saner forms of consumption and downsized their expensive lifestyle. Recently the French health minister argued that France could cut 50 per cent of its health budget to deal with the global AIDS epidemic without affecting France's health standards. Philosopher Peter Singer told Americans that they spend too much on themselves and should give away income above the US$30,000 needed to cover necessities. He maintained that money spent above that was effectively killing children in poor countries and wrote that there is 'no escape from the conclusion that each one of us with wealth surplus to his or her essential needs should be giving most of it to help people suffering from poverty so dire as to be life threatening' (Romei 1999:6). Peter Singer's far reaching agenda calls for rich countries to lower their living standards. He argues that rich countries have a moral duty 'to bring about a drastic decrease in the standard of welfare of their own citizens in order to bring aid to the citizens of poorer countries' (Singer 1972).

Yet it is clear that the necessary transfer of resources and changes in global governance will not take place. Such shift in economic policy and capital allocation would threaten the viability of existing liberal democracies. Any government advancing a political agenda based on tax hikes and wealth reduction would soon lose power. A global policy of downsizing consumption for the rich and a transfer of resources to the poor would threaten the existing capitalist global economy and the sustainability of G7 pensions funds and hence be resolutely opposed by powerful economic and political global lobbies. Mel Gurtov makes the point that foreign affairs in liberal democracies is controlled by a small clique of realists who prefer 'to treat the symptoms of global disorder rather than search for the basic cures [because] they recognize and fear the revolutionary potential of deeper structural change. Aid programs, arms sales, food relief, and repression of unrest are more appealing as political tools than are programs that address fundamental inequities in landholding, political power, law, and income' (Gurtov 1991:19–20). Henry Kissinger argued that the US should never make human rights 'a vocal objective of our foreign policy [because it] involves great dangers: you run the risk of either showing your impotence or producing revolutions in friendly countries – or both'.

The fourth world war began with the Gulf war of 1991 and has since involved a large number of military interventions culminating with the invasion of Afghanistan and Iraq at the beginning of the twenty-first century by US forces. Since the end of the Cold War the US and its key allies – the European Union, Japan and Australia – have moved to secure the rest of the world by military means in an effort to promote the political stability necessary for the expansion of global capitalism to protect their economies and societies. Control of the economic and political development of the rest in the world is vital if they are to safeguard their hold on the global financial market and secure their vast investment funds. Protection from 'dangerous classes', 'terrorist groups', and 'rogue countries' is therefore critical for the viability of the new world order. Subcommandante Marcos, leader of the Zapatista movement, argues that 'neoliberalism is a new war for the conquest of territory ... the unification of the world into one single market' (Marcos 1997).

Climate change is likely to impose restrictions on consumption and bring an end to an era of market liberalism. Herman Daly and others have argued that the present growth agenda and economic liberalisation is not sustainable because we live at a time when economic growth has caused irreparable environmental damage (Arrow et al. 1995; Daly 1996; Watson 2005). They warn that 'we are consuming the earth's resources beyond its sustainable capacity of renewal, thus running down that capacity over time – that is, we are consuming natural capital while calling it income'; and Daly calls for rich countries to consume less and become more self-sufficient to avoid war (Daly 1996:61, 157). China and India cannot aspire to a US-type consumption level without 'consuming natural capital and thereby diminishing the capacity of the earth to support life and wealth in the future', in other words without 'destroying the natural capital of the earth to support life in the future' (Daly 1996:4, 5). Despite these and other warnings about rising sea levels the US Bush administration is 'rolling back environmental protection' at home and abroad. US journalist Bill Moyers laments his government's failure to protect the environment and writes that what is happening 'is not right and we are stealing their [our childrens'] future. Betraying their trust. Despoiling the world' (Moyers 2005:10).

During an earlier debate on limits to growth Robert Heilbroner suggested that 'the limit on industrial growth depends in the end on the tolerance of the ecosphere for the absorption of heat' (Heilbroner 1988b:50, 72). This issue is now at the forefront of the climatic-change debate with claims that global warming is a bigger threat than terrorism. Sir David King, the UK government chief adviser, suggests that there is a clear possibility that the ongoing melting of the ice caps would submerge cities such as New York and London (Brown 2005). A report by the former head of planning of the Royal Dutch/Shell group for the US security agency claims that 'major European cities will be sunk beneath rising seas as Britain is plunged into a "Siberian" climate by 2020' (Townsend and Harris 2004). The Institute for Environment and Human Security at the United Nations University in Bonn claims that rising sea levels, desertification and shrinking freshwater supplies will create up to 50 million environmental refugees by the end of the decade.

Climatic change and the demands of the developing mega-economies of China and India are likely to change the nature of the world order. John Gray writes that the US global free trade agenda is 'setting sovereign states against each other in geo-political struggles for dwindling natural resources. States become rivals to control resources that no institution has a responsibility in conserving' (Gray 1999:20). In the absence of reform, he suggests, 'the world economy will fragment as its imbalances become insupportable. Trade wars will make international cooperation more difficult. The world economy will fracture into blocs, each riven by struggles for regional hegemony' (Gray 1999:218). Moreover, US hegemony is likely to be challenged in the coming decades. Paul Kennedy makes the point in *The Rise and Fall of Great Powers* that the US will eventually make way for another hegemon because it cannot preserve its existing position, 'for it simply has not been given to any one society to remain *permanently* ahead of all the others' (Kennedy 1989:533). The US will make great efforts to maintain its role as the world's hegemon and pre-eminence in the world economy by focusing on lead industries, particularly information technology and biotechnology (Chase-Dunn and Reifer 2002). The danger is that the US will become more militaristic with more sophisticated weapons systems and predatory policies in relation to the global economy, and will demand compensation from its allies and dependencies for the cost of a protective military shield.

US imperialism has gone through different phases, as Victor Kiernan explains with the evolution of US imperialism from white settlement to world hegemony (Kiernan 2005). Neil Smith analyses the same phenomenon and shows how US policy was shaped by the need to expand and control global trade, and how the manufacture of global liberalism became the ideological vehicle to propel US economic expansion without direct political or military control of new markets (Smith 2004). The US imperium serves the interests of what John Galbraith once called the contented majority of those who vote for a system which delivers them great wealth. US affluence and mass consumption have come at the price of a juggernaut military-industrial mega-machine which has become largely autonomous and 'standing above and apart from democratic control' (Galbraith 1992:126). The power of the US military culture was clearly demonstrated during the Vietnam war when a US Marine Corps commandant warned that 'America has become a militaristic and aggressive nation ... it is this influential nucleus of aggressive, ambitious professional military leaders who are at the root of America's evolving militarism ... the military is indoctrinated to be secretive, devious, and misleading in its plans and operations ... our militaristic culture was born of the necessities of WWII, nurtured by the Korean war, and became an accepted aspect of American life during the years of Cold War' (Shoup 1969).

Thirty years later the US military machine invaded both Afghanistan and Iraq and planned more military actions in Asia. In the aftermath of the destruction of New York's World Trade Center, US democratic foundations are being eroded by legislation that further restrict citizens' human rights. Basic freedoms are gradually eroded by a powerful homeland security establishment which could in the near future ease the seizure of power by undemocratic forces. Norman Mailer has suggested that the 'combination of the corporation, the military and the complete investiture of the flag with mass spectator sports has set up a pre-fascist atmosphere in America already' (Mailer 2003). The new imperialism is built on the destruction of the republic, 'for an empire to be born the republic has first to die' says historian Tony Judt. West Point graduate Andrew Bacevich maintains that the

US is becoming a military society 'a country where armed power is the measure of national greatness and war or planning for war, is the exemplary (and only) common project' (Bacevich 2004; Judt 2005:16). US imperialism, Johnson argues, is moving into a new and dangerous phase in which the US ceases 'to bear any resemblance to the country once outlined in our Constitution' (Johnson 2004a:285). US imperial sorrows are mounting and Johnson laments the decline of democracy in the US and the loss of 'constitutional rights as the presidency fully eclipses Congress and is itself transformed from an executive branch of government into something more like a Pentagonized presidency' (Johnson 2004a:285).

Challenge to US hegemony is likely to emerge from East Asia and probably from China, and the US is responding with a major military commitment to militarise space and deter China from challenging its vision of a world 'safe for democracy'. President George Bush made it clear in 2002 that freedom

is the non-negotiable demand of human dignity. Throughout history, freedom has been threatened by war and terror; it has been challenged by the clashing wills of powerful states and the evil designs of tyrants; and it has been tested by widespread poverty and disease. Today, humanity holds in its hands the opportunity to further freedom's triumph over all these foes. The United States welcomes our responsibility to lead in this great mission. (Bush 2002)

THE LUCKY COUNTRY?

As US sheriff, Australia is committed to US plans for regime change in Iran and North Korea and the containment of China. Australia's continent is being militarised and integrated into the US global missile defense system and strategy to control space. The militarisation of northern Australia continues with the emplacement of large military capabilities to protect Australia's resources and borders and provide a US launching platform for likely military action in Asia. Darwin is becoming a military city as part of the Army Presence in the North (APIN) and the realignment of Australia's military establishment northward. Northern Australia is also the location for several major air bases, training areas for regional war games, weapons testing areas, and radar and intelligence installations. The construction of a rail link to Darwin is largely a military project to move military equipment and logistics from southern bases, such as tanks and armoured personnel carriers, to the northern territory. The line subsidised by the federal government was built and is operated by Halliburton, a major US military contractor.

As a close military and economic ally to the US, Australia has become a major actor in the war on terror and military intervention in many parts of the Asia-Pacific region. Australia is likely to find itself involved in more dangerous military actions in the coming years. Seymour Hersh claims that President Bush has 'an aggressive and ambitious agenda' against Iran and other countries (Hersh 2005). There were reports that Australia's special forces were already in Iran running covert operations with their British and US counterparts. Australia's military actions have already led to attacks against Australian interests and play in the hands of those engaged in the domestic politics of fear. The war on Iraq has highlighted the problem of resource scarcity and the view that the world is running out of cheap oil and water. With rising demands from China and elsewhere there is more concern over new geopolitical conflicts for energy resources focusing in West and Central Asia (Klare 2003).

Global free trade will intensify competition among nation-states and lead to trade wars and geopolitical conflict over scarce natural resources. Climatic change and sea-level rises in the Asia-Pacific could displace millions of people. Former World Bank president James Wolfensohn has warned Australia to prepare itself for the prospects of large numbers of people coming to the continent. He said 'rich countries such as Australia failed to understand the dangers to their own security of the explosion of the world's poor' (Eccleston 2004). China and India may one day put pressure on Australia to let millions of their refugees settle in Australia's empty north. This highly risky environment will further draw Australia into the US orbit because of the nation-state's sense of insecurity; its great wealth, high living standards and politics of greed will force it to make further concessions to the US.

The situation in Australia will be largely dictated by developments in East Asia and the probable formation of a regional economic bloc centred on China. This will affect the nature of Australia's trade relations as well as its commitments to democracy. At the same time Australia is likely to become more involved in East Asia's challenge to US hegemony, and China as well as India's demand for a greater role in world affairs. Australia's gamble in acting as US sheriff and the growing US military presence in Australia are going to be difficult issues to negotiate in view of Australia's growing dependence on the Asia-Pacific for economic growth and living standards. These and other demands will lead to the further growth of military expenditures and of the power of neo-right forces in domestic politics. Threats of environmental refugees seeking refuge in Australia are likely to lead to a resurgence of nationalism. Recent developments in Australia question the compatibility of Australia's civil and political liberties with the needs and purposes of an overdeveloped capitalist society.

This book argues that Australia should cut off the US umbilical cord and strike out on its own as an independent country. It should abandon the British crown as its ruling family, start anew as a republic, and move towards full reconciliation with the Aboriginal owners of the land. Australia's democracy needs a new life with a bill of rights incorporating the right to know and free education for all. All government agencies must open up to public scrutiny. The funding of elections by corporations and powerful economic interests must end and political parties be deregulated under a new proportional voting system. Australia's economic relations with the world should be based on the same principles that govern commerce in Australia. Relations with countries that abuse human rights and engage in corrupt practices would be restricted under a charter setting clear guidelines about improving governance and the welfare of people, and the protection of the environment. Australia should lower its level of consumption to help bring an end to poverty in the world, and extend its democratic charter to include a number of nearby countries. People of the Solomon Islands, Bougainville, PNG and East Timor should be offered the option to join the Australian federation as full citizens. The process of inclusion is a necessary pathway to reaffirm and consolidate democracy at home.

2

The US in Australia

Colonies do not cease to be colonies just because they are independent.

Benjamin Disraeli

GREAT POWER DEPENDENCY

Prime Minister John Howard was in Washington DC on 11 September 2001, and days after the destruction of New York's World Trade Center committed Australia to the US planned invasion of Afghanistan and Iraq. Australia's support for the US geostrategic role in the Asia-Pacific began much earlier, perhaps in 1908 when Deakin invited the US Fleet to visit Sydney to remind Europeans that 'they were engaged in a climatic struggle between the white and yellow races' (Day 2001:161). WWII finally brought Australia within the US political orbit when, in 1941, Japan invaded Southeast Asia, took Singapore and subsequently bombed Broome, Darwin and other coastal cities. So great was the panic that the military planned to abandon the country north of a line cutting across from Brisbane to Melbourne.

The job of saving Australia was given to the US, and specifically to General Douglas MacArthur who, having fled the Philippines, landed in Darwin in 1942 to be given command over all Australian military forces (Edwards 2001). After the Coral Sea and Midway sea-battles the US became Australia's saviour and thus began the alliance with the US and dependency on its power for protection from the country's greatest fear of invasion from the north. The alliance grew in strength during the Cold War as Australia played a critical role as a close US ally in the war against communism in the Asia-Pacific region. A key agreement was the 1947 UKUSA Treaty which linked the intelligence agencies of Australia, the UK, USA, NZ and Canada, and established Australia's Defence Signals Directorate (DSD).

With the help of the British the country formed the Australian Security Intelligence Organisation (ASIO) and Australia's Secret Intelligence Service (ASIS). The 1951 Australia–New Zealand–US (ANZUS) treaty and the Southeast Asia Treaty Organisation (SEATO) further consolidated the alliance. The development and integration of spying agencies in the Anglo-Saxon world was the key to the future strengthening of the alliance. Defence analyst Des Ball speaks of signal intelligence sharing (SIGINT) as the tie that binds (Ball 2001:237), and Dennis Phillips points to the spying club membership as the association that 'fixed Australia firmly in an American-dominated defence and intelligence web' (Phillips 1983:30).

Vietnam was another turning point in the alliance with Prime Minister Harold Holt proclaiming 'all the way with LBJ' as he offered troops to support the Americans and sent advisers as early as 1962. Eventually close to 10,000 military personnel fought in Vietnam's civil war while tens of thousands of US servicemen came to Australia on rest and recreation leave. Historian Stuart Macintyre calls it obeisance and payment to a powerful protector 'for defence on the cheap' (1999:209). Australia's intelligence agencies worked closely with the Central Intelligence Agency (CIA). John Pilger claims that the CIA ran 'fifteen black airfields in Australia' and massive drug shipments were made from Vietnam to Australia using these facilities. Drugs were then shifted to other destinations as part of the CIA fund-raising operation and payment to criminal organisations (Pilger 1992:200). Historian Alfred McCoy recounts the CIA banking operation in Sydney, the Nugan-Hand Bank, which financed the traffic in narcotics between Southeast Asia and Australia. Heroin flown to abandoned airfields in northern Australia was sold to organised crime in Australia to finance CIA operations in many parts of the world (McCoy 1991). During that period the Australian government ran covert operations in South and North Vietnam, in Chile, and in Indonesia as part of the 1965 coup to destabilise and replace the Sukarno regime with one friendly to Western interests.

At the time of the Vietnam war the US military establishment had gained a firm foothold on the continent with communication facilities built for US nuclear submarines at North West Cape in 1963, the Nurrungar 1971 US spying installations in South Australia, and a British MI6 station operating from Kowandi south of Darwin. According to Pilger, Australian facilities were used by the US during the Vietnam war to mine Haiphong and other harbours and to bomb Cambodia (Pilger 1992:202). The cornerstone of the intelligence organisation however, was at Pine Gap, built between 1966–69, and located on extra territorial grounds close to Alice Spring in central Australia. Pine Gap was until recently entirely run by the CIA and Australia's parliamentarians had no access to it nor could they find out the contents of the treaty which set it up. Pine Gap picks up information from many satellites and other sources and transmits data to and from command posts located in the US and elsewhere in the world. Pine Gap provided coordinates for all the targets during the first 1991 Gulf war and probably played a similar role during the 2003 invasion of Iraq.

With the end of the Cold War, the disintegration of the Soviet Union, and the end of the socialist alternative, Australia became an important partner in the US plan for a new world order. Part of the scheme was to deregulate economies and introduce market reforms to minimise the role of government, privatise public assets, and push for a free trade agenda. Another was the role of military intervention in the region to make the world safe for the expansion and sustainability of market capitalism. For Australia it marked the Americanising of the economy and the end of egalitarianism. Society became more fragmented and replaced with a ruthless individualist competitive culture dominated by an ideology of greed marketed by big corporations, universities and government. Australia became more assertive and interventionist in the region's economic and political affairs. Military action took place in Iraq, Cambodia, Papua New Guinea's Bougainville, and Indonesia in what Australia's Prime Minister boasted as the 'liberation' of East Timor in 1999.

The attack on New York's World Trade Center in 2001 and the events which followed confirmed Australia's role as US sheriff and its closest ally after the UK. In the aftermath of 11 September, Australia joined the US in the illegal invasion of Afghanistan and Iraq, and sent its military to a number of central Asia states. Australia was involved in military operations closer to home in East Timor, the Philippines and Papua New Guinea (PNG), and in 2003 led an armed intervention in the Solomon Islands. A year later it put the PNG government on notice that Australia would send a police force to reestablish order in the country. Australia was also beginning to play a more important role in East Asia's security and organising with Japan a series of sea-based interdiction exercises as part of a US-led process to bring down North Korea's political regime. After the bombing of a Bali night club which killed 202 people including 88 Australians in October 2002, Howard announced that Australia would carry out preemptive strikes in Southeast Asia without notice if it had information that terrorist organisations were endangering Australia's national interests.

BINDING KINSHIP

Australia's continent plays a critical role in US global geostrategy and hegemony. Control of Australia enables the US to have a full reach over the earth and to project its power everywhere. Since the 1989 fall of the Berlin Wall the relationship has advanced to a higher stage of political and military integration. US military presence has become more visible with more than thirty bases or stations in Australia and unlimited access to many Australian military facilities such as the bombing range near Katherine in the Northern Territory and the jungle training school near Queensland Rockhampton. US naval ships have berthing facilities in many ports. Freemantle in Western Australia is a major transit facility for the Pacific Fleet where crews are rotated and flown in and out of the country. Aircraft carriers and other nuclear-armed ships are often in Sydney harbour after long cruises in the Pacific and Indian Oceans. Air Force units train in Australia and have unlimited access to airbases for support and training. There are plans to provide the US with facilities for the permanent deployment of F-16s at Tindal airbase near Katherine and a brigade of more than 5,000 marines either near Townsville or Darwin. The stationing of US land forces is part of a shift of US forces from Japan and South Korea to Australia, Malaysia, Singapore and possibly the Philippines.

Pine Gap is probably the most important US installation in Australia. It plays a vital role in the US Star War system based on a new generation of space-based infrared missile defense system (SBIRS). It relays missile launch data from satellite infrared sensors permanently stationed on this side of the planet which can detect missile activities and launches. This role will become even more important once the US places laser-based interception platforms in space. Another function for Pine Gap is to 'spy on one half of the world's population' (Caldicott 2002b). Pine Gap receives information from geostationary satellites which act as giant airwave vacuum cleaners. The information is then forwarded to various US locations including CIA headquarters at Langley, Virginia.

According to Helen Caldicott, Pine Gap's other roles are 'spying on radar signals of other countries and detecting missile launches and nuclear explosions [and it] is deeply involved in nuclear-war planning including first-strike winnable nuclear war' (Caldicott 2002a:195). Pine Gap played an important role in the 2003 invasion of Iraq by collecting Iraqi communication and relaying it to the US and to command posts in the Persian Gulf. Missile strikes on Iraq, including one on a restaurant where Saddam Hussein had been reported to be, were linked to Pine Gap interception of radio communication between Iraqi leaders. Professor Ball of the Australian National University

Strategic and Defence Studies Centre said that Pine Gap 'would have had involvement in intelligence and targeting' (Ball 2003).

Australia's treaty covering the operations at Pine Gap has been extended to 2010. The contents of the treaty have never been released to the public and Australian parliamentarians are barred from reading it. Access to the facilities are restricted and while some Australians are now employed there, most are in menial jobs working as gardeners, waiters and clerks. Caldicott writes that 'Australia has virtually no responsibilities, nor access to most of the crucial and secret information. Much of the material and information collected and analysed at the Signals Analysis Section is never conveyed to Australian officers' (Caldicott 2002b). Pine Gap is part of an extensive spying consortium run by the US and the UK with the junior partnership of Canada, Australia and New Zealand. It is directed by and linked to the US National Security Agency (NSA) at Fort Meade, Maryland.

Australia's major contribution is largely directed by the Canberra-based Defence Signals Directorate (DSD), one of Australia's five intelligence groups. Other Australian agencies contribute to that effort and operate bases and installations around Australia including Pearce and Geraldton in Western Australia, Shoal Bay in the Northern Territory, Canberra, and Wagga in New South Wales (Caldicott 2002a:199). The Anglo-Saxon intelligence brain is a grid of supercomputers known as Echelon which scans vast areas of communication. The network intercepts land-based and satellite-based fax, phone, e-mail, and telex communication traffic and will soon be able to tap into undersea fibre-optic cables.

Australia's alliance with the US calls for compatibility in doctrine and operations of Australia's military machine with that of the US. For Australia this had meant large-scale procurement of US military hardware and software and the integration of its armed forces into the strategic and combat operations of the US. Military collaboration has been accelerated since 1995 with large-scale joint war exercises. Dubbed 'Tandem Thrust' the 1997 military version in Australia's north involved more than 20,000 US troops and was the largest military exercise with the US since the end of WWII. Held every two years these interoperability military ventures have become progressively more sophisticated in scale and aims. The 2001 operations tested the collaborative effort in a simulated seaborne invasion somewhere in Asia.

Dependence on US military weapons systems began in earnest with former Prime Minister Robert Menzies' decision to buy the US F-111 in 1963. It took ten years for the plane to be delivered to Australia at more than four times its original cost. This was followed by the purchase of the FA-18 Hornet in 1982. When Prime Minister Howard was in Washington in June 2002 he sealed a deal with President Bush for Australia to buy a plane that has yet to be developed. Australia was the only country to buy the Texas-based Lockheed-Martin fighter F-35 in a deal worth more than A$12 billion. Lockheed's management were 'absolutely flabbergasted' that Australia abandoned its own competition and declared it wanted the F-35 years ahead of time'. The head of Swedish Saab said that it was 'a modern-day case of all the way with LBJ which went further than they needed to for the sake of the strategic relationship with America' (Stewart 2002).

A similar development was taking place with Australia's naval forces and the integration of the country's naval shipbuilding programme and procurement within US operational requirements. This will mean additional billions of dollars in Australia's military expenditures moving to US corporations. Interoperability with the US navy is now the main objective of Australia's naval strategy. Australia's new submarines, for example, are to be equipped with US weapons systems. Moreover, the army announced in 2003 that it would retire its British-made Leopard tanks for American Abrams which are more suitable for the army's new role as part of expeditionary forces with the US. All these developments clearly indicated how far the US–Australia military alliance had travelled towards the integration of Australia's defence within the US imperium.

Military collaboration extends to important research areas where the US has access to many research facilities including those of universities. A recent example is the role of Australia Defence Science and Technology Organisation (DSTO) in the development of the global Hawk remote-control aircraft which can fly for some 36 hours without refuelling. This jet plane is the world's most sophisticated aerial surveillance plane and a prototype for future unmanned fighter bombers. More important is the involvement of Australia in the US programme on anti-missile defence, the National Missile Defense (NMD) system. Collaborative efforts involve Australia's DSTO working with the US Ballistic Missile Defense Organisation (BMDO) to build a missile defence system in the Asia-Pacific region. The project operates with South Australia's Woomera missile range and the Northern Territory Jindalle-over-the horizon radar, and the missile testing system at Jervis Bay in New South Wales. A recent addition to the programme is a missile interception test range north of Broome, a project named 'Dundee' (Down Under Early Warning Experiment) which makes use of a ballistic testing and tracking station between Port Hedland and Broome in Western Australia.

AUSTRALIA IN THE EMPIRE

US geostrategy to control Eurasia has its genesis in the geopolitical work of Halford Mackinder at the height of the British Empire and became US policy at the beginning of the Cold War in 1945. Former US secretary of state Henry Kissinger outlines the basic principles of US global geostrategy when he writes that:

Geopolitically, America is an island off the shores of the large landmass of Eurasia, whose resources and population far exceed those of the US. The domination by a single power of either of Eurasia's two principal spheres – Europe or Asia – remains a good definition of strategic danger for America, Cold War or no Cold War. For such a grouping would have the capacity to outstrip America economically and, in the end, militarily. That danger would have to be resisted even were the dominant power apparently benevolent, for if the intentions ever changed, America would find itself with a grossly diminished capacity for effective resistance and a growing inability to shape events. (Kissinger 1994:813)

US hegemonic role is always expressed in the context of a threat to its territory and to its mission to construct a capitalist world system. In the aftermath of the Cold War new threats have been popularised in books such as Samuel Huntington's *The Clash of Civilizations* and also in many films such as the epic action movie based on Tolkien's fascist-minded mythology of *The Lord of the Rings*. Huntington's book is an attack on Islam and China and a call for the West to prepare for war against the new barbarians (Huntington 1997). He praises the West's glorious history and civilisational burden, and the leading role of the Anglo-Saxon people in their mission against evil forces. Huntington suggests that human rights and democracy are essentially Anglo-Saxon cultural products unlikely to graft outside the Western world. Western civilisation is now threatened by what Huntington calls the Sinic-Islamic alliance. This was the essence of President Bush's 2002 message to Congress when he outlined US plans to reshape the world and use its hegemonic power to attack those who 'hate the United States and everything for which it stands'

(Bush 2002). The US wants to reconfigure the political map of most of Asia but the main focus is on China whose aspiration to great power status is seen as incompatible with US hegemony.

Australia has a major role to play as regional sheriff in US hegemonic strategy. Australia is a principal member in a regional security alliance with Japan, South Korea, Taiwan, Pakistan and a number of Southeast Asian states. This grouping is an expanded security architecture of the Cold War's Southeast East Asia Treaty Organisation (SEATO). Singapore has replaced the Philippines as a key US naval base. The Changi naval base is the new home for US aircraft carriers and became fully operational in 2003. Singapore will provide support for the US Seventh fleet based in Japan's Yokosuka and the San Diego-based Third fleet. These two battle-groups operate in the Indian Ocean, Western Pacific and Arabian Gulf. Meshed within this geographical alliance of Asian states is a US-controlled weapons system based on the control of space.

The US is building a defensive and offensive military structure to strike at any target on earth with deadly accuracy. In that scheme the US and its allies are placing weapons systems on land, at sea and in space that will destroy missiles anywhere on earth whether on the ground or soon after lift off. This is the Star War plan also known as National Missile Defense (NMD) and Theater Missile Defense (TMD) systems. Weapons including land-based anti-ballistic missiles are being positioned in the US (Alaska and California) and in a number of other countries such as Israel, UK, Greenland's Thule, Japan, South Korea, Qatar and Australia. Continental Australia is an integral part of US space war strategy to control Eurasia. Pine Gap, for example, can track missiles launched from China and North Korea, and provide targeting information for missiles to destroy them. Pine Gap plays a similar role to the US–UK facilities at Fylingdales and Menwith Hills in the north of England in tracking incoming missiles.

Land and sea-based missiles are integrated with satellites equipped with infrared sensors to detect missile launch, and to land-based X-Band radar stations which use advance signals processing to track missiles. Japan has been asked to develop and install ballistic missile defence systems to counter threats from North Korean missiles. North Korea has deployed some 100 Rodong missiles which have a range of 1,500 km. Japan has been developing such a system since the 1998 missile scare when a North Korean missile flew across northern Japan. The US is developing space-based weapons such as laser guns positioned in space or carried out in large planes; it has already operated an airborne laser which consists of a high-energy chemical oxygen iodine laser (COIL) mounted on a modified 747–400F freighter aircraft that can shoot down missiles in the boost phase, and destroy satellites.

The ties that bind with the US are getting stronger and have implications for Australia's democratic regime and relations with the region. Recent developments in the world, particularly the attack against New York's World Trade Center, have moved domestic politics further to the right. The Australian government has made a commitment to serve the US and wage war against all those who stand against it. The politics of fear and the war on terrorism have allowed an alliance of neoconservatives and technocrats to capture the state apparatus. This new elite is closely attuned to the US in spirit and ideology and stand to benefit financially. The prime minister and government of Australia lied to its citizens about Iraq's threats and the reasons to go to war. Australia's mass media failed to investigate government claims and generally supported its action. There was no parliamentary debate or vote on Australia's decision to invade Afghanistan and Iraq.

The politics of fear have dominated the domestic agenda. Australia's national security elite have hidden behind President Bush, warning that 'either you are with us, or you are with the terrorists' in order to introduce the equivalent of the US Patriot Act and move the country towards a sophisticated surveillance society where everyone is monitored and a potential suspect. Security agencies have received substantial additional funding, and new powers that restrict civil liberties, human rights and basic freedom of citizens, and further curtail rights of resident aliens. New laws give secret agencies increased powers to search and spy on people. People can be detained for a number of days without access to a lawyer merely on the grounds that a person 'might substantially assist the collection of intelligence that is important in relation to a terrorist offence'. Australian citizens have lost their right to remain silent and the failure to answer a question is punishable by up to five years in prison. US military commissions have gained legitimacy under Australian law and their rulings equate that of an Australian court. Australia's terrorist legislation has in effect abandoned 'fundamental principles of the rule of law: they dilute the prohibitions of arbitrary detention, they obliterate the right to habeas corpus, they remove the right to silence, and they reverse the onus of proof' (Michaelson 2004:30).

Close ties with the US military establishment and a shared view of Western civilisation under threat have politicised Australia's military elite and their counterparts in government. This is particularly dangerous to democratic life because it questions the allegiance and role of the military leadership and intelligence agencies. Their increasing weight in the country's political life has shifted the debate away from the more fundamental politics of a fair and egalitarian society to one more concerned about internal security, terrorism and military intervention in the region to sort out their affairs. It has encouraged the manipulation of the national psyche to support aggression and war, and to seek a military solution to what are essentially social and economic problems. Governance transparency and accountability have severely diminished because of the increased use of secrecy and confidentiality in government dealings and restrictions imposed on mass media content.

A close military alliance with the US is an important factor in Australia's growing militarism. The military budget passed the A$14 billion mark in 2003, acquiring new weapons and building up a major expeditionary combat force which could join US overseas forces. Despite the increasing cost to society, the government has argued that US protection saves a great deal of money since Australia has access to US technology, weapons and intelligence for a relatively small public outlay. There are nevertheless some hidden liabilities to Australia's military alliance. Notwithstanding the implications to the country's democratic process and ideals, Australia has developed an unhealthy dependency on the US which has serious implications for the future. The strategic analyst Ball has written about the dependency aspect of the US alliance in terms of access to information, equipment and technology: 'privileged access to the highest level of US defence technology' means that the US is 'indispensable to Australia's self-reliance. The defence of Australia requires high technology ... which the US provides' (Ball 2001:237).

Australia depends on US military supplies for any sustained operation which allows the US to control Australia's operations. More importantly, the high cost of US technology is a major burden on a small economy with a substantial current account deficit and a weak currency subject to speculative operations by the international money market. Gary Brown argued in 1989 that the US alliance inhibits self-reliance and leaves the country open to 'misinformation', that 'self-reliance' and 'alliance' are incompatible and 'this will either bring down the alliance or return Australia to the subservient condition of the 50s and 60s' (Brown 1989:152). Reliance on US intelligence shapes Australia's view of the world and carries the danger that Australia's foreign policy is shaped by flawed intelligence or information that has been dramatically altered or concocted to influence government policies. The problem was amply demonstrated in the months prior to the 2003 invasion of Iraq when the US passed on intelligence to Australian agencies which turned out to be false or based on grossly exaggerated claims. This was in turn manipulated by Prime Minister Howard to sway public opinion and justify Australia's illegal war against Iraq.

Australia has become overdependent on US high-tech military gadgetry to defend its vast continent and small population. The US military umbilical cord has serious repercussions for the Australian economy. Dependence on US weaponry has a direct bearing on the decline of Australia's manufacturing sector and the problems faced by the information technology sector. A more independent pathway such as the Swedish model would have led to a strong manufacturing industry and the rise of an important and innovative electronic sector capable of providing all of Australia's military needs. Such a policy would have been a serious boost to university research and the training of scientists. In turn research and development would have added value to Australia's natural resources and turned them into valuable exports. Sweden, with a population a third of Australia's, has today one of the world's most innovative and lucrative manufacturing and information technology sectors. Instead, dependency on US protection has weakened Australia's economy and its capacity to compete in the region, and put more reliance on the export of raw mining and farm products. This has been costly in terms of environmental degradation. Australia's reliance on food exports has put enormous pressure on land and water resources. Environmental degradation is a major national problem and the cost of repairing the environment has been estimated at more than A$60 billion (Wahlquist 2000).

Asia-Pacific is a more dangerous region because of US imperial politics and the war on terrorism. US policy to develop an anti-missile system, put weapons in space and construct a regional balance of power will increase the danger of war and fuel an armament race. A policy of military intervention to address what are economic and social problems will have serious consequences for the political stability of many countries in the region. Anti-ballistic defences will destabilise the Cold War understanding reached between Russians and Americans when they both accepted the logic of the destabilising effects of such a move and signed the 1972 anti-ballistic missile (ABM) treaty. The US repudiation of that treaty in 2004 can only mark the beginning of a new Cold War. Former prime minister Malcolm Fraser warned that:

An antiballistic missile defence shield would upset the delicate nuclear balance, it would halt the impetus to nuclear disarmament and create the possibility of a new nuclear arms race. In a desire to achieve security for themselves, the US is now putting world stability and world security at risk. It is a policy of selfishness, of short-sightedness and of ignorance of the motivating forces behind national decisions. (Fraser 1999)

Of concern is a possible conflict with China over the issue of Taiwan's independence, and Australia's participation in the development of the Star War system targeted at China. Australia could be directly involved in the event of a war over Taiwan because of its military treaty commitment to the US. Australia's role as US regional sheriff has damaged its reputation according to public opinion polls carried in the Asian region. In relation to John Howard's speech about Australia's right to strike at Southeast Asia in response to a perceived threat of terrorist attack, some Asian leaders have spoken of a new period of neo-colonialism. A doctrine of preemptive strike encourages other countries to do likewise and could escalate an already tense situation in many parts of the region. Australia's boast of liberating East Timor and its war against Afghanistan and Iraq are interpreted in Indonesia and elsewhere in Southeast Asia as Australia's war against Islam – another crusade by the West to fight Islam and deny Islamic countries and people their rights to a better life.

Australia's military alliance with the US is shaping its foreign policy. What particularly stands out is Australia's scepticism towards multilateralism and the role of the United Nations in addressing world problems. Australia is moving away from the multilateral human rights system in the name of community security and has made significant retreats from its international treaty obligations. Spencer Zifcak argues that there has been a disengagement from countries and cultures 'that do not resemble our own. A new unilateralism deeply popular here because it returns Australians to a more secure and comfortable identification with nations and peoples like us' (Zifcak 2003a:8). An anti-internationalist stance and close alignment with the US and UK has led Australia to support US policy to divide the European Union and vote against the Kyoto protocol on reducing greenhouse gas emissions. Former diplomat Malcolm Booker has argued that the events of WWII created a psychology of dependence on the US which continues to this day. He says 'we lapsed into the status of a dependency of America after WWII, while our economy was arrested at a primary producing level. Consequently, our destiny remains, as for the past 200 years, in the hands of others' (Booker 1988).

ECONOMIC DEPENDENCY

The US has become Australia's most important trading partner followed by Japan and accounts for more than 9 per cent of Australia's total exports and some 23 per cent of Australia's imports. Merchandise trade to the US is primarily made up of bovine meat, crude petroleum, alcoholic beverages and aircraft parts. While imports include aircrafts and parts, telecommunications equipment, measuring and controlling instruments and internal combustion engines. Australia's merchandise trade deficit with the US has been rising and reached more than A$11 billion in 2002. Trade in services is a growing area of commerce with the US, particularly in regard to transportation and travel services and contributed to Australia's deficit in its service trading account for some A$1.6 billion in 2000.

The pattern of merchandise trade shows a developing pattern of reliance on the US for high-value and high-technology content goods in exchange for Australia's mine and farm products. The US is Australia's largest market for beef and takes in about 30 per cent of the country's beef exports. Each month 'Australian farmers ship 700 tonnes of high-grade chilled beef worth A$7 million and 6,300 tonnes of frozen beef worth A$25 million to the US' (Macfarlane 2002). Exports to the US often originate from US controlled investments in Australia such as beef from US agribusiness holdings ConAgra. Access to the US market for Australian goods can change dramatically when the US decides unilaterally to impose quotas or other restrictions as in the case of lamb and steel in 2001, and in 2002 when the US threatened to halve Australia's A$450 million annual steel exports to the US.

Australia has the highest level of foreign investment of any industrialised country. Most sectors of the economy are dominated by foreign companies. Foreign control increased in recent years with the privatisation of important government assets. More than 40 per cent of companies listed on the Australian stock exchange are owned by foreigners. As a former British colony, capital from England formed the basis for the capitalisation of the Australian economy, but with the impact of globalisation in recent years the US has moved swiftly to become Australia's major investor with some A$297 billion, as shown in Table 2.1, followed by the UK's A$178 billion, with Japan in third place with more than A$49 billion.

Table 2.1 Australia and US investment, 1994 and 2003 (A$ million)

	Australia in US	US in Australia
1994	38,493	86,656
2003	211,004	297,311

Source: Australian Bureau of Statistics, various years, series: 5363.0, 5352.0 – the US was the largest investor in Australia in 2003 (30%), UK (26%) and Japan (4.5%).

US investment covers a wide range of areas beginning with large land holdings such as the Queensland and Northern Territory Pastoral company which owns Australia's largest land holding of some 2.7 million hectares. Some US land investments are integrated with agribusiness such as the US giant ConAgra and Meat Holdings which run cattle businesses and abattoirs. Others are linked to the development of the Australian cotton industry in which American farmers have played a big role attracted by cheap land and water. They brought with them irrigation techniques and helped expand Australia's cotton production to rank as the world's third largest exporter after the US and Uzbekistan. Cheap water has attracted food producers such as US food giant JR Simplot, producer of pasta sauces and tomato-based products, and Heinz baby-food. Both companies are located in Echuca northern Victoria, a service town for the vast irrigated agricultural land of the 4,500 km2 Campaspe Shire.

Australia's privatisation of public assets has attracted many foreign companies to buy into water, electricity and gas production, transmission and distribution systems. US companies have been at the forefront of this campaign buying out a large share of the Australian market. Mission Energy purchased Victoria's giant energy generator Loy Yang B and US giant NRG energy has some A$10 billion in Australia's energy assets, including Victoria's Latrobe Valley Loy Yang A power station with US-based CMS Energy. NRG controls Flinders station in South Australia, and a major power-generating plant in Queensland's towns of Gladstone and Collinsville. NRG and

Epic Energy also own a large share of Australia's gas transmission network, some 4,000 km of pipeline in Queensland, South Australia and Western Australia. Epic Energy, owned by US corporations El Paso Corp and Consolidated Natural Gas Co., managed to accumulate by 2003 a A$3.5 billion business as Australia's biggest gas transmission company. More recently it has shifted focus towards Australia's gas reserve and joined US Phillips Petroleum, which controls the Bayu-Undan gas project in the Timor Sea, to build and operate a 2,000 km pipeline from the Timor Sea gas fields to Darwin's processing plant, and on to Moomba in South Australia. Moomba is a critical hub in the distribution of natural gas to the large urban markets of Sydney, Brisbane and Adelaide.

Other US energy players are Xcel Energy, American Electric Power which owns Melbourne's Citipower, and Duke energy's pipeline and power stations in Queensland and Tasmania among its A$2 billion Australian assets. Another is Enron which until recently was the biggest electricity trader in Australia. Enron's funding in Australia came from a US$7 billion US public assistance programme. The collapse of the US-based company has exposed Australia's energy-trading market to higher risks and the potential for substantial increases in the cost of energy. By 2003 the biggest stake, some A$4.7 billion, had been put together by Dallas-based Texas Utilities (TXU). These assets included Victoria's gas and electricity distribution assets and the control of more than 45,000 km of electricity and 8,045 km of gas pipeline networks, and close to a million customers. Many of these assets have since been sold by TXU to Singapore to realise huge profits made possible by Australia's privatisation policy, and to position itself to capture future privatisation opportunities in New South Wales and Queensland's energy assets.

US investments in Australia's services are sizeable and wide-ranging. The most recent and visible investment in the transport industry was the construction of the 1,410 km rail line from Alice Springs to Darwin by Texas-based Brown and Root Engineering. This offshoot of the US-based Halliburton Corporation built, owns and operates the rail line. US company Fluor Daniel has a number of contracts for rail and power stations maintenance. Rail America became a major operator of the country's rail infrastructure when it purchased assets from the Australian National Railways Commission, including the operations of the transcontinental Indian Pacific, Ghan and Overland, and the Brisbane-to-Cairns lines. US-based Genesee and Wyoming Inc. have recently purchased the assets of Western

Australia's Westrail freight business. Another lucrative line in service investment for the US is in the incarceration industry. Companies such as Correctional Services of America (CCA) and Australasian Correctional Management (ACM) operate 80 per cent of Australia's jails, and six Immigration Department detention centres for illegal refugees in Australia and on the Islands of Nauru and Manus in Papua New Guinea.

Some US companies such as Halliburton have been particularly successful in making fast inroads in Australia's economy. In recent years Halliburton has managed to capture the Adelaide-to-Darwin railway and the management of Melbourne's Grand Prix. Less obvious have been the company's more than 150 contracts with Australia's defence (Calacouras and Bacon 2005). Halliburton's subsidiary United Water has been buying up water assets such as Adelaide's water distribution and Perth's water assets. Another subsidiary, Kellogg Brown and Root (KBR), has gained a substantial share of AusAid overseas work, supplied environmental impact surveys for major Australian projects, and successfully tendered for engineering and design contracts for major energy projects, including work on the A$11 billion Gorgon gas development in Western Australia.

Australia has largely sold its future in the information technology (IT) sector. Billions of dollars of public expenditures in IT have not built an indigenous industry that could have been the platform for important benefits elsewhere, particularly in high-value exports for Australia. Instead, most of the benefits have accrued to foreign investors, mainly US-based companies such as EDS, IBM and CSC. Texan computer services EDS, for example, has become a major player in the field. It all began when the company gained a major foothold in South Australia's public service. From there the company moved into federal government business and won billions of dollars worth of outsourcing contracts with the Australian Taxation Office (ATO) and Australian Customs Services (ACS). The Australian government Office of Asset Sales and IT Outsourcing (OASITO), under former liberal minister for finance John Fahey, paid fortunes to US law firms, including A$20 million to Shaw Pittman, to provide expert advice on how the government could outsource government services. Peter Thorne, a computer science expert at Melbourne University, argues that Australia failed to develop a local IT industry and that despite government 'rhetoric about the clever country and the information economy, Australia is a colony in the global information society' (Thorne 2002:55).

Australia's resource sector is dominated by US companies. US holdings extend from the country's gold fields to the iron and coal mines of the continent. The process of takeover continues: in 2002 Australia's biggest gold producer, Normandy Mining, was sold to US Newmont Mining, the world's largest gold producer, and the last big Australian diversified mining company WMC was taken over by Alcoa. More critical to the economic future of Australia is the US control of energy resources. US companies are major operators of Australia's oil and gas resources. Some of the world's biggest gas fields are in Australia. Phillips Petroleum is the principal operator in the Timor Sea gas reserves of Bayu-Undan. Chevron-Texaco is a major partner in Australia's largest North-West Shelf (NWS) gas project off the coast of Western Australia, which won a A$25 billion contract over twenty-five years to supply China with liquefied gas from 2005. NWS is a major provider of liquefied gas to Japan and South Korea. Chevron-Texaco is also involved with ExxonMobil in the development of the Gorgon gas project for markets in China and the US. The field off the coast of Western Australia is said to be Australia's largest gas reserve estimated at 20 trillion cubic feet of gas, the equivalent of 3.3 billion barrels of oil, or twice the size of the NWS. Chevron-Texaco plans to build a processing plant on Barrow Island, directly south of Montebello Island where Britain exploded nuclear weapons in the 1950s. ExxonMobil is also a major operator of the southern Bass Straits gas fields.

In recent years the US has gained more control over Australia's transmission of domestic energy. A major project planned by ExxonMobil and Oil Search is to build a gas pipeline from Papua New Guinea (PNG) to Queensland. The pipeline would deliver gas to TXU Australia and other customers in direct competition with domestic companies such as Santos Petroleum. The deployment of Australian police to PNG highlands in 2004 is partly to lower the political risk of the project. It is likely that in the near future there will be further pressure by US companies to bid for additional Australian energy assets and companies. Foreign control of Australia's energy exploration and production is directly linked to a decline in Australia's energy self-sufficiency. Australia's import of oil is increasing and in 2004 reached more than 40 per cent of oil needs. Oil exploration and domestic refining is largely in the hands of US-based companies which make more profit importing oil and refined products because of what they call Australia's 'punitive tax regime' for local producers.

A recent report by the Committee for the Economic Development of Australia points out that foreign companies do not necessarily bring competence, knowledge and innovation into their Australian operations (Nicolas and Samartino 2003). US-based companies among others can take advantage of many loopholes which greatly benefit their business operations in Australia. These would include low or negative tax liabilities because companies use debt to finance their Australian operations so that they can claim tax breaks. Companies can also take advantage of Australia's generous business welfare scheme and gain a major share of industry's corporate welfare which was worth more than A$10 billion in 2003. Philip Morris received more than A$1 million in tax concession claims in the late 1990s to research and develop a high-tar cigarette for export to Africa. Among other cases is Dupont's closure of their operations in the mid 1990s despite receiving A$60 million in federal money in 1990 to stay in business; or US-owned King Gee using A$6 million of taxpayers' money to 'upgrade their warehousing facilities so they could import from Indonesia more efficiently' (Verrender 1996). A more visible subsidy to US corporation is the gift to Rupert Murdoch of a large prime site in the centre of Sydney worth some A$100 million to run his Hollywood-type movie studio and entertainment centre.

Table 2.2 **Australia current account, major trading partners, 1993 and 2003 (A$ million)**

	Total	US	ASEAN	Japan	China
1993	−16,416	−15,080	4,410	3,858	−547
2003	−46,633	−15,648	−8,875	2,111	−5,196

Source: Australian Bureau of Statistics, various years, series: 5363.0 and 5338.0.

US operations in Australia contribute to Australia's sizeable current account deficit. The country's trading losses have been increasing steadily over the years from more than A$16 billion in 1993 to more than A$46 billion in 2003 as shown in Table 2.2. The income flow to US investors accounted for some 24 per cent of the current account deficit with the US. Overall the US is the largest debtor in Australia's total trade. More than 35 per cent of Australia's trading losses in 2003 are accounted for by commercial links with the US. US business operations in Australia are well organised in their efforts to lobby government for more tax breaks to improve their profitability and maintain their operations in the country. Companies shop around to meet their wish list of 'tax breaks, relocation assistance, permits, road and utilities [and] ... more controversial requirements of low or zero income tax' (Baragwanath and Howe 2000:9). The weight of US business activities in Australia exerts political pressure powerful enough to change state and federal policies. The business lobby has been instrumental in the deregulation of Australia's financial market and the introduction of economic rationalism which in turn has been responsible for growing inequalities in Australian society.

US FREE TRADE AGREEMENT

Australia's satellite status was confirmed with a free trade agreement (FTA) sealed prior to Australia's 2004 federal elections. Labor, the main opposition party, failed to oppose the FTA fearing the loss of business support and US retribution. Negotiations which began in 2002 were largely driven by a number of powerful US and Australian lobby groups. No public debate was held on the issue and the mass media supported government efforts by providing extensive coverage to supporters of the FTA. New Zealand, joined to Australia by the Close Economic Relations agreement (CER), has not been a party to the negotiations because of its opposition to the US invasion of Iraq. Bill English the leader of New Zealand's National Party accused Australia's prime minister of waging war in Iraq for a free trade agreement with the US. The US told NZ's prime minister in 2003 that it was not an ally of the US and unlikely to be considered for an FTA by the Bush administration.

One of the more controversial aspects is the US attack on Australia's Pharmaceutical Benefits Scheme (PBS), which is an important component of Australia's public health system. Under this scheme the government subsidises the cost of a range of essential pharmaceuticals by fixing prices and reimbursing patients. The US pharmaceutical industry wants the PBS changed so that Australians pay full price for their drugs. Pfizer, for example, the maker of Viagra, wants the scheme scrapped so that it can sell Viagra and other drugs at market price. This would mean paying an extra A$4 billion a year to the industry from public and private sources (Lokuge and Denniss 2003). US businesses want better business conditions in Australia including a reduction of the dividend withholding tax on royalties from 10 per cent to zero. Such a concession would reduce Australia's tax revenues by more than A$200 million yearly. Other US demands focus on the further deregulation of the labour market, and rights for US companies identical to those of Australian firms including the right to sue government if they fail to get equal treatment.

The US is gaining more access for their investors through the elimination of other 'means of restricting trade' such as rules imposed by Australia's Foreign Investment Review Board and restrictions on foreign ownership of any Australian assets including key companies such as Telstra and Qantas, and in sectors such as public schools and universities, postal services, water and electricity supply, and rail and communication. Hollywood's lobby is keen on lifting local-content quotas in television and advertising and enforcing stiff copyright and patent protection for American products such as video, music recordings and computer software, including criminal penalties for pirating in such goods. There is fear among Australia's artistic world that Australia's culture and entertainment will fall under the control of US giants, namely Time Warner, Rupert Murdoch's Fox Studio, and the Motion Picture Association of America.

Australians have been told that a free trade agreement with the United States will lead to a substantial increase in Australia's exports and gross national product. Prime Minister Howard claims that a trade agreement is worth A$4 billion to Australia while the US negotiator Bob Zoellick has up the ante to A$7 billion. There have been many warnings that an FTA with the US will not be to Australia's benefit. ACIL Consulting's major study, commissioned by the government's Rural Industries Research and Development Corporation (RIRDC), rejected government claims of a A$4 billion gain for Australia and warned of repercussions for Australia's trading ties with Asia particularly in regard to beef and wool exports. It concluded that an FTA would cut Australia's Gross Domestic Product by about US$100 million a year by 2010. This raises many questions about the motives behind a process which is likely to compromise Australia's future.

Powerful political and economic groups covet a closer and more permanent relationship between Australia and the United States. It is often claimed that Australia's small economy, continental size, and dependency on foreign investment and capital would benefit from close ties with the world's largest economy. These matters are often discussed at the Australian American Leadership Dialogue, a privately organised gathering funded by Australian businessman Phil Scanlan, a former head of Coca Cola, which brings together every year in Washington DC influential members of both countries. Major US companies with interests in Australia including Caterpillar, Boeing, Cargill, Citibank, Ford, Motorola and Halliburton have declared their support for the FTA.

Australia's elite support for the FTA has less to do with trade than with Australia's political and economic insecurity as a nation in the Asia-Pacific region. Australia's considerable problems with its raison d'être are compounded by cultural isolation and fears of exclusion from the Association of Southeast Asian States (ASEAN), and the larger community being formed through ASEAN's closer relations with China, Japan and South Korea. Behind the business facade there are more irrational motivations driven by greed and racism. Many members of Australia's business community want a close US partnership in the economy as a counterweight to the growing presence and economic clout of the Asian business community. There are fears that Asian capitalism will displace Anglo-American global economic dominance. Australia could emerge as a major faultline in the conflict among the major participants of the capitalist world system.

Australia's FTA is similar to the US agreement with Mexico and Chile in that it leaves out major agricultural sectors such as sugar, builds in a transition period or phase-in conditions over 10 to 15 years, and refers to clauses that allow for negotiations to continue in bilateral and multilateral venues. These could be empty promises given the nature of the US economy and the political power of American farmers and agribusiness. The US 2002 Farm Bill increased government subsidy to farmers by some 80 per cent with a promise to deliver more than US$100 billion over the next five years. Protection of US agriculture is extensive. Most subsidies under the Farm Bill are directed at wheat, corn, cotton, soybeans and rice. Sugar and dairy products receive large subsidies through price regulations and tariffs. A US farm policy specialist estimates that consumers will pay US$271 billion in higher prices to support milk and sugar in the next decade and that together with the Farm Bill's supplement, support to farmers will come to some US$451 billion in the next ten years (Hartcher 2002; Oxfam 2002; SBS 2002).

Australia's farming lobby has been sweetened into the deal by generous government subsidies such as big handouts to Queensland's cane growers who have been offered access to a A$400 million fund to leave the industry. The government plans for more than 2,000 growers to diversify to other crops or leave the land in the next two years. Released land will likely be rezoned to meet the needs of

Queensland's rapid urban growth. Australia is paying Queensland farmers to get out of cane production at a time when the government is subsidising the expansion of the cane industry as part of the Ord irrigation scheme in the far northwest of Western Australia. Other well-funded packages have been offered to farmers who have missed out on land clearing, and handouts offered to rationalise the dairy industry and allocate water rights. Important exporters with political clout have been well looked after, as illustrated in a recent government decision to guarantee a disproportionate share of the US beef quota in the lucrative A$4.2 billion export beef industry to the Consolidated Meat Group owned by Australia's richest family.

The FTA will increase the US influence over Australia's economy and politics. It will give further impetus and momentum to the process of liberalisation and open up Australia's economy to a new round of privatisation with the public school, university, health and other public sectors being opened up to the bidding power of multinationals. US investors are likely to challenge any legislation which protects workers and the environment as an unfair restriction on free trade. The possibility exists that branches of government could be privatised, such as quarantine and customs, to be replaced by private organisations. Australia's public health system will be weakened and slowly privatised with the entry of US health companies into the market. In addition, the price cap on pharmaceutical products which gives Australians access to needed drugs at reasonable prices will come to an end as pharmaceutical companies take the government to court for imposing price regulations on their industry in breach of the FTA. A primary focus of the US is the protection of US intellectual property (IP) covering patents, trade marks and copyrights. Australia will pay a heavy price in future years as the intellectual property market increases the outflow of profit to the US and becomes a big earner for law firms. Australia will also lose out on manufacturing exports because of strict US rules of origin and the expense of administering export requirements.

The social costs of the FTA will be passed on to taxpayers, such as public expenditures to take dairy farmers, cane growers and other primary producers out of production. Australia's self-sufficiency aims in oil and gas supply will be further compromised by the US energy consortium's global policies. Cheap food exports from the US will threaten Australia's farm income and put pressure on farmers to mismanage land to compete for the world's food markets. Canada's experience with the US suggests that NAFTA has been costly to that country's economy and society. Brian Mulroney, Canada's former prime minister, said that the 'US–Canada free-trade agreement was like falling down a gold mine' (Kerr 2002). Canadian society is losing control of what happens to local communities as US multinationals claim the right under NAFTA to buy and manage their assets and pollute the land. Cities and towns in Canada pay the price of free trade which has uprooted people from the land and created new waves of homeless people because of cuts in federal employment programmes and deregulation of rental markets (Klein 2001).

Australia's trading links with Asia will come under pressure. Professor Ross Garnaut of the Australian National University (ANU) warns about the costs of trade diversion and that an FTA with the US 'would amount to Australia practising systematic trade discrimination against Asian economies which accounted for a majority of Australian exports' and that 'Australia will be damaged directly and indirectly by the increasing importance of trade discrimination in East Asia' (Davis 2003a). An FTA with the US sends dangerous signals to Asia that Australia's economic and geopolitical interests are with the US. Australian trading links with South Korea and China are likely to be affected, and Australia could expect retaliation from Asia in terms of market access and role in regional affairs.

The FTA may be detrimental to Australia's economic position with other important trading partners. The EU, for example, will put pressure on Australia for equal rights in trading and investment access. There are already signs that the EU is responding to the FTA by asking Australia to eliminate a raft of barriers to competition in local service industries and to foreign investment. Already there are demands on Australia to dismantle barriers to trade in services and to end monopolies held by universities and Australia Post. The EU will also retaliate against increased US farm protection by demanding that Australia opens its market to agricultural products from poor countries for sugar, bananas and rice as part of a global plan to reduce world poverty.

US hegemony is being fought on the trade front. The US is expanding its free trade agenda through multilateral and bilateral trade deals. This offensive is partly to counteract the emergence of economic and political forces that compete with US global power. The European Union is a potential threat to the US and so is the rise of an East Asian economic grouping centred on China. The European Union and China are the main challengers to the US empire. To counteract and weaken forces of regionalism the US has been constructing its own all-Americas trade agreement expanding the North American Trade Agreement which includes Canada, Mexico and Chile to the rest of the Americas. Moreover the US is on the offensive in the Asian region with bilateral trade deals with South Korea, Taiwan, and a number of Southeast Asian countries. Australia is a major asset on the US geoeconomic chessboard. The FTA with Australia is not simply a trade deal but locks Australia in the US sphere of influence and impedes advances by the European Union and East Asian countries. The FTA will further impose on Australia the economic and political policies of US imperial rule.

SHAPING POLITICAL CULTURE

In the aftermath of WWII large amounts of money came into Australia from Britain and the US to finance anti-labor campaigns, undermine the Labor government, and fund the electoral win of Liberal Party leader Robert Menzies in 1949. Wilfred Hughes, Menzies' minister for the interior, declared in 1950 that Australia 'must become the 49th state of America' (Pilger 1992:164). This was a time when US spying operations in Australia became more extensive, particularly on Canberra's politicians, under the UKUSA Cooperative Intelligence Agreement whose contents continue to be a secret to this day. By then Australia's ASIO, ASIS and states special branches were spying on large numbers of Australians and collaborating with US intelligence agencies. Fear of communism, and the activities of ASIO in the defection of a Russian embassy secretary, assured Menzies election victory in 1954 and prepared the grounds for Australia's war against Vietnam.

An anti-war movement and the Liberal government's racist policy put the Labor Party in power in 1972. Gough Whitlam, the new prime minister, pulled Australian troops out of Vietnam and sent Australia's first ambassador to China. He was suspicious of US activities and concerned about the operations of Australian and US intelligence agencies, and began to question US activities at Pine Gap. Whitlam removed the heads of ASIO and ASIS after he found out they were using Australian agents in CIA operations in Chile, and lying to his government about their activities. Journalist Brian Toohey has exposed ASIO's role in passing potentially damaging information on prominent Australians and politicians to the US (Toohey 1983). According to Des Ball, Whitlam did not know of the existence of the Defence Signals Directorate or the UKUSA Cooperative Intelligence

Agreement (Ball 1980:153). Whitlam suspected that Pine Gap was used to gain information on Australia's political, trade union and commercial life, and he threatened not to extend its lease. Whitlam's government was also critical of US multinational control of Australia's natural resources, and Rex Connor, the minister for minerals and energy, had plans for the government to buy out foreign-owned resource assets. The turning point came when the prime minister of Australia was 'declared' a security risk by the US; by then there were serious efforts to destabilise the government and get him out of office.

Dirty tricks were used to dismiss the government including the use of CIA-front banks to compromise it in a major loan scandal (Pilger 1992). Australia's governor-general John Kerr, who dismissed Whitlam's government, was said to have CIA and British intelligence 'associations' (Caldicott 2002a:197). Malcolm Fraser won government for the Liberal Party in 1975 and intelligence agencies continued to interfere in Australia's domestic affairs during his leadership. Particular efforts were made to cultivate ties with the right-wing of the trade union movement. Eventually Fraser lost the support of the business community when he refused to adopt market fundamentalism to resolve Australia's deepening economic crisis. In the 1960s CIA agents posing as labor attachés in Australia were grooming Hawke to become president of the powerful Australian Council of Trade Unions (ACTU). According to historian Humphrey McQueen the US informed Australian right-wing union leaders in 1969 that the 'US embassy favoured Hawke for the ACTU presidency against [his opponent] Harold Souter' because Hawke's leadership would support US corporations (McQueen 1998:44). Hawke became particularly close to George Schultz, the head of the Betchel Corporation – a California-based construction conglomerate which continues to have close connections with the CIA with many of its key employees rotating between government and business.

By 1980 the Fraser government faced major economic problems and rising unemployment. The opposition under Hawke's leadership of the Labor Party began to negotiate with the business sector about ways to boost economic growth and create jobs; in exchange for their support he would freeze union militancy. His election as prime minister in 1983 assured the taming of the Labor Party and the unions and set the stage for the neoliberal restructuring of Australia's economy and society. During Labor's reign of power until 1996 the government introduced the most far-reaching political and economic reforms in

Australia since the act of federation of 1901. Market reforms were introduced along the lines of the UK's Margaret Thatcher and Ronald Reagan's US administration. Neoliberal market reforms and the deregulation of the financial market were instrumental in furthering US economic and political interests in Australia. The fall of the Labor government in 1996 came as a result of damages to Australia's social fabric caused by economic rationalism, corruption within the party and growing discontent among Labor supporters that the party had lost its way. Labor policies gave rise to widespread resentment about the unfairness of the system. One outcome was the emergence of Pauline Hanson's One Nation party, which crystallised marginalised Australians resentful of the large intake of Asian migrants, loss of employment and rising inequality.

John Howard's new Liberal coalition government moved the country firmly within the US orbit declaring Australia's role as the US regional sheriff. Under Howard, US influence in government has increased. The decision to invade Afghanistan and Iraq was made without consultation of parliament. Australian intelligence agencies were fed information from the US and the UK to support the prime minister's claim to the nation that Iraq was a threat to world peace and had to be attacked. Howard lied to the country about Iraq's weapons of mass destruction, Iraq's supply of uranium from Niger, and Iraq's involvement in the attack on New York. The government further dismissed the United Nations' usefulness in resolving the crisis and joined with the US unilateral decision to invade Afghanistan and Iraq. Under Howard the equivalent of a US Patriot Act was passed by parliament restricting Australia's civil and political rights. The powers and budgets of Australian intelligence agencies have increased and their activities meshed with those of US intelligence and military administrations.

US interference in Australia's political life continues. Australia's conservative think-tanks and mass media frequently invite US personalities to attack Australians critical of US policies. Targets have included former prime minister Paul Keating, who warned Australians that US policies are fuelling a nuclear arms race and leading the way to a 'Mad Max world' and declared that the Labor Party 'will not be thugged by US officials' (Keating 2003 and 2004). Another recipient of US criticism is former prime minister Malcolm Fraser, who told the country that the US cannot be trusted to protect Australia's interests. In recent years the US has manipulated the Australian Labor Party (ALP), exploiting divisions within the party in a strategy called 'wedge politics'. Among the many targets have been members of the left-wing faction such as former party leader Simon Crean who opposed sending Australian troops to Iraq and supported the UN pathway to resolve the Iraq problem; and former Labor leader Mark Latham who told parliament that 'Bush is the most incompetent and dangerous President in living memory'.

Keeping an eye on labor politics is an old tradition dating back to WWII. The US has spied on Australian politicians to destabilise labor politics in the past and more recently passed information collected on Australian soil to the government during the 1999 East Timor crisis about Laurie Brereton, at the time foreign affairs opposition spokesman. Labor strategist Brereton had earlier warned Australians that US missile Star War plans 'had the potential to severely damage world prospects for nuclear disarmament and trigger a vicious spiral and proliferation – a new arms race'. Former US ambassador to Australia Tom Schieffer, President Bush's political appointee who said he came because 'I've never been to Australia but I hear it's a lot like Texas', received front page coverage when he accused Crean of anti-American activities and of deepening the rift between the ALP and Washington. Crean called Schieffer's 2004 public attack an 'unprecedented interference in Australian politics and unacceptable'.

Attacks against the then leader of the opposition Mark Latham were part of a successful US strategy to shift the leadership to Labor's right-wing faction and undermine Labor's electoral strength at the 2004 Federal elections. President Bush accused Latham of 'emboldening terrorists and endangering the alliance with the US'. Within months the Labor leadership had passed into the hands of Kim Beazley. A former defence minister in the Keating government, Beazley is a friend of US media mogul Rupert Murdoch and a strong supporter of Australia's military alliance with the US and its unilateral military action and preemptive strike policy.

Press reports in 2002 hammered on about Australia 'embracing America's values' and highlighted the government love-fest with the US. In his speech to a special joint sitting of the US Congress, Prime Minister Howard spoke of the common values shared by both countries, and of Australia's commitment to fight alongside the US to preserve 'the fundamental values and liberties that characterised the United States' (Davis 2002). Howard's speech in America's heartland of power confirmed the hold and command of US culture on Australian society. While cultural products such as US movies and music tend to dominate Australia's popular culture, more critical is the influence of US capitalism on the country's political and economic culture. Australia's import of neoliberalism has changed the distribution of political power and damaged the nature of social relations.

Much of the ideological framework of market economics, also known as Anglo-American capitalism or economic rationalism, was formalised in US and UK think-tanks funded by neoconservative and business groups. Neoliberal policies became the mainstay of politics in the UK and the US under the leadership of Thatcher and Reagan in response to a deepening crisis of capitalism which they both faced. During that time, market fundamentalism was brought into the fold of Australian politics and became the mainstay of economic reforms during the Hawke-Keating labor government. The selling of market capitalism in Australia has been the work of a number of neoconservative think-tanks and universities, and mainly US-trained economists who gained control of key ministries and converted ministers and bureaucrats to market fundamentalism.

Selling state assets and the deregulation of the state's traditional functions have transferred political power away from civil society to a small domestic and international business and managerial elite. Moreover, the money politics of the business community has corrupted the political process by giving business groups control over the country's resources and planning process. Non-governmental organisations (NGOs) which provide the links between the state and the people have been co-opted into a managerial and technocratic state structure. The dissenting voice and power of unions, universities and the mass media have largely been neutralised and incorporated into Australia's corporatist structure. Economic rationalism has altered in fundamental ways Australia's social fabric and has generated mechanisms to exclude most Australians from deciding about their country's future. The impact of US-style capitalism has reconstructed levels of inequality in the distribution of income and wealth unseen since the 1920s and 1930s.

The foundations of economic rationalism are a mixture of social Darwinism and eugenics, and claims that the pursuit of self-interest in the marketplace leads to a successful and happy humanity. An extreme version was popularised by Alissa Rosenbaum, a Russian who settled in the US in the 1920s, changed her name to Ayn Rand and began a movement preaching the goodness of laissez-faire capitalism. Her public success played on the human predisposition for selfishness and greed in human relations, and the attraction and benefit of get-rich-quick schemes driven by human appetites and miseries. Among her many famous followers was Alan Greenspan, the Chairman of the US Federal Reserve Board, who wrote a number of articles praising her doctrine and vision. Unlike Buddhism her teaching unburdens humanity of any social obligation except to oneself, and removes constraints on predatory behaviour: to be rich is glorious and the poor deserve their fate for lacking initiative or the will to power. Rand's laissez-faire capitalism anticipated the coming of a postmodern society driven by greed and the need for the market to expand its tentacles to a new range of goods and services. The commodification of new areas of human life and relations under the guise of market forces has proven to be a life-saver for the recurring crisis of capitalism faced with economic slowdown and increasing social and environmental costs.

Australia has become fertile ground for Rand's brand of predatory capitalism. This process has been helped by the new gospel for prosperity, a brand of Christianity also imported from the US. It teaches 'that God shows his approval by dispensing cash, success and good looks on those who obey his laws as interpreted by his preachers' (Macken 2005). A US-based business culture and management model dominates Australia's education and mass media. The country's new heroes are those who make it on Australia's *Business Review Weekly* (BRW) yearly richest 200 list. Remuneration for company directors has reached astronomical sums, while millions of low-wage workers are unable to afford housing in Sydney and Melbourne. Australia's business culture has encouraged business failures and fraudulent activities. The Enron syndrome has been part of Australia's corporate scene since the 1980s. A predatory business culture has led to the collusion of business managers, auditors and supervisory agencies. The mass media has failed in most instances in their responsibility to educate and inform the public, and investigate and expose criminal business activities. Economic rationalism has become a new sophisticated postmodern instrument to plunder the country's resources.

FEAR OF FREEDOM

Australia's integration into the US military and economic empire has important implications for the country's political future and relations with the Asia-Pacific region. Economic and military dependency on the US has put more pressure on Australia to rely on exports of mining and agricultural products at the expense of developing manufacturing and high-technology sectors. The intense use of land and water resources and the resulting environmental degradation are not likely to be sustainable. Dependency on food exports, for example, means that the country is vulnerable to drought, or a situation like an increase in salinity where productivity and yields decline sharply. A reminder of this problem was the 2002–03 tumble of Western Australia's wheat harvest and the importation of feed grain to meet domestic needs. Global warming will increase Australia's cost of production and reduce its competitiveness for food exports. An Australian economy built largely on exporting natural resources to pay for increasingly expensive high-value imports must rely on a large intake of rich migrants to further populate the main southern coastal cities. At the 2004 Sydney's Futures Forum, scientist Tim Flannery, author of *The Future Eaters*, said that global warming and water shortages would turn Perth into 'the twenty-first century's first ghost metropolis'.

Australia's model of development and role as US regional sheriff will put the country on a continued path of confrontation with Asia. Conflict with Asia is an integral aspect of US geostrategy to respond to global economic and social problems by military means. Demands for the good life in Asia and rising frustration among the young will cause anger and the targeting of rich countries like Australia who will be blamed for growing inequality and lack of progress. The militarisation of Australia's continent against China will fuel a new Cold War and a costly regional armament race. Australia's increasing reliance on Asian markets for its livelihood makes it more vulnerable to external political pressure and to demands to settle large numbers of migrants in what is widely perceived in the region to be an underpopulated continent.

Inclusion in the US imperial orbit bears on Australia's political process and democratic regime. Interference in domestic affairs can be expected if Australia shifts away from US expectations. Mel Gurtov reminds us that 'indirect US pressure proved sufficient to cause changes of government in Guatemala (1954), Chile (1973), and Australia (1975)' (Gurtov 1991:17). Australia's role as US sheriff has redefined its relations with the region and emboldened it to threaten its neighbours with the right to preemptive strike. Australia's 'liberation' of East Timor and invasion of Afghanistan and Iraq have damaged its relations with Southeast Asia and China. What happens if multilateral trade negotiations die a slow death because of incompatible demands and the world economy breaks down into regional blocs? What are the consequences if East Asia forms an economic bloc and discriminates against Australia?

There is the suggestion that Australians are now happier than before as measured by the Australian Unity Wellbeing Index, because of the knowledge that the US is their protector (Unity 2003). Bonding with the US gives Australians the feeling that their continent is secure because they know they are backing the winning team and people can get on with the business of getting richer. A recent parliamentary paper suggests that without the US alliance and security Australia could have 'developed as an inward looking, less open and more xenophobic society, a sort of apartheid-era South Africa in the South Pacific' (Brown and Rayner 2001:6). It is more likely that free of US ties Australia would have shaped into a vibrant and independent republic endeared to its indigenous people and with influential and beneficial relations with the region.

3
A Corporate State

Fascism should more properly be called corporatism since it is the merger of state and corporate power.

Benito Mussolini

Australia's liberal democracy is metamorphosing into a form of corporatism which cannot be called fascist in the old sense of the term but nevertheless contains some of its seeds. What is clear, however, is that the country is in transition to a new form of authoritarianism. Social and political development show symptoms that an era of liberalism in Australia has come to an end. Reforms towards a more democratic country and the expansion of civil and political rights and more political equality have stalled while the forces of repression and police power have become more visible and coercive.

FOUNDATIONS OF CORPORATISM

Australia's constitutional foundations are instruments of colonisation. The constitution which formed the basis for the merging of separate colonies into a self-governing federation was an instrument of British power and not the reflection of a free people seeking liberation, independence or some vision of happiness. Australia's constitution was more of a corporate strategic document to legitimise the invasion and occupation of a whole continent, and manage a growing number of white settlers into a viable commercial enterprise. In contrast, the United States constitution incorporated legal instruments to advance and protect human rights and built-in checks and balances to minimise political corruption. These clearly implied that government could not be trusted and that power and integrity resided in the people. To this day, Australia's constitution reflects a particular bias towards a benign form of natural authority, it has no bill of rights and there is little in it that encompasses a vision for its people and their role in advancing the common good.

Australia's colonial modality in modern politics was clearly demonstrated early in the twenty-first century when Australia went to war against Afghanistan and Iraq without a mandate from parliament. In 2002 Prime Minister John Howard committed Australian troops to the US invasion of both countries without the support of elected representatives and against the wishes of the majority of people. This was at a time when UN Secretary General Kofi Anna warned that an attack on Iraq without UN endorsement would be illegitimate under international law. In March 2003 Howard told the country that he had received legal advice that his decision to commit troops against Iraq was his to make because the power to go to war in Australia resides with the executive power of the commonwealth which is vested in the Queen of England's representative in Australia: the governor-general. According to Australia's constitution the governor-general who is nominated by the prime minister but appointed by the Queen of England is the commander-in-chief of Australia's armed forces and also the final arbiter in the country's political life.

The governor-general's office is symbolic of the authoritarian character of the country's democracy. In 1975 the governor-general used his power to dismiss the Whitlam government in what has been called a coup against the Labor Party leader. Journalist John Pilger claims that the governor-general's office was used by conservative forces to dismiss a prime minister who had been declared a threat to Australia's security by the Australia-UK-US intelligence consortium (Pilger 1992). Anglican archbishop Peter Hollingworth's short tenure as governor-general and commander-in-chief of Australia's armed forces clearly demonstrated the continuation of an authoritarian regime, and that the country had yet to establish its secular credentials. Hollingworth's appointment indicated that the ties between church and state were alive and well; this was interpreted in the region as a political statement that Christianity is an integral part of the nation-state's identity and foreign policy.

Australia's military tradition was further advanced when former army general and special services (SAS) commander Michael Jeffery became the new governor-general in 2003. He distinguished himself for bravery in Vietnam's civil war. In recent speeches Jeffery claimed that the Vietnam war was a just war and preached Australia's right and duty to intervene in the domestic affairs of its neighbours. He publicly supported Howard's doctrine of preemptive strike against threats to Australia's national security. Prime Minister Howard's choice as governor-general was in keeping with his government's clash of civilisation foreign policy and Australia's role as US regional sheriff.

The absence of a bill of rights constitutes a major mechanism to exclude citizens from participating effectively in the decision making process. Such regime empowers government to promote apathy among the electorate and to easily dismiss key issues that have to do with Australia's historical situation. In the first instance, government is relieved of the responsibility to implement processes of debate on important issues and educate the public through major budgetary intervention in education and the mass media. Essentially it allows government to make key decisions at the executive level with little or no reference to parliament or the electorate, and to ignore a situation where an increasing number of people are marginalised or excluded from the benefits of economic growth.

A missing social contract between the people and their rulers is a major obstacle to reconciliation with Australia's Aboriginal population and to coming to terms with the country's brutal history and holocaust. The dismissive attitude of government to reports on the stolen generation and other important inquiries regarding past and present harm to Aborigines represents a grave omission in Australia's human rights record. Australia has not signed a treaty which recognises the seizure of the continent from its indigenous people. The nation-state needs to apologise and make amends with the recognition of their status and sovereign rights. Professor Marcia Langton said that the lack of a national treaty 'remains a stain on Australian history and the chief obstacle to constructing an honourable place for indigenous Australians in the modern nation state' (Langton 2002).

Effective participation and political equality are further restricted by the preferential voting (PV) electoral system. Preferential voting denies representation by smaller parties, as in the case of the Australian Greens, and minority or special interest groups such as the Aboriginal and Torres Strait Islander communities. In the 2001 elections, 2.2 million voters or 19.2 per cent of the electorate voted for independent candidates but they won only 2 per cent of the seats. Almost 2 million voters were disenfranchised in favour of the major political parties. Attempts to change the system to a more representative one such as the mixed member proportional system adopted in New Zealand have been strongly opposed by the business community and leaders of the main political parties who see it as a threat to their political power. The political elite is also firmly against giving the electorate the right to a citizen-initiated referendum.

A colonial elitist culture continues to oppose the view that Australians should be trusted to challenge major decisions made without their consent. Attempts to increase citizens' participation in the political process by removing colonial constitutional burdens have failed. The 1996 referendum on whether Australians wanted a republic failed because it was a political exercise manipulated by an elite intent on advancing narrow racist and corporate interests. The process of formulating a referendum on the republic was flawed from its inception by giving control of the process to a small group of people whose intention was to maintain an oligarchy under the British crown.

CORRUPTION OF POLITICS

In Australia's market democracy politicians are entrepreneurs who deliver political goods to the highest bidders. The suppliers occupy privileged positions in society because they maintain a monopoly situation in the supply of such goods. It follows that social justice will not be served if the main political parties do not differ in any meaningful way in what they propose to do. Both Labor and Liberal parties have been captured by neoconservative interests and offer essentially the same menu of neoliberal policies to manage the economy and society. Both parties want a bigger population and encourage migration by the rich, young English-speaker, well educated and preferably white. All stand for preemptive strike and a strong Australia in a close embrace with the United States. There is no longer competition for an alternative society but largely a competition among elites wanting a bigger share of the pie. Politicians are well paid with a range of pension plans and perks which compares well with corporate executives. Politics is an attractive option to gain power and wealth, and, once on the job, there is strong motivation to do what it takes to stay in employment for as long as possible, and encourage your kinsfolk and cronies to join in the business of delivering political goods.

Politicians and their parties need large sums of money to gain and stay in power. Most funds are donations by corporations, business associations, some unions and wealthy individuals. Mainstream politicians are addicted to money from the corporate sector. This is the money that maintains a Labor and Liberal party monopoly on power. More money is moving through this political machine than ever before to meet mounting advertising costs and rising expenditures in networking, vote buying and patronage. There is a bidding war going on among the political elite to deliver political goods to the corporate sector and the wealthy which requires a considerable cash flow. Money involved at the time of the 2001 election was in excess of A$100 million, in addition to more than A$30 million in public funding. At the national level the Liberal and National Party receive more money than the Australian Labor Party, but the situation is reversed at the state level where the ALP controls all state governments. The Greens is the only political party in Australia that does not accept corporate donations.

Large amounts of money pass through the formal system but much more enters the political system indirectly either through loopholes in the legislation on political donations or unlawfully. Mechanisms exist and are devised to channel cash and services to political entrepreneurs and their parties such as the use of think-tanks and trusts, front companies, and the gift of services such as advertising, food, accommodation and software. Other more devious means involve cash in 'brown paper bags', defamation payouts in bogus court cases, and lucrative positions in the private sector in post-politics retirement, the Japanese equivalent of the golden parachute. Political parties are always on the lookout for new means of bidding for their services and employ professional fund-raisers to boost their income. In more recent times the marketing of politicians has been a big fund-raiser. Key figures such as ministers are now accessible for meetings, briefings, conferences, with or without food, for substantial sums. The Liberal Party, for example, has created an organisation called the Millennium Forum which provides access to Howard and his ministers for between ten to twenty thousand dollars a short meeting. Essentially ministers and others sell their time to anyone willing to pay the market price.

Donors expect a return on their investment. Graham Richardson a former Labor minister and power broker in the New South Wales Labor right, and now a friend and employee of the very rich, was honest enough in his book *Whatever it Takes* to say that you are unlikely to get what you want from politicians unless you bid for their services. Your influence on the political machine depends on the amount of money you offer. The mechanisms are varied, some more open than others. One pathway is to change the rules of the game through legislation which favours a particular industry. Another is to provide funding to subsidise various sectors. Those in power have also recourse to other means such as regulatory bodies which enforce and arbitrate compliance. They can change the nature of the regulatory regime to change the level of supervision of various industries. Favouritism is part of the game with the appointment of cronies to commissions, tribunals, committees and various bodies which administer the country. Money politics directly influences the distribution of the costs and benefits of economic growth through taxation and the level of social services such as public health, education and transport.

In the past twenty years money politics and economic rationalism have transformed Australia's society and economy. The election of a Labor government in 1983 marked the beginning of this change. Labor came to power as the result of a deal between the party and the business sector: in exchange for funds and support the party would bring the unions under control and restructure the political and social environment to boost economic growth in favour of the corporate sector. This was the beginning of a symbiotic relationship between business and Australia's leading political party. It brought the ALP firmly under corporate control. From 1983 onwards, Australia witnessed a great wave of deregulation which opened up the economy to new sources of profit. Many valuable public assets were privatised and wealth transferred into a few private hands. The commonwealth was sold at bargain price to the few and made many bankers, lawyers and other insiders instant millionaires. Politicians doing deals with their business mates have become common fare. Under the Hawke government, ministers became close mates with some of Australia's biggest corporate robbers such as Alan Bond and Laurie Connell. Under the Keating administration some ministers extended their influence to business deals in Australia and Asia. Since the 1996 election of a Liberal coalition the relationship between business and politics has gained in strength. Under Prime Minister Howard a symbiotic relationship between corporate money and government policy has been firmly entrenched, and Australia's electorate has been effectively disenfranchised in favour of a corporate oligarchy.

The acceptance of corporate money by political parties is essentially a corrupt practice. Money is received with the understanding that favours will be rendered. Large amounts of money have changed hands in ways which affect politicians behaviour in the design of the political agenda and the legislative process to favour donors. Big sums get big rewards while small donations may help in regard to migration visas. Money politics encourages cronyism with the appointment of major donors and friends to regulatory agencies such as the Reserve

Bank. With every administration many major donors have been found
involved in dishonest practices which cause considerable damage to
society. The scandals of the 1980s and 1990s are being repeated in
the first decade of the twenty-first century, exemplified by the A$5.3
billion collapse of the insurance giant HIH in 2001. Directors of
the company had paid themselves extravagant salaries and bonuses
and days prior to the collapse HIH moved millions of dollars to
their friends. HIH was the largest contributor in the insurance
industry to the Liberal Party and lobbied hard to ease the regulatory
regime of their industry, and to benefit from changes in workers'
compensation, third-party insurance and financial regulations. The
industry succeeded in convincing the government that self-regulation
was good for everyone and this led to the formation of the Australian
Prudential Regulation Authority (APRA) staffed with appointees from
the industry and fellow travellers. APRA has been described by the
former Australian Securities Commission chairman as 'one of the
most useless regulatory bodies on earth'.

Australia's corporate democracy is more discernible and observable
at the state level. Big-city politics provide a full version of the working
of the system because more than 90 per cent of Australians live in
urban areas and mainly around the large and growing urban cores of
Sydney, Melbourne, Brisbane, Perth and Adelaide. At the beginning
of the twenty-first century the ALP controlled all state governments
and every state government had a symbiotic relationship linking
corporate money to the ALP machine. ALP politics is mostly about
economic growth based largely on construction, but also gambling
and sports. The driving force behind the country's political economy
is population growth fuelled by yearly intakes of more than 200,000
new settlers and long-term residents. Most settle in principal cities, and
mainly in Sydney, Melbourne and Perth. There are other important
factors in the model such as the cheap credit. Under economic
rationalism, banks and other institutions are free to print money
by simply offering low interest loans on residential and commercial
property. In addition, a major share of superannuation cash flow of
more than A$50 billion a year has been captured by developers and
construction companies eager to make fast money. But this is not
enough and developers and builders want states to borrow money
to fund bigger infrastructure projects in partnership with the private
sector. The deregulation of the financial and investment sector also
brings more billions of foreign money eager to buy into the country's
real estate market.

New South Wales is Australia's most populous state, and Sydney is Australia's largest and only global city. Sydney has a booming economy with housing prices to match those of other global cities such as New York and Tokyo. The ALP has been for many years reliant on corporate funding to maintain its power hold on the state. In exchange it has delivered a political regime very generous to business. The entire premise is based on fast population growth and the demand for housing and infrastructure and all the ancillary needs linked to rapid urban expansion and coastal development. The ALP has been good for business over the years, particularly with the 2000 Sydney Olympics. New South Wales premier Bob Carr was re-elected for a third term in 2002 under the banner 'Bob the builder'. Sydney's population is in excess of 4 million, and more than 5 million with its adjunct satellites of Newcastle and Wollongong, or 27 per cent of the country's total population. In recent years, Sydney has undergone a massive construction programme worth in excess of A\$10 billion a year. Much of this has been built to accommodate a growing population in urban sprawl suburbia, and medium to high density housing in the city's core and along transport corridors. With this has come important infrastructure work with many new toll roads, tunnels and sport venues.

The state government has been a great friend to developers and builders by making substantial changes to planning legislation, altering zoning, and staffing regulatory bodies with party cronies and friends of the industry. Development controls have been diluted and eased so that builders can bypass local councils and certify their work as complying with state and local requirements. The result is often shoddy planning and work, and the making of tomorrow's city slums. Members of some of the biggest construction companies serve on the state's planning boards that regularly make decisions such as the rezoning of Sydney's harbour foreshore to favour developers who give generously to the party. Premier Carr has been accused of closing Sydney harbour as a working port to free the waterfront for land developers who fund the party machine. Under his leadership the state's Local Boundaries Commission has been instrumental against the wishes of local residents in redrawing boundaries in response to business pressure for fewer councils to simplify and lower their cost of the planning and development process. The people of Sydney have lost their power to control the planning and development of their city. These powers have been largely transferred to a political and technocratic machine which responds almost solely to the bidding process by domestic and foreign business concerns.

Developers and builders are the ALP's major donors followed by union and gambling interests. Money is passed on directly or through other means meant to obscure the process such as fund-raising activities and ministerial briefings. The gambling industry has been successful in the deregulation and the expansion of their industry. The state is increasingly dependent on gambling revenue to fund social services and other budgetary commitments. Sydney's casino is a dominant feature of Sydney's skyline, taller and bigger than the Anglican cathedral, and many reports of large-scale money laundering and other rackets have marred its history. Poker machines have been allowed in pubs and clubs and totalled more than 100,000 in 2003. Pub owners and their powerful lobby, the Australian Hotels Association, hold major fund-raising events for the ALP with big name performers such as former US president Bill Clinton. Many social clubs have become big business by linking their interests with professional sports and gambling activities. Many large public clubs have become more like casinos and their management linked to companies run by insiders. Public campaigns and the mass media encourage people to gamble and considerable numbers of Australians are in trouble because of their gambling habits and the rackets associated with it.

New South Wales (NSW) Liberal Party is also in the corporate money game. The party receives substantial donations from builders, developers and the gambling industry. Business groups use the Liberal and National parties as leverage against their Labor opponent. Major parties compete for power on a common neoliberal platform and fast-paced economic growth for the city and state. There are big rewards for members of the political machine and the competition for funding is intense. Both parties play the game of electoral gerrymandering to improve their chances at the poll. The absence of alternative politics allows the business sector to use the major parties to advantage in a strategy that maximises their profitability and return for their investment in the state's political machine. When Labor can no longer offer what business wants, corporate funding switches to the opposition. The possibility of bringing the Liberal Party back into power assures another cycle of profit for the corporate sector, and continues the growth of Sydney as Australia's primate city.

Capitalism combined with money politics corrupts democracy. Many state and council politicians have received payments from developers and other business interests. Some politicians and their spouses have invested in the gaming and alcohol industry and have benefited from land sales to and from government, and many are linked to companies on the receiving end of state disbursements through directorship of family companies and trust funds. New South Wales parliament ethics committee appears powerless to deal with the situation. Its chairperson Helen Sham-Ho has labelled the government's inquiry into corruption of members of parliament as a cover-up, and as 'inadequate, politicised, unpleasant, frustrating and divisive'. Sham-Ho concluded that the report 'will no doubt be looked at as a precedent for subsequent considerations of failures to comply with pecuniary interest disclosure requirements, not only in this parliament but also in other parliaments throughout Australia and overseas' (Sham-Ho 2002). The powers of the Independent Commission Against Corruption (ICAC) have been diluted in recent years and its independence compromised by the power of the state's money politics.

At the national level the job of regulating money politics comes under the jurisdiction of the Australian Electoral Commission (AEC). The commission is largely ineffective because of limitations in its terms of reference, power and resources. There is also an unwillingness of the political class to change a system that benefits them. Political parties often fiddle their books by logging donations as payments for services rendered by the party, or to one of their front organisations, such as a trust, holding company or a think-tank. Donors also cheat with the nature of their contribution, often omit reporting cash flows to political parties and politicians, or fail to disclose their identity. The overall result is that the commission's records are incomplete, and difficult to access and research. In recent years the AEC has not penalised companies for failing to report donations or submitting false declarations.

Underway is a process to normalise corporate money as having a legitimate political function and community service including the right to move money in ways that do not require reporting to the AEC. Fees paid to ministers and shadow ministers, for example, are not donations and therefore disclosure to the AEC is not required. Other ways include channelling money through entities controlled by political parties such as the Liberal Party's Free Enterprise Foundation or the use of businesses independent of political parties such as the Trustees of Greenfields Foundation and the McKell Foundation.

Markson Sparks company and Labor Holdings both shift millions to both Liberal or Labor parties.

Attempts to limit donations, or move to a full disclosure of the amounts and the identity of donors, have been defeated by politicians. What has been forgotten are the findings of Western Australia's commission which investigated state corruption in the 1980s. Among its final conclusions were the words that 'Ministers have elevated personal or party advantage over their constitutional obligation to act in the community's interests. Public funds have been manipulated to partial ends. Personal associations and the manner in which electoral contributions were obtained could only create the public impression that favour could be bought, that favour would be done'. Recent developments demonstrate that parties and politicians want to be less accountable. In recent years, rules have been changed to further restrict information on political donations and to legitimise the system of money politics as part of Australia's democratic process. The Australian Greens Party policy against corporate funding is a threat to the system and a major reason why the mainstream parties want to destroy the Greens as a political force in national and state politics.

Australia's main political parties have become self-perpetuating oligarchies competing for the same pool of corporate money and offering their services to the highest bidder. Money politics imposes major restrictions on the democratic process by linking corporate money to the political agenda. Under such conditions there can be no political equality for voters who to a large extent are excluded from the decision making process and disenfranchised from political life. In contrast the corporate sector and rich individuals whose fortunes are closely linked to business are given greater control and access to a political regime which works in their favour. Giving the franchise to businesses is a dangerous path to take. In recent years with the extensive privatisation programme carried out by both Labor and Liberal governments, corporations have been given more political power. They now stand as the major source of influence in the political market. It is ultimately the willful denial of the one person, one vote principle on which an open society is founded and survives. The political model of power and funding cannot respond to Australia's most pressing social and economic problems. In Australia as in the US the rise of corporate power has altered the balance of power and corrupted the political process in favour of an oligarchic regime.

CAPTURE OF CIVIL SOCIETY

Power in Australia is controlled by those who dominate the economic and political life of the country. The ideological basis of hegemonic power lies in an anti-democratic form of neoliberalism which pervades Australia's postmodern society. A silent witness to the powerful influence of economic rationalism is the ideological merging of main political parties and the almost total absence of dissent or debate regarding a set of ideas as radical as communism was once. The Productivity Commission has become Canberra's thought police of what Clive Hamilton calls the 'repository of ideological purity' (Hamilton 2003a). Economist Peter Brain has argued that economic rationalism has flourished because Australia is an 'undemocratic society' which he describes as more of a 'dictatorship by special interests' (Brain 2001). What is it about postmodern Australia that has allowed special interests to capture the state and manufacture consent with so much ease, and accept a politics of fear with slogans such as 'be alert but not alarmed' to define its vision of the future? Why do Australians consent to wage an illegal war on Iraq?

Neoconservative forces have been in the process of taking over or destroying civil society. William Kornhauser in his classic *Politics of Mass Society* puts forward a model of political change where the individual is increasingly isolated from an all-powerful state machine. This situation arises because of the absence of genuine intermediary institutions which stand between people and the state. In this process the state captures or destroys intermediary organisations. The state becomes more powerful and tyrannical once it can control the mass media, universities and unions. These and other key organisations can then be used to mobilise, manipulate and control the citizenry. Australia's megamachine is in the process of capturing civil society, and the politics that accompany this profound change are essentially anti-democratic, authoritarian in character and a pathway towards a benign form of fascism.

A clear change is evident in the marginalisation of the Australian union movement in recent years. Membership has fallen from 50 per cent of the labour force in the 1980s to less than 25 per cent in 2003, and is expected to further decline to around 15 per cent. Many workers left the union movement in the 1980s because of the Labor government's accord, and other deals with the corporate sector and business mates to freeze wages and adopt market fundamentalism to deregulate the labour market. Under both Labor and a Liberal coalition, union power to organise and campaign for better work conditions and wages has been sharply reduced. New legislation limits the right to strike, restricts union power to a specific enterprise, and further limits union militancy and capacity to expand its membership. Rights of employers have been enlarged with alternative individual contracts and expensive payouts for union breaches of new labour laws. Some sectors such as the mining industry are trying to get rid of unions altogether by signing workers on individual contracts and refusing to bargain with unions. The process of reducing union power was initiated by London-based mining giant Rio Tinto, which successfully introduced the individual work contract. Rio Tinto's wedge politics of its workforce was given power of the law in a January 2001 federal court's decision in regard to the right of BHP, another London-based mining giant, to offer individual agreements to its workers. In the BHP case, Justice Kenny gave the green light for companies to get rid of unions by providing individual employment contracts.

A Liberal coalition has made substantial progress since 1996 to further deregulate the labour market. Recent legislation further restricts employees' right to strike. The Workplace Relations Amendments Bill of 2003 stops strike action at the enterprise level if one person in the workforce complains to the Australian Industrial Relations Commission. The bill targets the hospital and university workforce as part of a process to further privatise the health sector and bring tertiary education firmly under corporate control. Decline in union power has been concomitant with the restructuring of Australia's economy and major shifts in the nature of employment and work. During the 1990s the percentage of permanent employees fell from 74 per cent to 61 per cent of the workforce, while casual jobs grew from 16 per cent to 27 per cent of all employees. Two-thirds of the job growth in that period came from casual jobs. Pay differentials have increased dramatically with senior management remuneration reaching absurd and obscene heights while nine out of ten net jobs created in the last decade paid less than A$26,000 a year. Decline in the role of unions is also linked to a shift in the politics of the ALP. From a party representing the workers, the ALP has moved to the right of the political spectrum. Since the 1980s it has been a major force in the restructuring of Australia's economy and the adoption of market fundamentalism in politics and social and economic relations.

Universities have failed to act as a counterweight in the attack on democracy waged by neoconservative forces. Tertiary institutions have become integrated into the corporate state to further advance policies of neoliberalism in Australia and the region. The rapid expansion of tertiary education has been accompanied by the transformation of public universities into corporations which respond to business needs and government management directives. Universities' operations have been taken over by a powerful managerial and technocratic elite and transformed into large shopping malls driven by profit and the need to grow big. Many departments and staff are now engaged in business activities which corrupt the integrity of their teaching and research. Management models from the US have introduced a vast array of organisational control techniques directly derived from the military. The establishment of bureaucracies, hierarchies, divisions, censorship and a culture of subservience have seriously endangered academic work and freedom of speech. Academics are now employees selling a product and an image, and their promotion depends on entrepreneurship and marketing. University management is de-unionising and casualising its workforce. Senior managers have organised nationally into a powerful team to lobby government about the best way to fully corporatise and de-unionise their campuses in the name of efficiency and international competition.

Universities have become key centres for the teaching and propagation of neoliberalism. Economic rationalism is the bible of management and dominates teaching in the fields of economics, commerce, law and management which have become the mainstay of university life and funding. Political culture on campuses has moved to the right partly because of the dominance of conservative faculties and the hiring of large numbers of overseas trained economists and other technocrats indoctrinated in the teachings of market fundamentalism and the pursuit of greed. Another trend is the rise of postmodern studies in lieu of the traditional humanities. The deconstruction of the social sciences has been a dominant function with the emergence of postmodernism in Australia's populist culture. The celebration of nothingness, cyberspace and cyberbabble typified by the work of academic McKenzie Wark suggests a postmodern recycling of Filippo Marinetti's 1930s futurist manifesto in praise of Italian fascism.

A key instrument in the pursuit of democratic ideals is the role of the mass media. The concentration in the ownership of the media in Australia should be of great concern to all citizens. Most of the print media is controlled by Rupert Murdoch's News empire and Fairfax. Kerry Packer's Publishing and Broadcasting (PBL) has a substantial share in Fairfax, and controls television stations and some 46 per cent of the country's major magazines. Packer's interests are keen to gain control of Fairfax which would put all major sources of news in the hands of two of the most powerful people in the country. Concentration in the ownership of the mass media has been the policy of both major political parties. Labor leaders in the 1980s helped Murdoch purchase the Herald and Weekly Times Group and lifted restrictions on ownership of television and radio stations. The ALP has made media barons very rich; according to journalist John Pilger Labor policies gave Packer's company and Murdoch's News Corporation a A$1 billion tax free gift (Pilger 1992:286). The process has continued under a coalition government to lift remaining obstacles to what controls are left over media ownership, and further weaken the power of regulatory agencies. Since the 1980s, many independent and alternative sources of news have disappeared including the *National Times on Sunday*, Brian Toohey's *The Eye*, Max Suich's *Independent Monthly*, and more recently *The Republican*.

Dissent is further restricted by defamation laws which restrict free speech. The absence of legal protection of freedom of speech and libel laws are major deterrents to investigative journalism. High defamation costs put fear in anyone bold enough to expose political and corporate corruption. Other restrictions on publishing information are imposed by government censorship of information which it claims threaten national security. New legislation by the Howard government make it illegal for public servants to leak information and for journalists to use such information in their work. A liberal coalition has largely succeeded in changing the content and direction of the Australian Broadcasting Corporation (ABC) which operates the country's only non-commercial television and radio station. ABC's management is so fearful of being critical of government and corporate interests that it has moved ABC's format to harmless discussion and entertainment.

Government has made major inroads in controlling non-governmental organisations (NGOs) with the help of right-wing academics and think-tanks. Neoconservatives want the role and policy of NGOs to be more attuned with conservative thinking. As a result many NGOs have been transformed into providers of government welfare and social services. Australia's public welfare is being downsized and subcontracted to charities such as the Smith Family, the Salvation Army, Wesley Mission and other church-based organisations. Issues of social exclusion have been shifted into the private realm, and religion is seen as a solution to inequality and social problems in Australia. Christian organisations and churches are becoming part of government in the implementation of welfare policies and as a strategic response to the plight of the disadvantaged and needy. Many have been incorporated into government business networks securing large contracts to deliver employment, legal and welfare services. In exchange these charities have given up their right to dissent and criticise government policies. Thanks to the Howard government the Salvation Army has more than A$1billion in assets and earns more than A$300 million a year delivering government services to the poor and needy while discriminating in their hiring policies against homosexuals and non-Christians. Others such as Anglicare and the Uniting Church have gained multi-million dollar contracts to deliver legal aid to society's disadvantaged while building up their tax-free wealth in real estate and commercial investments.

Other NGOs are being incorporated into government management through legislation which redefines the meaning of a not-for-profit organisation and its tax status. Organisations which receive government subsidies have come under government scrutiny about how they use their money and their right to engage in public advocacy. The proposed legislation to control the status of NGOs follows the UK model which denies organisations such as Amnesty International charitable status because of 'excessive' advocacy. A number of organisations are being targeted, such as the Australian Council of Social Services (ACOSS), Greenpeace, Care, Oxfam, and groups that represent women and refugees advocates. The government is also suppressing dissent against their policy by encouraging big corporations to sue individuals and bankrupt them. In 2004 the Tasmanian timber group Gunns, served writs on 20 environmental activists demanding A$6.4 million in damages.

Australia's neo-right think-tanks have helped government muzzle NGOs by supplying research policy papers and media coverage on the issue. The campaign against NGOs has been masterminded by think-tanks such as the Melbourne-based Institute of Public Affairs, and the Sydney Center for Independent Studies. Both have close ties with US neoconservative think-tanks such as the American Enterprise Institute and the Cato Institute. Strategies for muzzling NGOs and for a church-based solution to economic problems have been developed in the US where the Bush administration has a faith-based welfare programme agenda, and provides millions of dollars to Christian groups to support attitudinal change through conversion to fundamentalism. The Howard government has offered A$2.5 million to fund a new supervisory body, or a GONGO (government organised non-governmental organisation), for not-for-profit organisations to enable them to speak 'with one voice'. Another US-based reform is the plan to reshape funding of charitable bodies through tax-free neoconservative philanthropies to encourage the rich to fund bodies similar to the Ford Foundation. Australian neoconservative groups are promoting philanthropy to encourage a more resilient society less dependent on government welfare. Australia's new philanthropy is a mechanism to provide the rich with new avenues to minimise their taxable income and provide funding for groups and political parties preaching market fundamentalism and the virtues of a less egalitarian society.

Aboriginal organisations are a key target in the government's effort to shape and control Australia's intermediary institutions. Government's long-term plan is essentially to integrate indigenous people into a market economy and ease the capitalisation on their land holdings by non-indigenous corporate partners. Land councils and the Indigenous Land Corporation (ILC) have come under much external pressure to link up with corporate interests. One of the key organisations building a future for minority groups has been the Aboriginal and Torres Strait Islander Commission (ATSIC). In recent years ATSIC has become more political and independent with its agenda of self-determination, and even talk of sovereignty. In 2003 the government dismissed its chairman Geoff Clark and moved to disband ATSIC and introduce a new system more attuned to financial, mining and pastoral interests. The model is based on the US Harvard project with native Americans who used land holdings and special legal status to develop natural resources and build tourist and gambling resorts. The government's policy is to privatise indigenous land and integrate Aboriginal people into the market economy.

In Australia as in other postmodern societies, the capture and control of intermediary institutions between the state and the people has been facilitated by the fragmentation of society and the atomisation of individuals. This has been an ongoing process over many generations with major changes in social relations, the socialisation of the young, and the sources of social cohesion. Technology has played a major part in isolating individuals from each other. Sociologist Jacques Ellul has described the process in the context of France's history as social plasticity 'which involved the disappearance of social taboos and natural social groups' (Ellul 1964:49). In a more contemporary context the atomisation of society has enabled a powerful government and an economy based on mass consumption to manipulate individuals and create images of a civil society which no longer exists, and to promote wants and needs which are illusory. In this climate, neoconservative forces can ascend with relative ease and efficiency without a sufficiently strong challenge to reclaim democracy.

Social movements are no longer powerful enough to oppose the rise of neoliberal forces in Australia. The anti-systemic movement is disorganised, fragmented and largely ineffective in confronting a powerful and well-funded neoconservative front. Some movements tend to dwell on cultural or sexual matters which focus on the self and are narcissistic in nature. Many are consumer oriented and too often based on single issue platforms. Most have no political agenda that address inequality and the nature of democracy and power. Many are oriented towards widening the role of litigation and compensation in resolving social problems. Consumer groups that strive in conditions of political apathy reinforce the existing status by encouraging greed and selfishness as worthy social goals. Only the Greens movement and political party provide an alternative in today's political climate. The Greens party has gone beyond environmental issues and embarked on an ambitious social and economic agenda which clearly contests neoconservative hegemony. Only the Greens Senators had the courage to criticise President Bush during his visit to Australia's parliament on 23 October 2003 and to protest against Chinese President Hu's address to parliament on the following day. Neoconservatives are sufficiently threatened by the Greens that they have made several attempts to destroy the integrity of the party. More recently in opening the campaign against the Greens, Queensland Liberal Senator George Brandis called the Greens a sinister force and likened them to the Nazis in their 'hatred of globalisation'.

Most people in Australia's postmodern society are sufficiently pliable and atomised to function effectively in various public and private organisations throughout their life stages. People move through schools, work and living environments, using skills and information generated by market needs. Individuals have become cogs in an efficiently working megamachine run by a sizeable army of experts who manage individuals' existential and physical needs. Australia's therapeutic society provides experts to manage individuals' compliance with the demands of a postmodern society. Technocrats resolve the contradictions imposed by a society which encourages narcissistic and greedy lifestyles. Experts also create false needs to resolve the psychological anxieties they create. A therapeutic culture depoliticises society and shifts economic and social issues to problems of individual behaviour and personality. This allows for behavioural modification rather than changing how society works. A similar process channels political dissent into mass sports and entertainment, the consumption of more goods and services, and harmless social movements or cyberspace Dadaism.

Neoconservative power in Australia relies on a sizeable technocracy which manages and coordinates the country's sizeable administrative and planning machinery but also caters to a wide range of individual social and psychological needs. People in Australia's postmodern society are in the hands of experts who are the repository of knowledge as to why things must be the way they are. Frank Fisher describes technocracy as a 'system of governance in which technically trained experts rule by virtue of their specialized knowledge and position in dominant political and economic institutions' (Fisher 1990:17). The experts have scienticised social and economic life and decide for us what society should and must do. A technocracy takes away from people their needs to participate and make decisions about issues and events that are critical to their well-being. Instead of promoting feelings of security, emotional dependency on technocrats leads to a mood of powerlessness that can easily translate into moods of anxiety and fear. These problems also fall within the realm of a regime of experts in human management.

What is seldom appreciated is what Robert Putnam calls technocracy's 'deep-seated animosity towards politics'. Putnam argues that the technocracy mindset is particularly antagonistic to democratic politics because of beliefs that 'technics' should replace 'politics', that what they do is apolitical, and that social and political conflict are unnecessary. Technocrats are often hostile towards politicians and political institutions and believe that policy is a question of pragmatics not ideology. Moreover, technocracy views technological progress as necessarily good and that issues of social justice, political openness and equality are unimportant (Putnam 1977). Australia's technocracy has become part of a neoconservative governing political culture. Sociologist Michael Pussey has chronicled Canberra's capture by economic rationalists. He tells how technically trained economists gained control of key federal institutions in Finance, Treasury and the Prime Minister's Office, and how policy making became the realm of hardline fundamentalists (Pussey 1991).

CULTURE OF SECRECY

'Knowledge is power' writes Jeremy Pope, 'and those who possess it have the power to rule' (Pope 2003). A culture of secrecy keeps Australians from finding out too much about their government, society, and the state of the country. It keeps the electorate docile and excludes citizens from engaging in informed debates about issues of local concern and national importance. Secrecy corrupts state and society and allows state power to be captured by anti-democratic forces which proceed to further erode society's right to know.

State and federal governments have adopted a culture of secrecy in their operations and in their relations with the public. Australians are increasingly denied access to information to which they are entitled. With the widespread privatisation of public assets, state administrations are keen to hide their dealings with the corporate world from the public. Government outsourcing of services is often by way of confidential contracts whose content cannot be made public. The use of commercial-in-confidence (CIC) contracts is a major mechanism to hide information from parliaments. Other types of information are kept out of the public realm by restrictions on the Freedom of Information Act which enable public servants and politicians to deny access on various grounds. Most government funded research by university and other research organisations, for example, is not published nor made available for public use. Scrutiny of governance is also limited by imposing restrictions on regulatory agencies such as the Auditor-General or Ombudsman.

New South Wales main watchdog, the Auditor-General, has condemned government for refusing him access to documents and allowing elected officials to evade accountability on issues ranging from secret deals with construction companies to matters concerning the police, public hospitals, and jails. The same has been said by the federal government's Commonwealth Ombudsman who in his 1999 report concluded that government was 'misusing the extensive exemptions of the [Freedom of Information] act often enhancing these powers with imaginative reasons to deny access to documents'. Since 2001 government powers to deny information to the public have become more widespread and obtuse because of Australia's war on terrorism.

While government is less transparent and keeps more secrets from the public it is granting powers to the corporate sector to find out more about what people do and think. Under the Privacy Amendment

Bill new powers have been given to data-mining companies to access information about individuals and businesses. The entire recorded history of individuals available in public and private data banks can now be assembled into one profile by large corporations and marketed for a substantial fee to government and business. More dangerous are the expanded power and role of spying agencies to fight the war on terrorism. The Australian Security and Intelligence Organisation (ASIO) can now arrest, detain and question individuals on 'suspicion of involvement in or have knowledge of a terrorist act, or have information about terrorism' (NewMatilda 2005). Under the New South Wales Terrorism Bill the police have been given extensive powers of interrogation, search and seizure without adequate checks and balances against abuse, and the power to use covert warrants to search properties without telling the occupants they have done so. Justice Michael Kirby, the only outsider in Australia's conservative High Court, has warned of a decline in civil and political rights in the wake of Australia's Orwellian terrorism laws.

A campaign waged by the government and media for a US-like Patriot Act has already led to a wave of fearmongering about 'Middle-Eastern and Asian looking types', and attacks against Mosques and women wearing a head scarf in public. Australia's spying agencies and the Australian Federal Police (AFP) can now spy on and punish those who disclose information deemed to be prejudicial to 'national security', or individuals 'who can substantially assist the collection of intelligence that is important in relation to a terrorism offense'. New powers potentially target a large range of organisations and individuals including community-aid and environmental groups, journalists and teachers, while prohibiting media access or coverage of spying and police actions.

Under the Intelligence Services Act, Australia's top secret satellite spy agency, the Defence Signals Directorate (DSD), has the right to spy on Australians on grounds ranging from national security and foreign relations to Australia's economic well-being. Politicians have been on the receiving end of the DSD's attention. One recent operation targeted Laurie Brereton when he publicised East Timor's militia close links with Indonesia's military. Brereton, then foreign affairs opposition spokesperson, told the press in 1999 that the government knew that the East Timor militia movement was an extension of Indonesia's Kopassus. Brereton's harsh criticism of the Indonesian military became an embarrassment to the government. The DSD's operations against Brereton involved the Australian Security and

Intelligence Organisation (ASIO), and the Australian Federal Police (AFP) which used intelligence obtained by foreign governments probably from the US and possibly Singapore.

Two years later the DSD was used by the government to intercept communication to and from the Norwegian ship *MV Tampa*. The ship had rescued 438 asylum seekers near Australia's Christmas Island in August 2001 but the government refused to let the ship disembark its human cargo on Australian territory and ordered Special Air Service (SAS) troops to board the vessel. Telephone calls were intercepted between the ship's captain, the Maritime Workers Union of Australia and other parties including Australian-based lawyers and Norwegian foreign ministry officials. This saga took place weeks before a federal election during which the government ran a fear campaign that the country was under threat of invasion by asylum seekers from the Middle East and other parts of Asia.

The role of Australia's overseas spying agencies has been expanded in the name of national security. Organisations operated by military and civilian authorities run covert operations in a number of countries in cooperation with the US and UK, and involve dirty business which would be deemed unlawful and criminal under Australian law. Some operations have targeted the movement of refugees from Southeast Asia to Australia. Indonesia has been a focus for covert work to sabotage refugee boats. There have been allegations that the asylum-seeker vessel code-named SievX (suspected illegal entry vessel) by Canberra, which sank off Christmas Island in October 2001, had been sabotaged before leaving Indonesia. Canberra had detailed intelligence about the boat's journey and probably the time and place of its sinking, killing 353 refugees including many women and children.

Spying leads to deceitful behaviour by politicians and bureaucrats and the corruption of power. A culture of secrecy encourages government to lie about what they know and do. Government officials have lied to the public in recent years about important issues which have a bearing on Australia's democracy and foreign relations. Government lied to the public about refugees seeking protection in Australia in order to generate a climate of fear and swing the electorate behind them in the November 2001 federal election. A prime minister, ministers of the crown and leaders of the defence force lied to a parliamentary inquiry in their claims that refugees had thrown children overboard in October 2001 in an attempt to force the navy to bring them to Australia. The lying in the children overboard case involved senior officials including senior public servants from the Defence Department, the Immigration Department, the Office of the Prime Minister and Cabinet, along with navy officials and intelligence officers from the Office of National Assessments. The manipulation of the *MV Tampa* and children overboard affair by the government and mass media created a climate of fear and hatred against Asians, and was a decisive factor in the re-election of a neoconservative government in 2001.

Government secrecy and deception of the electorate compromises the country's foreign policies and relations. In 1999 the government knew that Indonesia's military-backed militia was preparing to cause havoc in East Timor after the December UN-sponsored referendum. Had this information been made public much of the destruction and killing which took place after the referendum could have been prevented. Australia's foreign affairs department kept secret their intelligence about a possible terrorist attack on Bali, four months before the October 2002 Bali nightclub bombing which killed 88 Australians. In 2002 Prime Minister Howard lied to the public in regard to Iraq's weapons of mass destruction and why Australia had to go to war against Iraq. Senior former bureaucrats have accused the prime minister of knowingly using discredited information to justify an attack on Iraq in 2003.

Some have argued about a culture of fear in the bureaucracy. Employees of the Office of National Assessments, Foreign Affairs and the Defence Intelligence Organisation knew the case for mounting an invasion of Iraq was based on poor evidence or false intelligence yet did not prevent government officials lying to the public about Iraq's weapons of mass destruction and other evidence used by the government to invade Iraq. Retired major-general Alan Stretton has argued that ministerial staff put firewalls to prevent information reaching ministers. Moreover, ministerial staff including the Prime Minister's Office are involved in manipulating information to manufacture consent. Former intelligence analyst Andrew Wilkie testified that the dossier on Iraq was significantly altered by senior bureaucrats close to the prime minister to fit into the US/UK public spin and make a case to sell Australia's war on Iraq to the public.

Australians show a great deal of apathy about fundamental questions of government accountability and transparency. Few questions have been raised about the greater powers given to spying agencies and the new laws that undermine the country's democratic process. There have been few signs of public outrage about government lies and deceptions in recent years, and no formal condemnation of a prime minister misleading the country to invade Iraq. Have Australians become cynical about politics or simply do not care, or is the electorate sufficiently in tune with the neoconservative leadership to support its policies? Secrecy leads to a decline in trust in the system and to post-retirement outbursts such as that of former deputy governor of the Reserve Bank John Phillips, who declared at a 2003 Sydney meeting of Australian Business Economists that 'financial institutions are not to be trusted, that they are rapacious and not particularly ethical'. Secrecy in business as well as in government is the enemy of democracy and leads to public disquiet and the erosion of trust.

Secrecy is democracy's greatest enemy. A fundamental test in politics is the extent to which the public knows what government does. Australia's situation has worsened in recent years as more government business becomes confidential information and is conducted in secrecy away from public scrutiny. An apparatus of secrecy is being built at both federal and state level to reduce the accountability of politicians and hide their transactions from public eyes. Governments have become increasingly obsessed with secrecy in the name of commercial or national interest. This allows the subversion of checks and balances on power and the corruption of public life.

POLITICS OF CONTROL

All major parties use fear and hatred to manipulate public opinion and gain support for their proposed market remedies to social and economic problems. A culture of fear creates anxieties, paranoia and demands for security which in turn promotes aggression and mass killing. Fear and hatred have been major elements used to manufacture Australia's social cohesion and political hegemony. The construction of the nation-state was founded on hatred of Asians and the ethnic cleansing of Aboriginal people. Later came the yellow peril, the threat of Red China and fear of invasion by boat people. Presently, Australia is waging a war on terrorism and radical Islam. Politicians have warned the electorate that the war on terrorism will last decades. Some Christian religious leaders have denounced Islam as the work of the devil and Australia's leading Catholic George Pell, Archbishop of Sydney, told the Acton Institute for the Study of Religion and Liberty in 2004 that Islam could be the new communism.

All these images and events have imprinted on the mass psyche a siege mentality which has been carefully nurtured by politicians and mass media to advantage. Social cohesion has been maintained on the basis of turning domestic aggression against other people. In recent years hatred has been manufactured against those seeking freedom in Australia. The majority of asylum seekers who have landed in Australia without an entry visa arrive from Asia fleeing war conditions, persecution, and conditions of economic despair. In Australia they are incarcerated under harsh conditions in remote detention camps for long periods of time. Refugees including many women and children have been badly treated and traumatised by their experience in Australia and some have committed suicide. Among Somalian asylum seekers some have asked to be returned because they would prefer possible death and torture in their country than to endure the conditions of Australia's detention camps. Most refugees caught by Australian authorities have been deported and there are known cases of returnees who are killed for their religious or political views.

Government and mass media have successfully demonised refugees in the minds of many Australians. This campaign generates ethnic hatred linking Asians and people of 'Middle Eastern appearance' and Muslims to threats of terrorism and Islamic fundamentalism (Poynting 2004). Before the 2001 federal election, Prime Minister Howard made a point of warning of public anger if boat people were let in and claimed many Australians blamed Muslims for the attack on New York's World Trade Center. Australia introduced various measures to interdict access to Australia by refugees coming by boat from the north. A military security cordon has been put into place to patrol northern approaches to the continent linked with intelligence agencies' covert operations to sabotage refugee boats at points of departure in Indonesia. In a more recent development Australia has excised part of northern Australia and its off-shore islands from Australian territory. This clever legal device denies asylum seekers the right to claim refugee status in Australia and allows government the right to deport individuals to their country of origin, or to detention camps funded by Australian aid in Papua New Guinea and Nauru as part of the Pacific solution to the refugee problem.

Samuel Huntington's clash of civilisations thesis finds widespread support among Australia's middle class and intellectuals. According to Huntington's logic, Australia is on the front line in the battle between the West and the rest. The fault line lies on its northern approach which marks the great divide between Western and Sinic civilisations. The alliance between China and Islamic forces is part of the conflict going on in Australia's north and could easily spread to mainland Australia. Terrorism is an expression of the clash of civilisations in the minds of many and justifies Howard's preemptive strike policy in Asia if Australia's national interests and those of its US patron are threatened.

The terrorist threat to Australia has been medicalised by the media with images of a fast-spreading malignancy which undermines and destroys the organic integrity of the country. Medical imagery is a powerful means to manipulate public opinion and entice people to act badly towards others. Nazis ran entire academic and government departments to dehumanise some ethnic groups, and to study Jews and others as carriers of deadly disease. In the minds of millions of Europeans, Jews became rats infected with the bubonic plague intent on destroying the 'purer races' and had to be exterminated to save civilisation. Sixty years later, Australia's military top commander used similar terminology to describe terrorism as the new disease and plague of the century. Admiral Chris Barrie who became Chief of the Defence Force (CDF) in 1998 called terrorism a form of cancer which needs 'a combination of treatment. I like to think the military action that's underway is like radical surgery' (Wise 2001).

Australia's politics of control also promote fear about domestic crime. Fear for your personal security and the safety of your wealth because of widespread criminal activity is a useful tool to maintain social control and power. University of Western Australia's David Indermaur argues that the fear of crime in Australia is closely related to the nature of political power (Indermaur 2003). The political regime and the police have a close relationship beneficial to both parties. Fear of crime is used by politicians to maintain their power base and manipulate the voting public at election time. Political agendas are not focused on social and economic policies to address the crime issue but only to create community fear to maintain or gain power. The police force is also driven by power inflation and a demand for bigger budgets. The solution to crime through spending on education and employment opportunities is an unattractive political option because it requires substantial change to the marketplace and an increase in taxation which are likely to be unpopular and corrupted by the opposition to political advantage. Crime and the fear of crime wins elections, sells more products and services, and benefits both the market and the political regime that sustains it. State and federal law enforcement budgets are increasing and the country is building more jails to accommodate a rising prison population.

Neoliberal policies increase certain types of crimes as well as the community's levels of anxiety. A consumer culture and market approach to social issues encourages a wide range of destructive and anti-social behaviour. This situation in turn generates greater police powers and budgets, and the growth of low paid employment in the security sector. Drug addiction, an illicit drug market, and government dependency on gambling revenues create widespread crime against property such as break-ins and car thefts. Perpetrators are seldom arrested because the police force is not particularly interested in dealing with the problem and will complain about shortage of resources. New South Wales Solicitor-General Michael Sexton claims that 'housebreaking has been decriminalized in Sydney because it is frequently unreported and seldom investigated' (Sexton 2000). At the state level, political parties receive a large share of their corporate funding from interests linked to gambling and alcohol. In New South Wales, for example, much of the money funding the ALP comes from the gambling industry and the hotel lobby which represents some of the most violent pubs in the country.

Australia's culture of fear encompasses environmental and health issues. Threat of natural disaster and imminent death are being played out to the community on an almost daily basis. In 2003, for example, the mass media and government scared the entire population about the spread of Severe Acute Respiratory Syndrome (SARS) with hysterical headlines and absurd claims that tens of millions could be killed, at a time when the government was busy privatising public health and hiding the tragic state of health of Aboriginal people. Scaring the public to death is a game played by many parties with different agendas. Threat of death by fire or disease is largely diffused by academics and think-tanks funded by the insurance industry. Demographic anxiety is another theme in the politics of fear. An overpopulated Australia is a theme often captured by racist groups who disguise their neo-Nazi leanings in their discourse about environmental degradation and global warming. Another is the 'ageing crisis' and the 'war of generations' campaign under way in 2004 which claimed that the young are too poor and the old too rich, and that the young could soon be attacking the old for their money unless the young became richer. Much of that nonsense is spread by research funded by the financial industry and pension funds looking for new sources of income and more government handouts.

Australia's advanced capitalist society uses a wide variety of means to control behaviour, and chemicals occupy a special place as a major tool of human management. The health system has medicalised a wide range of situations which require drug therapy. An Australia Institute study shows that 'nearly one in five Australian adults reported that in the two weeks prior to the survey they had used medication to improve their mental well-being' (Hamilton 2003). The Australian Bureau of Statistics reported that 'nearly one in five adult Australians had had a mental disorder at some time in the previous twelve months and around the same proportion are expected to have a major depressive episode at some time in their lives' (ABS 1999). The Northern Territory had the highest prevalence of mental disorders affecting 26.5 per cent of the adult population (PC 2001). General practitioners write more than 500 scripts a year for every 1,000 Australians over the age of 15. More than 7 million scripts were written in the first eight months of 2002 for new generation anti-depressants Prozac, Aropax, Zoloft, Cipramil, Efexor and Serzone (Robotham 2002).

Among teenagers Retalin is increasingly used to control Attention Deficit Hyperactivity (ADHD) but there are other drugs on the market such as Dexedrine to meet what is a growth industry involving more and younger children. Australia came after the US and Canada as the third largest user of ADHD drugs in the world. Experts in alcohol and drug treatment are examining the possibility of legalising ecstasy for treatment of post-traumatic stress disorder. Ecstasy was widely prescribed in the US to couples undergoing marriage counselling in the 1970s and is seen as a potentially useful drug to help victims of rape and sexual abuse. Many Australians depend on alcohol and illicit drugs to cope with their mental state. A 2002 survey showed that some 27 per cent among 14 to 19 year-olds had used illicit drugs over the previous twelve months. The rate increased to 36 per cent for the 20 to 29 year-olds, and to 20 per cent for the 30 to 39 year-olds (AIHW 2002:36). Mass consumption of drugs indicate their importance in a market economy focused on economic growth rather than on democratic politics to resolve social problems. Eventually the cost of society's therapeutic controls is reflected in the increased consumption of health services and a health budget of more than A$60 billion in 2002, or an increase in health expenditures from 7.9 per cent of gross domestic product in 1990 to more than 10 per cent in 2002. This figure would probably double if it included the contribution of alcohol and illicit drugs to economic growth.

Multiculturalism has been a useful tool to re-educate the majority about a changing society and redefine Australia's image as a society made up of people from all over the world. A considerable effort has been made to create a new national image of a highly desirable and marketable identity which blends together what is best from all over the world within the colours and landscapes of Australia's continental geography. Multiculturalism nevertheless continues to embody a power distribution highly advantageous to the dominant culture and allows political power to stay firmly in the hands of an Anglo-Celtic minority. Multiculturalism has been successfully marketed by universities with the rise of new academic centres in cultural, media and postmodern studies. The study and emphasis of cultural differences leads to new forms of discrimination because it categorises people into ethnicities. An ethnic in Australian parlance is someone who does not claim British heritage and values, and is therefore not a member of Australia's dominant culture. This is a device which is particularly useful to disengage indigenous people from society and identify them within a special category of people. Categorisation leads to new forms of inequality and discrimination. Only non-Anglos suspected of a crime are described by their ethnic appearances as part of the state's bureaucratic classification of 'races'.

A process of pseudo-speciation is increasingly dividing Australian society. Erik Erikson has described the phenomenon as a form of cultural fragmentation where a group's source of strength and cohesion is based on the negative feelings for those outside the group (Erikson 1966). Social construction of identity however, harbours within it its own negative identity and becomes a source of friction in the socialisation process of youth and the reconciliation of peoples. The reassertion of ethnicity and race as a viable alternative has been facilitated by government and media policy to cultivate ethnic separateness, and more importantly by a search for meaning and self-esteem in an affluent postmodern society which is morally bankrupt because of the inroads of economic rationalism. Pseudo-speciation announces the resurgence of social Darwinian ideas in Australian political and economic life.

Social Darwinism has re-entered academic discourse and the curriculum in postmodern and environmental studies, and also in areas of management, commerce and economics. One outcome is that many young people have little understanding of politics, regional affairs and the meaning of democracy. Cultural relativism teaches the existence of so-called Asian values and denies the abuse of human rights by many governments in the Asia-Pacific region. Market forces have become the new credo to explain the social construction of identity and to promote one-world only for money and the rich. Business studies cleverly disengage greed and inequality from the exploitation of people and the abuse of human rights. Domestically, cultural relativism facilitates the intense marketing and profiting from Aboriginal culture and art among the white middle class while indigenous Australians live in poverty with a life-span some twenty years shorter than for white Australia.

The dominance and use of ethnicity in Australian society is misguided and destructive of the social fabric because of the failure of multiculturalism to provide shared core values to hold society together. Multiculturalism teaches cultural diversity and tolerance of difference without common and higher grounds for collective action and purpose. It weakens and fragments Australia's political culture because it promotes the competition of groups in the pursuit of consumption and pleasure, and the accumulation of more riches. Multiculturalism fails to promote social justice because it is essentially a mechanism to assure the hegemony of economic rationalism and market relations in Australian society. Missing are values about democracy and democratic ideals which clearly set out the foundations for the country's existence and aspirations both at home and in the world. These are nowhere to be found in the current political discourse except as propaganda by elected representatives. There is no constitution or bill of rights that sets out primary and core democratic principles. Australia's monarchist ties to Britain continue to advance a colonial mentality and pretension to political equality.

Government manipulates important issues of citizenship and civil society to divide and threaten the electorate. Wedge politics and the politics of guilt are used to advantage and consolidate the power of a small elite. Mass political advertising about civil society, social obligation and 'living in harmony', and campaigns about un-Australian activities and terrorism are meant to manufacture consent about domestic inequality and aggression against other countries, and more generally shift the country's political culture further to the right. Mass media and a sports culture are busy broadcasting images and myths about 'Aussies' and a national character based on 'mateship, and egalitarianism'. In these circumstances it is not surprising that nationalism and patriotism are on the agenda, pushed by well-funded neoconservative elements. Australian history is being reconstructed to obliterate images of invasion and the destruction of indigenous people. A new history is emerging to show the coming of the British as liberators and agents of progress.

Patriotism is encouraged by campaigns to glorify Australia's soldiering and wars. Anzac (Australian and New Zealand Army Corps) day, the commemoration of past military feats and failures has been attracting more young people. Gallipoli's Anzac Cove, where Australia lost thousands of soldiers in a futile attempt to gain a foothold on Turkish soil, is the site of yearly quasi-religious pilgrimages and rituals by Australian sports teams, backpackers and politicians. The cult of Anzac is being promoted by the government. In 2003 at the dedication of an Australian war memorial in London, Prime Minister Howard, who never saw a day of military service, glorified Australian war dead as defenders of justice and freedom. Howard's visit to London's Australian war memorial was symbolic of efforts to reassert Australia's Anglo-Celtic identity and geopolitical alliance, and also a call to arms to shape the new world order with the United States against the infidels.

NEW AUTHORITARIANISM

Australians have traditionally looked at the state to advance political and economic rights and further political equality. Liberal reform has been the work of the state in providing public services and social security, health, education and improvement in the quality of life. Only the state has the resources and the power to bring about macroeconomic reforms to advantage the majority of the population. One of the state's major instruments in achieving social betterment has been the power of redistribution through the tax system. This has been the social component of the state and the true essence of democracy.

The era of liberal reform came to an end in the 1980s with the election of a Labor government backed by big business with an agenda to introduce Thatcher-Reagan-type neoliberal reforms. Labor conversion to economic rationalism and the recession that Australia 'had to have' was followed by a Liberal government which further advanced market fundamentalism with its social Darwinian view of the world. Culture and society are being reshaped to commercialise and commodify every aspect of life. Pierre Bourdieu describes the process as the manifestation of neoliberalism's 'utopia of endless exploitation' (Bourdieu 1998). A key instrument used has been the privatisation of collective wealth which has transferred vast amounts of wealth into the hands of the few and further consolidated the political power of the corporate sector. This mechanism and other legislative changes to deregulate the labour and financial markets have shifted the balance of power from citizens to big business. Money politics and control of the mass media provides the leverage for business interests to control elections and the elected members of both houses.

The re-election of the Howard government in 2004 and its control of both houses clears the way for significant changes to further deregulate the labour market, sell off major public holdings such as Telstra and Qantas, and increase privatisation of education and the health sectors. Privatisation of public assets has continued under public-private partnership (PPP) deals to transfer ownership of public land and infrastructure into the hands of large corporations. The Australia Business Council and other influential lobby groups have given the government directives for tax cuts and labour productivity measures and the importation of skilled migrants to maintain profitability and Australia's export competition.

Australian society today is less egalitarian than it was in the 1970s. Economist Fred Argy argues that on four basic criteria of (a) effectiveness of welfare safety net, (b) shared incremental benefits of economic growth, (c) equality of opportunity, and (d) effective participation in the workplace, Australia is 'definitely a less economic egalitarian society than it was in the mid 70s' (Argy 2002:18). Justice is less accessible today because of high legal costs, and justice is largely a matter of what you can afford to pay. Whatever 'mateship' means it certainly does not apply to the rising number of homeless people, or to asylum seekers locked in detention camps or pushed back to sea. Argy claims that politicians can lie about the state of the country by clever opinion management and get away with it because of 'the high costs to individual voters of acquiring information; electoral apathy; the infinite capacity of politicians to manipulate the popular media; and the uneven ability of citizens to participate in political activity, with increasingly sophisticated and well-resourced global business and finance interests dominating the field' (Argy 2002:20).

Australia's policy of economic rationalism and narrowed focus on economic growth obscures rising social and economic problems reflected in statistics on health, crime, unemployment, land degradation, and rising inequality. Journalist Deborah Hope has written about the personal side of these issues because she was appalled by the treatment of the old and dying she observed while attending her father in his dying months. She writes 'whether you're talking about family relationships, the impact of longer working hours and downsizing, epidemics in stress and depression, the state of health, faltering community responsibility, teen suicide, aged care and public schooling, or our unwillingness to commit to voluntary service, I'm regularly confronted with evidence that a boom economy does not always equate with better quality of life' (Hope 2000:30). Clive Hamilton suggests that there has been a decline in the quality of life for most Australians because of the high costs of unemployment, pollution, accidents and land degradation, and other costs linked to economic growth in recent years (Hamilton 1997). Yet there have been few signs if any of political disruptions or counter-hegemonic social movements. Part of the explanation may be found in the effectiveness of social controls and repression of dissent in Australia's postmodern society.

4
Politics of Greed

The individual position is such that his egotistical drives are constantly being accentuated while his social drives progressively deteriorate.
Albert Einstein

Neoliberalism combines capitalism with neoconservative ideas about society and the world. It presents a modern version of social Darwinism because it justifies the market as the primary social space for the struggle of individuals over wealth. In this modern version of the survival of the fittest, market competition sorts out people and ranks them according to their success in getting rich. Those who succeed best at the accumulation of riches are also the most powerful and the natural leaders of society. According to the gospel of economic rationalism, this form of social existence propels economic growth and the accumulation of wealth, and maximises individual happiness.

Australia's postmodern culture is ensconced in the pursuit of pleasure and the gratification of needs and wants manufactured by an economy dedicated to greed. The message for all is to search for happiness and well-being in the accumulation of wealth and the consumption of goods and services; in the pursuit of happiness it is good to be selfish and a self-serving egoist. Market fundamentalism teaches that the aim of life is happiness and to be happy you have to win, and to win you need to get rich.

Neoliberalism is transforming Australian society on the basis of an ideology which preaches the virtues of self-interest, laissez-faire capitalism, and money as the root of all that is good. Neoliberalism became a mainstay in the politics of the UK's Margaret Thatcher and in the US under Ronald Reagan, and became firmly anchored in Australia with the election of Bob Hawke's Labor government in 1983. In all three instances, market politics was a reaction to an economic crisis and a push by the corporate sector to revitalise economic growth through market capitalism and a symbiotic relationship between the public and private realm. The merging of state and corporate business was refined in Western Australia and Queensland in the

1980s. In Western Australia the interests of the governing Labor Party soon coalesced with those of the corporate sector. So blatant was the problem that the state became known as Western Australia Inc. The main beneficiaries were a small political and business elite, and the state model of governance became outstanding for its absence of openness, integrity and accountability. Since the 1980s economic rationalism has made major inroads in all states promoted by a culture of greed.

CULTURE OF GREED

Civil society is stronger when there is a shared feeling that the system is fair to all. A sense of equity goes a long way in establishing social capital and the trust needed to minimise political corruption. The role of the elite is important because they represent to the electorate values and behaviour which consolidate society and to which all can aspire. Sociologist John Carroll makes the point that 'the good of a society depends on the quality of its elites. But when a self-serving elite wedded to an excusing culture allows a radical liberalism to flourish, we get an anarchic free-for-all without morality' (Carroll 2000:18). In recent years neoliberalism has undermined civil society by allowing the corporate sector to impose their values on society, and the country's elite to enrich themselves at the expense of the common weal.

Greed has become a pervasive aspect of elite behaviour and a major force in an economy of plundering. The political and corporate sector have merged for the financial benefit of a minority, thereby encouraging the widespread corruption of government and state institutions. The blending of private and public interests by many members of Australia's elite suggests a serious loss in the integrity of positions of trust in politics, education and business. Elite behaviour in contemporary Australia shows an insatiable drive which Robert Heilbroner would explain as the 'gratification of unconscious drives' which have to do with aggression, power and domination (Heilbroner 1988:37). Modern capitalism, Heilbroner argues, forms a larger and powerful social setting 'in which the pursuit of wealth fulfils the same unconscious purposes as did the thirst for military glory in earlier times'.

Chief Executive Officers (CEOs) are paid vast sums of money for the privilege of running the economy, and earn on average more than A$3 million a year when options and other bonuses are included. In the financial sector the level of greed reached new heights with the privatisation of public assets and the federal government legislation on compulsory superannuation. Compulsory savings transferred more than A$550 billion from 1987 to 2004 into the hands of wealth managers who became rich quickly on their guaranteed percentage and fat bonuses. This act transferred huge sums into the hands of financiers who received a fixed percentage and wrote themselves contracts guaranteed to make them fast fortunes. One of the record setters was Colonial First State's payout to its former head Chris Cuffe of A$32.75 million in 2002. Other CEOs received large payments for getting rid of most of their workforce, such as former BHP chief John Prescott, who received a payout of A$11 million, and A$20 million to the company's outgoing chief Paul Anderson in 2002.

In the case of AMP (Australia Mutual Provident) big payouts were made for the privilege of plundering the company's assets. AMP, once Australia's wealthiest company owned by its policy holders, was demutualised in the wave of privatisation of the 1990s. This was followed by directors dipping into shareholder funds and paying themselves fortunes while making disastrous investment decisions for the company. Its US CEO George Turnbull was removed from office with a payoff of A$23 million in 1998. From 1998 to 2002 the company's failed strategies cost shareholders some A$9 billion in assets. As a result a number of board members resigned and were given multi-million dollar payouts. In 2003 AMP shares sank to new lows with losses of more than A$4 billion in shareholder wealth and the company came close to insolvency. Soon after, AMP announced salary packages and bonuses of more than A$43 million for a handful of fund managers and in 2004, after suffering a loss of more than A$5.5 million for 2003, it gave its chief executive Andrew Mohl a A$1.95 million bonus as part of his total pay of A$4.2 million. Frank Cicutto, chief of Australia's largest bank, the National Australia Bank (NAB), was forced to resign in 2004 and received a payout of more than A$14 million for losing A$4.6 billion in NAB's US HomeSide debacle and A$360 million in foreign exchange bets. He was replaced with former Citigroup banker 37-year-old Ahmed Fahour who on top of his yearly salary of A$5.15 million received A$12 million in cash and bank shares upfront when he joined NAB in 2004.

The enrichment of the few is largely based on closing down productive sectors and downsizing the workforce with the social costs transferred to government in pensions and other public handouts. Another pathway has been the privatisation of public wealth accumulated over many generations to profit a minority of financiers and shareholders. Corporate carnivores have used other mechanisms to shift public assets into private wealth such as fraudulent or highly misleading financial statements issued by the business sector. This has allowed many business leaders to plunder for private gains. Business academic Frank Clarke has written that 'commingling creative and feral accounting practices within complex corporate structures ensures that the financial outcomes are almost impossible to unravel'. Accounting standards distort the real financial shape of many companies and are meant to deceive by using a range of 'creative and feral accounting practices' (Clarke 2003). Deceptive means were involved in Enron-like scandals with the collapse of a number of companies such as One-Tel and one of Australia's largest insurers, HIH, with losses of more than A$5 billion.

Greed has corrupted many politicians and their advisers. Most politicians are driven by self-interest. Major political parties have become self-perpetuating oligarchies dedicated to the welfare of their leaders and their mates. The National Party, a member of the ruling coalition, has been a more obvious and blatant case because of the leadership's vested interest in large landholdings companies in rural Australia. Former federal president of the National Party, Don McDonald, owns 3.08 million hectares, most of which is covered by pastoral leases. Another National Party leader, former minister for defence Ian McLachlan, is related to Hugh MacLachlan, Australia's biggest private landholder with 5.03 million hectares. Among key backers of the National Party are other large landholders who stand to gain in their confrontation with Australia's Aborigines. The National Party has been a key mover in amending the Wik legislation to enable crown land now under pastoral leases to be upgraded to freehold. This process of shifting land ownership to the wealthy was an important scheme in Queensland during the corrupt rule of the National Party in the 1980s under the leadership of Joh Bjelke-Petersen.

Politicians regularly vote themselves large pay increases and additional retirement benefits. Their pension and perk package is among the most generous among rich countries. Politicians and senior civil servants have their own remuneration tribunal which they staff with fellow travellers appointed by the prime minister. In a recent decision the tribunal decided to compensate politicians for the introduction of a national tax on goods and services (GST), something no one else received in the country. At the time the tribunal chief was a former politician and managing director of the Australian Stock

Exchange. The other two members were the director of Sydney's radio station 2UE, involved in a cash for comment scandal, and a well-known businessman recently raided by the police for his alleged involvement in a major fraud and tax evasion scam. Politicians often do business while in office and some have become very rich while representing their electorate. After leaving office many enter the private sector and go to work for interests they had advanced while in office. Some of the more lucrative aspects of post-political careers have been in the gambling industry, business development in East Asia, and defence work.

Under market fundamentalism, greed and profit fuels most of the not-for-profit sector leadership. Churches have been behaving more like corporations in their dedication to profit and desire to accumulate more wealth. Some major religious organisations have large tax-free business organisations. The Wesley Mission, the Anglican and Catholic churches, the Salvation Army and the Smith Family, among many others, have all become large and wealthy corporations. The Australian Red Cross (ARC) itself has been selling blood to private companies, a practice unknown in the past. Salaries of ARC blood business directors now exceed what the organisation spends on disaster service. Some of the worst offenders of the greed elite culture can be found in tertiary education. Public universities have become corporations run for profit and headed by senior managers with little or no teaching experience. Many have voted themselves extravagant salaries while pursuing policies which have led to a decline in academic standards. The Australia Institute's report on *Academic Freedom and the Commercialisation of Australian Universities* found that the push for growth and fee-paying students from Asia have undermined teaching standards (Kayrooz 2001). Academic freedom itself has been compromised by a neoconservative leadership in the pursuit of growth, profit and big salaries.

The public universities' corporate activities have endangered academic freedom and research. Many academics have compromised their integrity by becoming entrepreneurs and setting up private businesses, subcontracting their work and research, and tying up financially with the business sector, often passing on the cost of their private earnings to universities. In many instances, research and research findings have been kept out of the public realm because of a confidentiality clause by government or a business sponsor. Australia's universities have been on a US-type growth track with academics on million-dollar salaries doing corporate research and running their own companies. When Pierre Ryckmans in his 1996 Boyer Lecture declared the Australian University dead, he meant that the idea of a university had come to an end in Australia with the commercialisation of academe and its integration in the corporate sector.

MARKETING CHARACTER

Australia's affluent postmodern society socialises its young to be part of a system of production and consumption. Schools and families prepare children for the great adventure in the accumulation of wealth while the mass media bombard them with advertising about the virtues of consumption and making money. Greed is a mindset which characterises itself early in the behaviour of the young and in turn shapes the national psyche. Later in life adolescents are attracted to universities that advertise themselves as places for winners and future millionaires. Many students do economics or fields related to commerce and are taught that economics is a true science, and that economic growth and making money are what life is all about. Education prepares young adults to act as if they were commodities and to market themselves for sale in the big marketplace of society and the global economy. As commodities, individuals perpetuate Australia's religious fervour for economic growth, the velocity of the dollar, and the pursuit of wealth in competition with the rest of the world.

Erich Fromm linked materialism and consumerism to a particular pattern of behaviour and the shaping of a dominant social character in society. Fromm argued that behaviour was shaped by specific socio-economic and political environments. He maintained that the 'social character internalises external necessities and thus harnesses human energy for the task of a given economic and social system' (Fromm 1965:311). Greed and consumerism are shaped by a process of socialisation that characterises the behaviour of individuals and which in turn further sustains and advances the nature of a system of production and consumption. Greed manifests itself in society's consumption frenzy such as the property rush of recent years which has been the mainstay of Australia's economic growth. Banks and other lenders have been channelling some A$10 billion a month into housing. About half has been for investment properties. People are buying second and third properties using cheap loans and generous tax benefits. In the past six years the share of households into investment property rose from 8 per cent to more than 17 per cent, or well above the situation in the US, UK and Canada. Obsession with property has led to major price increases and to housing prices more than doubling between 2000 and 2003. How to get-rich-quick property seminars attract thousands of people willing to pay some A$15,000 to hear how to become a millionaire 'using little or none of your money'.

People are buying bigger houses for themselves. In New South Wales the average new home covers 267 square meters compared to 169 square meters in 1990. Big houses resembling small palaces have become part of Sydney's urban sprawl. They stand as symbols of achievement and statements of being winners in the marketplace. In the Baulkham Hills district in west Sydney, the average new home has been growing to more than 418 square meters in 2001. While houses have expanded in size, families have grown smaller. In Sydney the average household has shrunk from 3.7 people in 1981 to 2.7 in 2001. With bigger houses come all the internal gadgets and cars and boats. Australians have been buying large numbers of imported tank-size fuel-inefficient 4-wheel-drive vehicles to further congest city roads. Boat ownership is also increasing and many congested coastal marinas show all the signs of wealth accumulation and coastal degradation.

Overconsumption is driven by luxury fever which Clive Hamilton suggests is 'the desire to emulate the lifestyles of the very rich' (Hamilton 2002:viii). Sale of luxury goods, including cars, has been rising over the years. High-priced watch brands and A$1,000 handbags have been selling well, and so have expensive champagnes and beauty products, along with A$10,000 home entertainment systems. Marketers and advertisers claim that such purchases express the 'taking care of me' (TCM) trend. People are 'satisfied but not necessarily fulfilled' and buying TCM products 'provides emotional grounding. They can't do anything about Iraq but they can look after themselves' (Shoebridge 2003). The fashionable cocktail bar 'The Establishment' cannot get enough Dom Perignon 1959 'to keep up with A$2,000-a-bottle demand' (Harcourt 2003). Business at Louis Vuitton and other fashion groups like Gucci is booming because like Americans many Australians feel that they deserve to splash out on luxury goods.

Australians' affluent lifestyle has dramatically increased the consumption of water, power, food and other valuable resources. Food intake is the more visible sign of overconsumption with obesity afflicting many people. Australia now ranks with the US among the most overweight nations in the world (Cameron 2003). In the last decade the level of obesity has increased from one in ten adults, to one in nearly five adults with a further 34 per cent of adults classified as overweight. Queensland was the fattest state in the country and child obesity a major problem. Obesity among children has moved from one in forty in the 1970s, to one in five in 2001. A University of Sydney study of New South Wales in 2003 concluded that 26 per cent of primary school boys in poor areas were overweight compared with 22 per cent in other areas (O'Dea 2003). A 2005 survey concluded that obesity in children and adolescents has reached alarming levels with 20 to 25 per cent of children and adolescents overweight or obese (Batch and Baur 2005). Many overweight children in their teens show signs of obesity-related liver diseases, including cirrhosis, usually associated with heavy drinking or hepatitis C.

Food is cheap and people have been encouraged to eat more by a constant barrage of advertising and perceived low self-esteem. There is a link between watching television and obesity among children and adolescents. Reliance on fast food and soft drinks in the diet of people has contributed to the problem. Fast foods are heavily processed and contain large quantities of fats and sugars, and artificial flavours. Sugar in soft drinks is a major contributor to Australia's obesity epidemic. The rate of obesity in Australia has increased along with media expenditure on food and drink advertising. The cost of obesity is high. Overweight people are more prone to coronary disease, type 2 diabetes and some cancers. The cost to the health budget has been estimated at A$20 billion a year. Issues of weight have led to the growth of a multi-billion dollar weight-losing and body-profiling industry. Some of the prescribed weight loss diets can cause health problems such as cardiovascular disease.

The spread of gambling is a major feature of the greed culture. Desire for money taps into the mind in the same manner as food and drugs, and becomes contagious particularly if it is encouraged by government policy and mass media hype. Gambling takes many forms including stock market speculation. A large number of financial instruments such as warrants and derivatives gamble on the rise or fall of shares, currencies and commodities. The turnover of this market is many times that of the regular daily trading in shares. Traditional forms of gambling have expanded quickly in recent years with the opening of new casinos and the introduction of poker machines in many venues such as clubs and hotels. Poker machines exceeded 180,000, or 21 per cent of the world's total, in 2000. For those on low incomes and welfare the dream is to win the jackpot at the poker machine. Advances in communications have made other forms of gambling such as horse racing more accessible to the public. On-line gambling has been another innovation which has expanded the industry's reach into society. Australians lost more than A$13.8 billion in all forms of gambling in 2002 which included A$2.1 billion in Australia's 13 casinos.

POLITICS OF GREED

Government's main role in a market democracy is to provide a political climate and conditions favourable to investment profitability and the accumulation of capital and wealth that sustains economic growth. With the advent of neoliberalism the state's economic power has diminished significantly because of the privatisation of much of the commonwealth. However, the generation of a budgetary surplus has been used to shore up the value of the dollar and bribe the electorate with pre-election payoffs and pork-barrel projects. The state has placed a greater premium on the role of the private sector to sustain economic growth with the help of a generous programme of corporate welfare. One mechanism is a loose monetary policy which has enabled financial institutions to generate credit on demand and improve their profitability. The critical role of the Australian economy under economic rationalism is to increase the production and consumption of goods and services to maintain a rate of economic growth which keeps the electorate contented. It is in this context that the politics of greed is a dominant force to keep the system moving along within a relatively stable political environment.

Australia's government has relied on the housing sector in recent years to meet its economic growth target. Demand for housing has increased dramatically over the years and a frenzy of buying has pushed prices to new heights. Government policy has contributed to this construction rush by increasing substantially the level of immigration and bringing to Australia large numbers of relatively wealthy migrants. Migrant quotas under a Liberal government have risen to more than 110,000 people yearly. The government also operates a long-term resident scheme that allows into the country an even larger number of young professionals and business people. Most newcomers settle in Sydney and Melbourne and enter the housing market bidding the price of housing and land upwards. Demand to live in Australia has been high and promoted by images of a wealthy and sunny Australia which has made the continent a destination of choice among the well-off.

Government has opened the housing and land market to foreign investors who are keen to buy waterfront and coastal properties. It has become fashionable among the global rich to have an expensive flat in Sydney or the Gold coast. Taxation rules for foreign investors are sufficiently generous to make such an investment of considerable benefit to the buyer. Education brings more than 100,000 full-fee foreign students yearly. Most arrive from Asia and many contribute to the housing market growth directly via family investments in flats and houses in Australia's major cities. Frenzy in property buying has been largely driven by cheap money available from the financial sector. Under economic rationalism banks and other financial institutions create money by lending. The more money they lend the higher their profits and payout to shareholders and directors. Australian investors have been attracted to housing by generous tax benefits such as deducting the cost of borrowing from their taxable income and the lowering of the capital gains tax on investment property. The government has also offered first-time home buyers substantial cash grants. In two years the Howard government spent more than A$3.8 billion on first-home-owners grants which have inflated prices and encouraged many fraudulent claims by people buying multi-million dollar properties in the name of their children. Buying property has been encouraged by the stock market crash of the late 1990s, and major advertising campaigns by the financial sector which play on individual egoism, greed and fear of poverty.

Another major pillar of economic growth has been the growth of the gambling industry encouraged by government licensing policy and money politics tying political parties to gambling donations. State governments have become increasingly dependent on gambling tax revenues to provision their budgets. Net revenues in 2001 exceeded A$13 billion with most growth in takings coming from the expansion of poker and gaming machines in clubs, pubs, and casinos. In New South Wales gambling is the second most important source of state revenue next to payroll tax, or more than A$1.4 billion in 2002. Government policy has encouraged big-time foreign gamblers to play in Australia. The case of Chinese property tycoon Eddie Ye who turned over A$122 million at Kerry Packer's Crown Casino in Melbourne in recent years is not unusual (Lamont 2003). The gambling industry has been a major source of economic growth in Australia because of the use of gambling activities to launder black market, drug and other criminal revenues. Hundreds of millions of dollars have been moved through casinos by syndicates in recent years, including Australia's Christmas Island casino which was used by Indonesia's dictator Suharto family and cronies to move fortunes out of Indonesia.

Growing inequalities are built into the politics of greed and economic growth. Policies under economic rationalism encourage egoistical drives and undermine civil society because they expand inequalities in the distribution of the country's income and wealth. Neoliberal politics view economic discrimination as a positive social development because competition in the marketplace increases productivity, profitability and capital accumulation. The market fundamentalism mindset is that inequality is the natural sorting out of people within the marketplace. Inequality sustains economic growth by fuelling the desire of the have-nots to have what the rich have. Greed and envy feed on each other in an ever widening circle and frenzy of consumption, urban sprawl and the production of waste.

After more than 20 years of the politics of greed, Australia's richest 10 per cent owned 85 per cent of all shares and investments, 72 per cent of rental investment properties, and 60 per cent of business assets (Kelly 2001). Using the benchmark of A$416 a week for a family with two children the St Vincent de Paul Society said that 3 million Australians lived in poverty in 2003 and one in five households lived with constant financial stress. Nearly 15 per cent of children lived in poverty (ERC 2002). More than 800,000 children lived in a household where neither parent had a job. A report by the Dusseldorp Skills Forum found that 23 per cent of young people aged 20–24 years were not studying or in full-time work in 2003. Indigenous people lived a shorter life and experienced higher rates of infant mortality, and generally lower living standards than non-indigenous Australians. In 2003 indigenous life expectancy was some 20 years below that of other Australians. More than 29 per cent of Australia's elderly lived in relative poverty, this was the highest rate together with the US among rich countries (Therborn 2003:141). The Australian Bureau of Statistics estimated that almost 100,000 were homeless on census night 2001. The geography of inequality and poverty has become more sharply outlined in postmodern Australia between city and rural areas and within large cities such as Sydney (Paul 2001:26).

Australia's income differentials have been reaching new heights of avarice and obscenity. Remuneration to Australia's CEOs averaged more than A$3 million in 2002 as they received pay increases of some

38 per cent in addition to large bonuses, while about 30 per cent of Australian households had a combined income of less than A$20,000 according to social researcher Hugh Mackay. Frank Lowly, chief of Westfield shopping centres paid himself A$11 million – or what 400 of his cleaners received a year between them. In 2003 politicians received salary packages in excess of A$250,000 a year and refused to pass the Workplace Relations (Protecting the Low Paid) Bill of 2003 that would have granted workers a gross minimum wage of A$456 a week, or roughly A$25,000 a year. The University of Sydney vice chancellor has a salary package of more than A$600,000, while he paid his cleaners between A$8 and A$10 an hour, or less than the minimum wage. Judges who are on some of the highest salaries in Australia have been sending to jail people who are excluded from society, such as the mentally ill and the poor.

Greed creates and strives on inequality. René Girard describes the implications of covetousness, the desire to have what others have – property, territory, food, jewels, high paying jobs, expensive cars – and what happens in the competition for power and wealth (Girard 1977). Greed and envy rule in a capitalist society, people want what others have; the poor want what the rich have, and the rich want to become richer. According to a recent survey, almost half of the richest households in Australia said they could not afford to buy everything they really needed. The proportion of 'suffering' rich in Australia 'is even higher than in the US, widely regarded as the nation most obsessed with money' (Hamilton 2002:vii). An economy of overconsumption is promoted by advertising and the mass media, and more generally by society's celebration of money and the accumulation of wealth, and that life is all about winning in the marketplace.

Australia's culture couches and disguises the politics of greed in discourses of well-being and happiness. The social construction of happiness is built around constant visual stimuli, and the need to have and to consume things and people. Surveys on happiness and well-being are a regular feature in the press. Deakin University's Australian Centre on Quality of Life publishes a yearly well-being index based mostly on how much one has accumulated in possessions and personal relations. The Centre is sponsored by an investment company whose philosophy is about business competition, growth and higher profits for directors and shareholders. Happiness is a state of mind created by the market and linked to a particular lifestyle and specific achievements and these are usually measured by how much money one is making, one's possessions, and who you know. The mass media often features poor people to show how unhappy they are and how much they complain about how little they have. Happiness is an illusion created by the market. The closest thing to human happiness is probably peace of mind which requires a difficult inner struggle, but neoliberalism preaches that happiness is something desirable that can be purchased like any commodity, all you need is a degree and money, drugs, or a new car or partner.

Desire and envy are often generated by campaigns initiated by institutions which have some authority in mobilising mass opinion, such as universities and think-tanks. A typical case is that of recent national media coverage about a widening generational wealth gap. According to a study by the Canberra-based National Centre for Social and Economic Modeling (NATSEM) older Australians were getting richer while the younger generation was getting poorer (Kelly 2003). The Baby Boomers generation, or some 4.1 million Australians, born between 1946 and 1961 were the lucky ones, said Professor Ann Harding of NATSEM: 'they enjoyed cheap housing, free education, and the benefits of a welfare state and abundant jobs'. Generation Xers born between 1961 and 1976, or some 4.5 million, were not so lucky and its share of the country's wealth has been declining. Substantial rises in housing prices have further widened the gap between generations. AMP, which funds NATSEM, warned that the Xers generation could not afford to support older Australians who got a free ride, and declared that society was unfair to generation Xers.

At the same time Australia's Reserve Bank Governor Ian Macfarlane spoke of a possible damaging generational war if young people had to pay more taxes to support the lifestyle of richer older Australians. He warned in November 2002 of an 'intergenerational conflict because the young might resent the tax burden of supporting an ageing population and that older Australians owned most of the assets – housing is the most obvious example' (Cornell 2003). Research for the campaign on inter-generational envy and discontent came from the financial sector and investment funds such as AMP. Since demutualisation, AMP has suffered a series of self-inflicted financial disasters losing more than A$4 billion of shareholder funds and was on the brink of insolvency in early 2003. Companies like AMP need to enlarge their pool of superannuation funds to survive and their strategy is to cause public anxiety for government to come to the rescue with a business welfare plan to secure their financial future.

There is a synergy between greed and competition. Competition for profit and power is what drives and sustains economic growth and people compete for jobs and money to accumulate wealth and status. In a modern society such as Australia, individuals' mode of existence is increasingly centred on property and profit which produce the 'desire – indeed the need – for power', according to Erich Fromm. Fromm discusses this well-known mechanism in social relations about control over people and the need to use power to break their resistance. His analysis of modern society's material mode of life suggests that 'to maintain control over private property we need to use power to protect it from those who would take it from us because they, like us, can never have enough; the desire to have private property produces the desire to use violence in order to rob others in overt or covert ways' (Fromm 1982:68).

SOCIAL COSTS

Neoliberal economic growth generates substantial social costs which contribute to the growth of the country's gross domestic product. These are the costs linked to rising health problems, harm and aggression, and environmental degradation. Mental health has become a significant issue in postmodern Australia. A culture of greed and competition contributes to widespread discontent which is reflected in Australia's high level of mental illness. The continuous stimulation of the desire to have and consume more leads to restlessness and dissatisfaction and eventual mental disorder, often requiring hospitalisation. Modern depression may well be seen as the sickness of affluence. Mental disorder affected almost one in five Australian adults at the beginning of the twenty-first century (PC 2001). Professor Ian Hickie of the University of New South Wales School of Psychiatry suggests that 60 per cent of people who visited general practitioners had a mental disorder (Hickie 2001).

Underpinning the mental health crisis is a deep existential problem caused by postmodern conditions. The disintegration of community and family have been exacerbated by feelings of powerlessness in a society which pushes consumption as a way of life. Lack of control is a reflection of a weak democracy and an electorate without an effective say in the politics of greed. Mental illness is a form of rebellion of the mind. Psychiatrist Peter Breggin has described depression as another word for hopelessness (Smith 2001:86). There are nevertheless other important dimensions to the problem highlighted in studies on nutrition which claim that the modern epidemic of depression may have as one of its major causes a diet rich in animal fats (Small 2002). Depression and other mental disorders are increasingly treated with new, potent and expensive drugs. In the first nine months of 2002 some 7.24 million scripts were issued for anti-depressants such as Zoloft, Aropax and Prozac at a cost of more than A$236 million to the government (HIC 2002). Such high cost to society encourages the pharmaceutical industry to medicalise a range of behaviour to increase market share and profitability.

A neoliberal political and economic regime generates a high level of conflict and anti-social behaviour which undermines civil society and is destructive of the environment. Society responds with more regulations, policing and repression which must be paid for by increasing revenues or borrowings. Policing budgets have been rising over the years, more prisons have been built to house a larger number of criminals sentenced to jail terms. Private security has been another growth industry offering services which the regular police force is no longer willing or able to provide. Materialism directly affects the environment. Australia is the second largest waste creator next to the US. Australians throw away more than 1.1 tonnes of solid waste per person every year (EA 2002:124). Australia has the highest emission of greenhouse gases per capita among the industrialised countries. At 26.7 tonnes per annum, Australians emit twice the average per capita of industrialised countries, and more than the US's 21.2 tonnes per person (Turton and Hamilton 1999:vii).

Because of widespread land clearing practices over the years, some 5.7 million hectares of land are 'at risk or already affected by dryland salinity' and dryland salinity is likely to affect 17 million hectares of land by 2050 (ANAO 2001:74–5). Salinity is affecting Australia's infrastructure, damaging buildings, water pipes, roads and sewers. According to a 2003 federal government *National Land and Water Resources Audit*: 'One third of the world's extinct mammals since 1600 AD are Australians [and] such a record is unparalleled in any other component of Australia's biodiversity or anywhere else in the world' (NLWR 2002). Thousands more native animals face extinction this century. Widespread land clearing, bad farming practices, and the introduction of non-native species such as the rabbit and cat have been among the main culprits.

Australia's expensive lifestyle is based on the export of large amounts of cheap food and other agricultural and mining products to Asia. This partly pays for increasing quantities of manufactured imports, particularly automobiles and information technology goods and services. The export of food to Asia has put enormous pressure on land and water resources. Some 2 million hectares of agricultural land is affected by salinity, most in Western Australia, and half is no longer productive (ABS 2002). Agriculture uses 70 per cent of Australia's water consumption. Much of this has been available to farmers free of charge. Some experts have estimated the cost of reversing environmental damage at some A$60 billion to restore vegetation and remedy land and water degradation. Australia has been subsidising food supplies to Asia, a situation which could easily be affected by global warming and changes in the rainfall pattern, particularly in the southern half of the continent. A controversial Commonwealth Scientific and Industrial Research Organisation (CSIRO) report has warned of the possibility that Australia could face drastic curbs in the good life if the country did not resolve its greenhouse gas problem in the coming decades (Foran and Poldy 2002). CSIRO scientist Barney Foran added that consumers should be paying treble for food to cover the cost of water.

Neoliberal capitalism is in crisis because it is morally bankrupt. Religion no longer plays a critical role in compensating for individual greed and the country's leadership has been compromised by corruption, scandals and self-serving egoism. Richard Tawney identified capitalism's destructive potential in committing people and countries 'to a career of indefinite expansion, in which they devour continents and oceans, law, morality and religion and last of all their own souls, in an attempt to attain infinity by the addition to themselves of all that is finite' (Tawney 1961:47). Capitalism without restraints destroys those qualities necessary for sustaining democracy. Economic rationalism is morally bankrupt because it teaches that money is the only meaningful goal in life. It reduces society to a game where success is based on power over people and the accumulation of material goods. Unlimited individual appetites and insatiable wants undermine the egalitarian and social justice principles which democracy needs to survive.

Capitalism in postmodern Australia has unleashed the full forces of competition and individual greed with few restraints and obligations to contain its destructive tendencies. With the advent of economic rationalism in the 1980s, governments have attempted to contain social damage by orchestrating political myth-building campaigns about social obligations and volunteering, civil society and the role of social capital. These have had little impact in containing or reversing damaging social trends. The moral bankruptcy of economic rationalism has encouraged government and chauvinist elements to fill the void with a new nationalism to promote social cohesion and externalise internal aggression. There has been a resurgence in the construction of a national character in the post-Cold War era which builds on myths of mateship, fair go and egalitarianism. The Howard government has been particularly busy fabricating new images of Australians and Australia. Prime Minister Howard has become a major voice for a new nationalism with often repeated public pronouncements that 'Australians are down-to-earth people. It is part of our virtue. Rooted deep down our psyche is a sense of fair play and a strong egalitarian streak' (Brett 2003:20).

Australia's neoconservative power elite has exploited Australia's overseas military adventures. Those who fought and died in Gallipoli in a costly attempt to invade Turkey's shores have become national heroes. The Anzac dawn service at the Australian memorial at Gallipoli's Lone Pine ridge has become a place of pilgrimage. The death of Tasmanian Alec Campbell in 2003, Gallipoli last survivor, was made into a national day of mourning. Alec Campbell, who returned from the war to become an anti-war republican, a militant union leader and socialist, would have objected to claims made at his funeral that 'they fought to build a nation'; rather he would have argued that those who died were used and betrayed by British imperial incompetence. Sporting heroes have been added to the construction of an Australian psyche such as well-known cricketers and Olympic games medal winners trained at great public expense at Canberra's Australian Institute of Sports.

The process of building a new history has required the destruction of older sacred texts and contrarian narratives. This process began under a post-Cold War Labor government with attacks on historian Manning Clark, accusing him of being a Soviet spy and rubbishing his writings on the history of Australia because it contained many unpleasant truths about invasion and destruction, and the dispossession of indigenous people's land and culture. In recent years the deconstruction of Australian history has continued with the work of neoconservative historians headed by Keith Windschuttle (2001). Windschuttle's mission has been to dehumanise Aboriginal history and erase their struggle against colonial invaders. Australia's new history has extended to the newly constructed National Museum of Australia (NMA). Conservative government appointees to the NMA board ordered a review because the museum did not sufficiently reflect white colonial modern history and the exhibitions were too sympathetic to indigenous black Australians. The outcome was the sacking of the museum's director Dawn Casey, an Aboriginal Australian, and the removal of her supporters from the NMA board of directors. A revisionist history claims European settlers as heroes and Australia as the new America; it praises British civilisation and constructs myths of uniquely Australian national spirit and character.

5
Australian Imperialism

The simplest definition of empire is the domination and exploitation of weaker states by stronger ones.

Chalmers Johnson in *The Sorrows of Empire*

What has really changed is that we no longer habitually wait for someone else to take a lead. In East Timor, in Solomon Islands and in Papua New Guinea, Australia has been front and centre trying to restore and maintain the universal decencies of mankind.

Tony Abbott, Australia's Federal Health Minister, 2004

INVASION AND TERRITORIAL EXPANSION

When the British began their conquest of Australia in the 1770s the continent was home to more than 200 indigenous nations and millions of people who could trace their ancestry far back into ancient time. Language was the primary attribute of the culture and cohesion of each nation and shaped the boundaries which divided the continent into 230 languages and more than 500 dialect groups (Fesl 1993). Conquest of the continent by the British was quickly achieved by various means including mass killings, forceful evacuation and destruction of families, and forms of biological warfare with the spreading of diseases such as smallpox. By the middle of the nineteenth century British settlers had claimed an entire continent and Tasmania as theirs and created a new Britannia in the Asia-Pacific for the British Empire. Towards the end of the nineteenth century territorial conquest pushed north with the annexation of the Torres Strait Islands in 1872 and southern New Guinea in 1884 as part of Queensland. The conquest was formalised by an act of federation in 1901 which laid claim to a continent of 7.6 million km2 for the benefit of some 2.3 million white Anglo-Celtic colonists.

Australia's dominion expanded southwards taking over the 370 km2 Heard, McDonald and Macquarie Islands, and 42 per cent of Antarctica or about 6 million km2. Control of Antarctica became embroiled in the Cold War, and fears that the USSR would expand in Antarctica and gain an advantage in the East–West conflict led to Australia's sovereign claim incorporated in the 1959 Antarctic Treaty signed by twelve countries. Australia expanded northwards and acquired land bases close to the Indonesian and Melanesian archipelago. The Ashmore and Cartier Islands came under Australian authority in the 1930s, and the British controlled Cocos and Christmas Islands were transferred to Australia in the late 1950s. Australia claimed the Coral Sea Islands under the 1969 Coral Sea Islands Act. These land bases became the markers for Australia's claims and delimitation of its territorial sea and Exclusive Economic Zone (EEZ).

The transfer of Cocos (Keeling) and Christmas Islands enabled Australia to extend its northern maritime jurisdiction and gain control of substantial economic resources. Australia's sovereignty to these islands is disputed by other countries and Australia has taken steps in recent years to consolidate its claim to Christmas Island which is 400 km south of Djakarta. It has encouraged new settlers to dilute the Malay and Chinese population who are seen as too militant and separatist in their politics, and the government has been spending a great deal of money to build up the island's infrastructure. One major project has been the construction of a A$200 million detention camp capable of holding 1,200 people complete with soundproofed underground interrogation bunkers. Christmas and other islands have been excised from Australia for migration purposes since the 2001 *Tampa* crisis and refugees caught in the region will be processed on Christmas Island for their deportation. The government is also contributing more than A$100 million towards the development of a space station. The A$800 million project is run by Asia Pacific Space Centre Ltd run by a Korean entrepreneur and his Russian partners who will provide the launchers and expertise to orbit satellites in competition with places like French Guyana. Russian involvement, however, is conditional on their recognition of Christmas Island as Australian territory.

Australia's maritime boundaries with Indonesia were delimited in 1971. The treaty was based on Australia's underwater continental shelf rather than a midline between both countries' coastlines. This device greatly expanded the country's maritime sovereignty and exclusive economic zone and brought Australian jurisdiction close to Indonesia's coastline. It gave Australia an unfair advantage which was the price Indonesia had to pay for Australia's support of Suharto's dictatorship. By the stroke of a pen many Indonesian fishing villages lost access to their traditional fisheries. Australia signed a similar treaty with PNG in 1978 which brought Australia's jurisdiction within less than 4 km from PNG's coastline, thereby fracturing a population's history and culture. The 300 km gap between Indonesia and PNG was delimited in the 1989 Timor Gap Treaty which pushed Australia's maritime dominion further north into the Timor Sea giving Australia control over major gas and oil reserves. Again Australia used the continental shelf to establish the baseline for its territorial sea. The agreement signed under Paul Keating's government could be construed as a payback for Australia's support of Indonesia's takeover of East Timor in 1975.

At the beginning of the twenty-first century Australia had added more than 6 million km2 of territory to its continental base and gained an EEZ of more than 8 million km2, exclusive of the EEZ off Antarctica, rich in protein, minerals and oil and gas reserves. The process of expansion was continuing with Australia's case to the UN's Commission on the Limits of the Continental Shelf for an extension of its maritime jurisdiction beyond the continental margin claiming an additional 4 million km2 beyond its existing EEZ. The UN acceptance of Australia's claim in 2006 would increase Australia's maritime jurisdiction to more than 12 million km2.

Australia's zone of expansion extends across the Indonesian archipelago to the Melanesian and Polynesian islands of the South Pacific. What Australia labels as its arc of instability sways from Sumatra in the Indian Ocean to islands such as Fiji and Tonga in the South Pacific. This area became an important region in the British Empire and later in the development of Australia's sense of separateness as a nation. It was a source of wealth for traders and investors and continues to make a valuable contribution to Australia's economy. Australian nationalism was created by excluding people from the region and a fear of invasion from the north. These perceived dangers emanate from the arc of instability and are ingrained in Australia's foreign policy to secure and control the region.

Calls for the annexation of islands to the north of Australia have been part of Australian imperialism since the nineteenth century, and since the end of the Cold War, this mission has taken on new dimensions as part of the US strategic plan for a new world order. From the early 1990s, Australia's role has been to exert pressure on the region's political and economic agenda and this policy has become more public with President George Bush's announcement of Australia's role as US regional sheriff and Prime Minister John

Howard's preemptive regional strike doctrine in the pursuit of Australia's national interests.

INDONESIA

Much of Australia's defence strategy has targeted Indonesia as a primary threat to Australia's security and a white Australia policy. Labor leader Arthur Calwell warned the country in the late 1940s that Indonesia's imperial ambitions might extend to Timor, then Papua New Guinea and on to northern Australia. The Menzies government purchase of the US F-111 in 1963 was part of its defence against Indonesia. Australia's instructions at the time were for a F-111 designed to have sufficient range to reach Djakarta with nuclear bombs. In the 1980s the Defence Department Hamilton report on *The Defence of Australia* identified Japan and Indonesia as the main future threats to Australia. Interventions in the affairs of Indonesia have become more overt since the election of a coalition government in 1996 led by John Howard. Defence Force Admiral Chris Barrie stated that Australia's military action in East Timor was part of Australia's new defence role in a US coalition control of regional affairs. Howard's preemptive strike doctrine foreshadowed the possibility of direct intervention in Indonesia's domestic politics by Australian forces in the pursuit of the country's national interests.

During the Cold War Australia's Indonesia's policy was part of an Anglo-American strategy to eliminate both Sukarno and the communist party. In the 1950s Australia supported nationalist and Muslim parties to weaken Sukarno's communist support. Efforts to organise covert operations in support of anti-Sukarno regional separatist movements suggested a policy of dismembering Indonesia by supporting ethnic-based rebellious elements on Java's periphery. Australian intelligence was involved in the 1950s Moluccas rebellion and Australia shipped arms and ammunition to the region from Darwin. Australia's involvement in the uprising in Aceh and other parts of Sumatra and Sulawesi took the form of air operations, probably from airfields in Australia and Papua New Guinea to bomb Sukarno forces, naval logistical support, and the use of Christmas Island for US submarines working with regional separatist groups.

The 1965 military coup against Sukarno led by General Suharto was an operation jointly planned by Australia and the US. Australian spy Edward Kenny wrote that 'the government of Australia in cooperation with the US government embarked upon a plot to have President

Sukarno overthrown ... high ranking officers of the Indonesian forces were bribed to get rid of Sukarno and his followers' (Toohey and Pinwill 1989:105). The US provided funds, arms and communication equipment as well as information about the communist party (PKI) membership. As part of the Cold War strategy the US embassy in Djakarta provided Indonesian security forces with a list of names of PKI leaders and cadres as well as funds. Humphrey McQueen alleges that following the coup 'top CIA operatives poured into Indonesia and supervised a hit list of 5,000 cadres to be eliminated' (McQueen 1991:75). According to the National Security Archive at George Washington University, US ambassador Marshall Green 'endorsed a 50 million rupiah covert payment to the Kap-Gestapu movement leading the repression of the PKI' (Reuters 2001). Massacres followed the 1965 coup and between 500,000 to one million Indonesians are said to have been killed. CIA operations in Indonesia formed the blueprint for the fall of Chile's Allende some eight years later, and operation Phoenix during the Vietnam war when US directed death-squads eliminated some 50,000 Vietnamese (Scott 1985).

Suharto's new order for Indonesia was heralded in a 1967 Geneva business conference organised by the Ford Foundation on 'To Aid in the Rebuilding of a Nation' during which various sectors of Indonesia's economy were assigned to multinationals, mostly US corporations. Among the winners were the US Freeport Company which gained West Papua's copper and gold, and the Inter-Governmental Group on Indonesia (IGGI) including Australia, which gained control of Indonesia's finances (Pilger 2002:41). Australia's support was rewarded with a Seabed Boundaries Treaty which gave Australia extensive maritime resources by drawing the boundary with Indonesia using Australia's underwater continental shelf as the base line rather than a median line between the coastlines. Some published accounts claim that during the negotiations the Australian Secret Intelligence Service had information on Indonesia's position and that 'money influenced the outcome' of the negotiations (McDonald 2000).

At the time, Australia's liberal government was conspiring with Holland, the US and the United Nations to betray West Papuans and transfer power over their country from the Dutch to Indonesia. Australia collaborated in the 1969 Act of Free Choice which involved 1,025 West Papuans selected by Indonesia to transfer their country's sovereignty under the auspices of the United Nations. A US document showed that 95 per cent of the West Papuans supported the independence movement and that the act of free choice was a 'mockery'. Some Papuan leaders who attempted to go to the UN before the vote to present the facts were arrested by Australian authorities as they crossed the border into Australian-administered New Guinea, interviewed by Australian intelligence and flown to Manus island to a detention camp to join scores of West Papuan political prisoners. Prior to the 1969 vote, Australia was engaged in secret operations with Indonesia to neutralise the West Papua independence movement and Australian authorities knew of atrocities committed by the Indonesian military against the people of West Papua (Balmain 1999). Bolivian Ortiz Sanz the head of the UN team supervising the Act of Free Choice told journalist Hugh Lunn that like the Americans he feared a communist takeover of West Papua and that 'West Irian is like a cancerous growth on the side of the UN and my job is to surgically remove it' (Lunn 1999).

Australia gave Indonesia the green light to invade East Timor following the departure of the Portuguese in 1974. Labor prime minister Gough Whitlam said at the time that East Timor was not a viable country on its own. The takeover was part of a plan by the West to back Suharto's anti-communist crusade with the support of US president Gerald Ford and his secretary of state Henry Kissinger. Suharto's regime 'kept the Australian government closely informed about Indonesia's intentions and operations' (Monk 2001). The occupation of East Timor led to a takeover of the region's resources by military and other entrepreneurs. James Dunn, Australia's one-time consul to East Timor, said that some 60,000 East Timorese were killed in the first year of colonisation. Amnesty International and other organisations have estimated the numbers killed by Indonesian forces up to the 1999 UN-led military intervention at more than 200,000. The Australian government failed to support the plight of the East Timorese during years of repression in that province. After the 1991 Santa Cruz cemetery massacre, former foreign minister Gareth Evans managed to dismiss what had happened and refused to condemn Indonesia, referring to the events as an 'aberration' from state policy and subsequently denied that a second massacre confirmed in 1998 had taken place.

Under a Labor government Australia established strong defence ties with Indonesia's military (TNI) and supplied it with weapons and training. Until 1998 many joint military exercises were held in the region and elite troops were trained in special warfare in Australia. A security treaty signed in December 1995 committed both countries to mutual consultation and cooperation in matters affecting their common security. Under Prime Minister Paul Keating the culture of appeasement with Suharto was carried to extremes of subservience. While Australian ministers were cavorting with the dictator and his cronies, Indonesian military units were killing East Timorese in Dili and students in Djakarta, and Australian intelligence was passing information to their Indonesian counterparts on Indonesian students and East Timorese in Australia.

Less than a month after the July 1996 violent military crackdown in Djakarta, former prime minister Bob Hawke visited Indonesia in his new role as a business consultant and delivered a speech defending Indonesia's human rights record, and criticising Australians for not understanding and respecting Asian values. East Timor's leader Jose Horta said that Keating 'was a political ally of the corrupt and repressive Suharto regime. He must share the blame with all his past colleagues for the decades of appeasement and servility towards the Suharto regime, the collusion with a corrupt and arrogant army' (Horta 1999). Under a coalition government elected in 1996, Prime Minister John Howard continued the policy of appeasement and condoned human rights abuses in Indonesia. Under pressure from Foreign Affairs and Trade Minister Alexander Downer, parliament banned an East Timor photo exhibition because it 'included photos of the Dili massacre'. Australia's then deputy prime minister Tim Fisher made an appearance on public television praising Indonesia's Suharto as a great world leader.

Australia played an important role to promote US globalisation. The Hawke and Keating governments pushed Indonesia to deregulate the economy and open up the country to global funds searching for short-term gain. This encouraged the expansion of corruption in Indonesia by providing new avenues for the elite to siphon off public revenues and foreign aid. The massive movement of short-term funds into the region led to the Asian financial crisis of 1997. The crisis was essentially a modern form of piracy and brought human misery to the country.

Australia's participation in this debacle is well illustrated by what happened on Christmas Island between 1993 and 1998. Australia's Christmas Island became the playground for the Suhartos and their cronies. A joint company brought together Australian entrepreneurs from Western Australia and Suharto's in-laws among others. They became principals in a casino licensed by the Australian authorities. From 1993 to 1998 many well known Indonesians landed visa-free on the island from their 45-minute flight from Djakarta to be entertained and gamble big money. Transport was provided by the military and brought Indonesia's richest of the rich. Money from drug operations, arms dealing, military protection rackets and corrupt government practices was gambled and laundered through the casino's facilities. The casino turned over some A$3 billion in the first six months of operation. Turnover in its first year was bigger than all of Australia's mainland casinos. During its operations the casino is said to have moved more than A$13 billion (ABC 2002). Some of Australia's Labor politicians involved in this affair were amply rewarded in their post-politics career.

Suharto's regime was a military dictatorship centred on Java and ruled by fear and state terrorism. The use of violence by the military and their hired mercenaries including Muslim extremists and criminal gangs was widespread. During the 1980s the regime assassinated large numbers of individuals targeted as troublemakers and dissidents (Anderson 2001). Several human rights leaders were arrested and sent to Indonesia's gulag to join the many political prisoners held since the 1965 coup. Human rights movements were suppressed by the military in Aceh, West Papua, and other regions, and state terrorism in the provinces further mobilised separatist feelings. Indonesia's military (TNI) ran large business enterprises and protection rackets to fund their operations and build up the leadership's fortunes. Suharto and his family corrupted state institutions and accumulated a fortune estimated at some US$15 billion with large overseas assets. Suharto's regime systematically abused Indonesians' human rights and repressed their democratic aspirations (AI 1994).

The opportunity to build firm foundations for a viable multicultural society within a democratic federation has been missed. Levels of poverty have increased dramatically over the years, and more than 110 million lived on less than A$2.70 a day including 70 million who lived in extreme poverty at the beginning of the twenty-first century. The extent of the Suharto regime's economic and political corruption has dissipated much of the country's capital resources as well the good will of the people. Indonesia remains an empire built on Javanese political power and faced with a separatist pull from the periphery. The Javanese core has failed and in times of economic stagnation and despair people are likely to reassert their sovereignty based on ethnicity. Suharto's dictatorship has brought the Indonesian empire to the brink of disintegration. East Timor with the help of Australia succeeded in seceding from Indonesia in 2001. Demands for independence in West Papua and Aceh have grown over the years.

In other regions the lack of progress has turned into ethnic violence, each group fighting for whatever resources exist on the ground. The situation has been compounded with the settlement of large numbers of settlers from Java on land appropriated from indigenous people. Ethnic confrontation has become a dominant feature of political life in Kalimantan, since 1998 there have been pitched battles between Christians and Muslims in the Maluku island chain, particularly in Ambon the capital of Maluku province, and Central Sulawesi in the Poso region.

Lack of economic progress for the masses and Suharto's suppression of progressive political forces have given birth to religious fundamentalism as a major force in Indonesia's political life. Suharto's military dictatorship eliminated leftist movements and many nationalist groups. An outcome was a political vacuum which provided fertile grounds for fundamentalist movements. Radical Islam became a powerful attractant to many young men and women who had lost faith in the West's promises of progress. Young Indonesians who faced little or no educational and employment opportunities have been pulled in by promises of a religious solution to their militant expectations. Violence has been a major reaction to the absence of open political channels to mobilise discontent. The emergence of networks dedicated to the use of violence to carry their political message and foment religious wars took place under Suharto's benign fascism. Many members of groups such as Jemaah Islamiyah and the Laskar Jihad fought in Afghanistan in the late 1980s in operations funded by the US. Since the late 1990s radical Islamists have been busy organising to fight in various parts of Indonesia particularly against Christian populations. The bombing of a Bali nightclub in October 2002 killing 88 Australians was Suharto's political legacy and the price for years of corruption supported by the West.

Indonesia is now on the frontline of the Anglo-American war on terrorism. Australia and the US have identified Indonesia as another Pakistan in the making and linked the country to the axis of evil. Indonesia's terrorist problem is seen as a rebellion against the empire which need to be suppressed through a more assertive policy on the part of Australia. Many Indonesians, however, view Australia's involvement as a fight against Islam and accuse Australia's Christian fundamentalists of waging a war against their country. Australia has been accused by local Muslim groups of arming Indonesian Christians. Indonesia's religious conflict has been internationalised with Muslim groups coming from other parts of Asia and foreign Christian organisations intervening in the domestic affairs of Indonesia.

Some Christian groups in Australia are known to view Islam as a wicked religion and the work of the devil, and consider Islam as the final frontier in their war against false religion and in the coming of the messiah. Indonesia is seen as a war zone in their crusade to convert the world. Australia-based Christian groups are sending missionaries to Indonesia where they operate under cover of businesses, aid and educational organisations to market their beliefs, convert Muslims, and support local Christian populations. The Howard government leased northern Australia's Cox peninsula transmitter to Christian Vision, a British fundamentalist group to evangelise throughout the region. The UK-based organisation is 'committed to bringing people into a relationship with Jesus' and has developed a number of global strategies to achieve this, including 'Touch a Billion' and 'Impact a Nation'. Christian Vision operates a service in Bahasa Indonesia, English and Mandarin from their Cox transmission site in Darwin, and since November 2003 their newest radio transmission based in East Timor has targeted Indonesia's Sulawesi and the Maluku island chain. Among other Christian radio stations targeting the region is the *Hoy Cristo Jesus Bendice* (HCJB) facility at Kununurra.

An Indonesian nation-state based on Java alone is not a viable proposition because of Java's population density and lack of natural resources. Australia's policy has focused on Indonesia's territorial core around the Sumatra–Java axis and supports Indonesia's repressive policy and war against Aceh's popular secessionist movement. Aceh in northern Sumatra, where an estimated 40 per cent of the population live below the poverty line, has a long history of opposition to foreign rule from the time of the Dutch to the present day. Over the years the province has seen little of the wealth transferred to Djakarta from its oil and gas fields. In 2003 Indonesia's former president Megawati Sukarnoputri declared martial law in Aceh and the military embarked on major military operations in the province to crush resistance movements such as the Free Aceh Movement (GAM). There have been many reports of summary executions, torture and other hostile acts against the civilian population. Indonesia's military authorities have used the Anglo-American 'war on terrorism' and the Tsunami disaster of December 2004 to suppress and wage war on the country's dissidents, and Australia's foreign office has publicly supported Indonesia's military suppression campaigns in Aceh, identifying members of various groups as terrorists.

Australia colluded with the Suharto government to transfer West Papua to Indonesia in a sham UN supervised exercise called the Act of Free Choice in 1969. Over the years Indonesian authorities have moved many migrants onto tribal land. This process has been accelerated in recent years. Muslims now comprise about half of the province's 2.5 million people. A resistance and independence movement has grown as an outcome of Indonesia's brutal policy of repression and the lack of development in the province despite the transfer of great wealth in natural resources to Djakarta. Some 100,000 Papuans have been killed by Indonesian forces since 1969. In recent years Indonesian suppression has increased and many Papuan leaders have been assassinated. Indonesia's military has been moving Laskar Jihad fighters to West Papua's main transmigration settler centres and set up a number of training camps along the border with Papua New Guinea.

The West Papua Morning Star flag has been flying in Australia and many Australians support West Papua's independence movement. A number of institutions including universities, trade unions and some Christian churches have made commitments to West Papua's independence. Australia could one day support West Papua's secession and propose to unite the Melanesian island into some form of federation with Papua New Guinea (PNG). Australia's indirect control of PNG and recent military and police intervention in that country could be seen as preparation for such eventuality. With the excision of East Timor from Indonesia in 2002 the separatist momentum has accelerated, particularly in an area delineated by the Banda and Arafura seas. A main focus of activity is the independence movement within the Christian population of the Maluku islands, Ambon-centred Maluku Sovereignty Front (FKM).

TIMOR LESTE

Secret Australian foreign affairs papers released in 2000 show that Australia 'knew of Indonesia's plans to invade East Timor more than 12 months before the 1975 offensive, but avoided criticizing Djakarta because of the paramount importance of good relations' (Garran 2000; Monk 2001). During the 1975 invasion, five newsmen including two Australians were executed by Indonesian forces. Australia knew of the planned attack on their location and information about their murders was kept secret by the Australian authorities (Ball and McDonald 2000). Their lives could have been saved had the

Australian government acted on the information they had. Questions have been raised about the role of Australian intelligence in shipping ammunition from Darwin to Indonesian forces in Kupang several days before the raid on Balibo in 1975 where the journalists were killed (Woodley 1999).

The Australian government recognised Indonesia's incorporation of East Timor while the UN and most countries declared Indonesia's occupation an illegal act. Australia supported the US strategy to block UN efforts to force Indonesia to withdraw from East Timor. Whitlam told Suharto in 1982 that 'he admired what had been achieved in East Timor' (Stephens 1999). Australia and the US aided and trained Indonesia's military. The elite force Kopassus was 'built up with American expertise despite Washington's awareness of its role in the genocide of about 200,000' East Timorese (Vulliamy 1999). World Bank funds for Indonesia's social development were diverted by the military for their operations and the enrichment of their leaders thus depriving East Timor of the opportunity for a better life. Labor governments under Hawke and Keating were steady supporters of Suharto's abuse of human rights, and their policy of 'waltzing' with the dictator was Australia's rendition of a 'we are part of Asia' policy. Australia's military worked closely with their Indonesian counterparts passing on intelligence about dissenters in Australia.

Jose Horta wrote in 1998 that for much of the past 23 years 'Australian officials engaged in a cover-up of the East Timor tragedy, with omissions, half-truths and outright lies to protect their links with one of Asia's most despotic and corrupt leaders' (Horta 1998). One of the big payoffs for Australia's collaboration with Suharto's dictatorship was the 1989 Timor Gap treaty signed by former foreign ministers Gareth Evans and Ali Alatas over a glass of champagne flying high above the Timor Zone of Cooperation in a Royal Australian Air Force VIP jet. Under the treaty, Australia was able to extend its maritime boundaries and exclusive economic zone and incorporate huge oil and gas reserves. The treaty designated some 61,000 km2 as a zone of cooperation to be jointly developed. Soon after the 1991 Dili massacre the Indonesia-Australia joint authority signed a number of oil exploration contracts which gave the green light to multinationals to further explore and exploit the huge reserves of the Timor gap.

Indonesia's change of policy towards East Timor came with the end of Suharto in 1998. Habibie, appointed as interim president, decided with 'amazing haste and barely any consultation' to give East

Timorese a choice of staying in the union or opting for independence (Greenlees and Garran 2002). Habibie was Suharto's favourite and acceptable to the military, but his decision was controversial and Megawati Sukarnoputri, then chairwoman of the Indonesian Democratic Party of Struggle, said that Habibie's government did not have the legitimacy to call for a referendum on East Timor and called the decision 'irresponsible'. There were pressures from Australia to let East Timor go and some Indonesian leaders such as Amien Rais felt that East Timor was too expensive to keep. Singapore's patriarch Lee Kuan Yew claimed that Australia precipitated the East Timor crisis and the Howard government pushed the Indonesians into a corner over the issue. The US did not want the issue raised at that time but went along with Australia's deputy sheriff advice that this was in their mutual interests.

The TNI leadership were opposed to East Timor's independence and had put into operations a plan to train and arm a militia to fight against independence through a campaign of fear and violence. Australia knew of the TNI's plans and operations against pro-independence movements and its 'scorched earth' strategy in the event the referendum went against Indonesia (Birmingham 2001). These reports were passed on to UN officials and Australian diplomats who ignored them (Jolliffe 2001). Information came mainly from Australia's extensive electronic surveillance facilities in the region operated by Australia's largest and most secret intelligence agency the Defence Signals Directorate (DSD). Special reconnaissance missions had gathered extensive information about TNI's covert operations in East Timor including intercepts of Indonesian military leaders' communications with their East Timor militia leaders. Information was also coming from Australian agents working in Indonesia. Some working for AusAID contractors were sending valuable information to Australian intelligence. Indonesian government sources maintain that Australian forces were operating in East Timor before the 30 August referendum and were involved in support activities with pro-independence militias (Murdoch 2000).

Questions raised about Australia's motives for keeping vital intelligence from the US, the East Timorese and the United Nations have been linked to Australian Defence Intelligence Organisation (DIO) officer Merv Jenkins closeness to the US Central Intelligence Agency (CIA) and his 1999 suicide in Washington DC. Jenkins hanged himself when an investigator from the Department of Foreign Affairs and Trade (DFAT) threatened him with jailing under the Crimes Act.

One line of reasoning leads to a power struggle among Australian intelligence agencies, and the desire of the Indonesian lobby not to offend the Indonesians and disturb their cosy relations. Had the US been fully briefed it is probable that they would have insisted on an Australian military intervention early in 1999 to back the United Nations referendum. A more sinister scenario is the possibility that East Timor's situation became an opportunity for Prime Minister Howard to win the 2000 federal election and stay in power for another four years. Indonesia's military violence in East Timor in the aftermath of Habibie's referendum decision became grounds on which Howard and Australians became heroes in liberating the East Timorese from their Indonesian oppressors.

Singapore's Lee Kuan Yew maintains that Australia carried a sense of guilt because of former Labor prime minister Gough Whitlam acquiescing to Indonesia's annexation of East Timor, and that Australia had precipitated the East Timor crisis. Lee said that 'given Canberra's role in pushing for an act of self-determination, Australia would have lost respect if it had failed to restore order' (Skehan 2000). Indonesia's 1999 TNI killings provided the opportunity for Australia to wipe out its collective guilt and firm up its credentials as US regional sheriff. Behind this scenario, however, was the urgency for Australia to take military action on behalf of East Timor in order to secure the seabed oil wealth in the Timor Gap so important to Australia's economy and future well-being.

Australia's prime minister in 1920, Andrew Fisher, had a vision of taking East Timor from the Portuguese as 'a summer resort for the settlers of northern Australia'. This came closer to realisation when an Australian-led International Force East Timor (InterFET) landed on Timor in late September 1999 with contingents from the UK and New Zealand. The US provided naval cover and the positioning of an off-shore amphibious force of some 2,500 marines. At the time the US warned Djakarta not to interfere with the Australian landing and occupation of Dili, and threatened Djakarta with retaliation if Australian forces were interfered with by the Indonesian military. The US also used the IMF to put the Indonesian government on notice that IMF financial assistance would be denied in the event of problems in Dili. Eventually more than 5,000 Australians occupied East Timor. InterFET was replaced with the United Nations Transitional Administration in East Timor (UNTAET) with more than 9,000 troops from a number of countries.

The Australia–UN intervention led to a substantial inflow of foreign currency in the country and shaped an artificial economy based in Dili to serve an enclave of tax-free and well-paid foreigners in a situation reminiscent of Vietnam's Saigon in the 1960s. East Timor was developing a dual economy incorporating global capital mainly based on the UNTAET requirements including their tax-free shops, and international contractors linked to various international aid agencies headed by the World Bank and AusAID. The globalised economy marketed East Timor's only cash crop coffee export while its finances came under the control of an international donors consortium through a trust fund with the World Bank as trustee and joint administrator with the Asian Development Bank (ADB). The trust fund will look after money from donors and lenders and receive oil and gas royalties from the operations of multinationals in the Timor Sea. The East Timorian financial situation is likely to be difficult in view of the economy's weakness, the poverty of the population, and the costs of rebuilding the country. Many pledges made by rich countries at the height of the crisis have not been fulfilled because of more pressing demands from new and more urgent crises in Afghanistan and Iraq.

East Timor's other economy includes the majority of poor Timorese. On independence day in May 2002, East Timor with a young and growing population of more than 900,000 was one of the poorest countries in the world, half of its people living in poverty on less than A$1 a day. Unemployment was close to 70 per cent, and educational and training levels were low with half the adult population unable to read and write. Many young East Timorese have grown resentful of their predicament and probably envy the conspicuous consumption and lifestyle of the wealthy foreigners who govern their lives. The situation is a microcosm of the immorality of the new order. Expensive parties on the Australian-owned floating accommodations for expatriates watched by poor and unemployed youth held back by police forces have contributed to the growth of resentment which resulted in anti-government student riots in Dili in December 2002 during which police killed six protesters.

Whether Dili becomes another Port Moresby will depend partly on East Timor's revenues from the huge gas and oil reserves which lie just south of the country. Under the 2003 revised agreement of the 1989 Timor Gap treaty, Australia gained most benefits from the major gas and field reserves of the Timor Sea. Under pressure from the international community the agreement was revised in 2005 on more generous terms to East Timor. As it stands East Timor will receive about 90 per cent of the A$30 billion Bayu-Undan gas field and around 50 per cent of the A$50 billion oil-and-gas Greater Sunrise project. The signing of the agreement in May 2005 gives the US oil giant Conoco-Phillips and Woodside Petroleum the green light to start construction on a pipeline from the Bayu-Udan and other gas fields to Darwin for processing into liquefied gas and shipment to Japan and elsewhere. While East Timor will receive the lion's share of the royalties, Darwin and Australia generally will benefit most with the development of a major energy infrastructure in the Northern Territory. The new treaty leaves East Timor out of the Laminaria-Corallina oilfield, until recently Australia's biggest oilfield, and other major gas deposits in the immediate area, and defers negotiation over the disputed maritime boundary for 50 years.

East Timor is increasingly attracted by the continent's economic pull and becoming one of Australia's satellites. Australia's Northern Territory has been the major beneficiary of East Timor independence. Many entrepreneurs from Darwin have moved to East Timor to profit from the new environment. Dili has also attracted a small army of UN camp followers attracted by the easy money to be made in crisis situations. Some have promoted plans to transform East Timor into a Swiss-like tax haven and five star global resort. Darwin has become a major supply base for the InterFET, UNTAET and the dozens of aid agencies working in East Timor. Some northern businesses have moved to East Timor to take advantage of cheap labour and a more lax legal environment. The territory is also benefiting from a sizeable share of reconstruction contracts tendered by the Asian Development Bank and international aid agencies. There have been substantial gains for the Australian economy with major contracts such as Telstra's monopoly of East Timor's communications, and others to Westpac Banking Corporation and Australia's giant construction firm Multiplex. Development of the oil and gas reserves of the Timor Sea will generate major demands for steel and other construction material in addition to a range of engineering and other services. These projects will add considerable strength to the expansion of Darwin as a major industrial and energy centre in northern Australia.

Australia's regional policy is to tie East Timor into an economic regional grouping in which it plays a dominant role as in the Arafura Sea Council, the Southwest Pacific Dialogue linking eastern Indonesia and PNG to the Northern Territory, and the Pacific Islands Forum. Australia has established six military bases in the country and taken over the training and arming of East Timor's new Defence Force, a regular army of some 1,500 men and the same number of reservists. It is likely that Australia's military presence will be maintained in the years to come as part of its 'forward defence' strategy. Australia's efforts face many difficulties. Some are linked to East Timor's unsettled internal politics and growing inequalities, others are in the context of Indonesia's West Timor policy and the viability of East Timor's enclave of Oecussi-Ambeno. Regional and global competition and tensions will be played out in and around Timor involving Portugal, the European Union and Asian players such as China. All of these will further project Australia's power and ambition in the region.

PAPUA NEW GUINEA

In the aftermath of WWII, imperial nations came under pressure to decolonise and give independence to their dependencies. Like slavery, the colonial enterprise had become too expensive to administer. Decolonisation and independence were means to limit liabilities while putting into place a system of political and economic dependency. Many leaders in Papua New Guinea (PNG) wanted to stay as part of the Australian federation but were told that there was no 'seventh state option'. PNG negotiators went back to Port Moresby and told their people that Australia had rejected them and that 'Orli no laikim mifela' which means 'they do not like us' (Dobell 2003b:18).

Papua New Guinea's five million people have not benefited from the country's nationhood. Cities and many villages are worse off than they were thirty years ago, and living standards have declined since independence from Australia in 1975. PNG's infant mortality and levels of death of women in childbirth have reached levels which are experienced in sub-Sahara Africa (Manning and Windybank 2003). PNG's HIV/AIDS levels ranks fourth in East Asia after Burma and access to primary education is one of the worst in the world. Some 90 per cent of the population work outside the formal economy making a precarious living. Most adults are looking for work and some cash income and more people than ever live below the poverty line. PNG's population is expected to double within twenty years.

The World Bank acknowledges that 'despite considerable natural wealth and substantial and sustained external assistance, [PNG] has been unable to achieve tangible development outcomes in its 25 years as a nation' (Callick 2000a). The country's gross domestic product (GDP) has declined in recent years and its foreign debt had increased to more than A$3.4 billion by 2002, or almost half of the country's GDP. People have become more dependent on imported foods, particularly from Australia. Infrastructure is not being built or maintained. The highland highway, a critical artery in the country's economic life, has fallen into disrepair and trucks can no longer access the country's central and richest provinces. Much of the 2002 coffee harvest, one of the most important rural crops providing a cash income to more than 1 million people, failed to reach the market because of crime and poor roads. A recent report on the state of PNG says that 'presently there is hardly any trust between the people and the government ... health stations have no pharmaceuticals, schools have no books, roads and infrastructure are falling apart ... there is a general sense of insecurity because of the law and order situation' (Rohland 2003). A well-informed Australian resident in PNG has written about the 'deep, destructive seeds of decay, long germinating in Papua New Guinea's body politic' while the people 'persist with their struggle to survive; their provinces unfunded, their schools closing, their health clinics falling into disrepair, they wait too, though for what, they are no longer sure' (O'Callaghan 1999:367).

After 70 years as an Australian colony the country was unprepared for independence. In 1975 there were few educated indigenous people, and little in terms of human and physical infrastructure to provide citizens the opportunities to play a significant role in the modernisation and progress of their country. From the start, PNG became totally reliant on Australian help and funding. The growth model imposed on PNG has been largely based on the exploitation of its vast natural mineral wealth, and coffee, cocoa and oil palm and copra plantations mainly run by expatriates and foreign-led church organisations. Logging in the country's extensive forest by Malaysian and Singapore companies has become another major earner but destructive activity. The country derives about a third of its income from Australian-based companies such as Rio Tinto, BHP-Billiton, Orogen Minerals, Placer Pacific, Oil Search, Lihir Gold and Goldfields. A new phase in dependence on the resource sector is shaping up with a number of oil and gas projects. The largest is the proposed A$7 billion Oil Search and ExxonMobil project to pipe natural gas from PNG's highlands to Brisbane and feeding into Queensland industrial development particularly in Gladstone and Townsville. The project could expand and bring gas to Australia's most important national distribution gas hub of Moomba in central Australia.

PNG's resource development model has come at a high cost. The most obvious case was the Australian CRA Bougainville Panguna copper mine. The forcible acquisition of the land, and construction and operations of the mine, caused considerable human and environmental damage. The Bougainville Freedom Movement reported that '220 hectares of Panguna's forest were poisoned, felled and burnt and then bulldozed directly down into the river, along with tonnes of rich organic topsoil'. Millions of tonnes of poisonous tailings were dumped into the river system. 'Effluent from the mine poured straight into the Kawerong river, the toxic wastes were carried down the Jaba River to the coast, leaving a trail of death 35 km long. Fish died and the wildlife disappeared. Jaba River became choked with tailings and overflowed its banks, turning flatlands into contaminated swamps' (BLM 1995). Conflict over land and mine operations generated a secessionist movement on Bougainville which eventually closed down the mine. What followed was a costly and disastrous civil war with PNG from 1988 to 1999.

The Ok Tedi mine, which until recently contributed about 10 per cent of PNG's revenue, turned out to be another disaster. The site in western PNG was in 1968 the world's largest copper and gold deposit and owned by Broken Hill Proprietary (BHP), Australia's largest company at the time. Mining started in 1981 but the project proved to be an environmental disaster. Mining the mountain released '70 million tonnes of waste a year flushed down the river system to the sea' (Pheasant 2002). Over the years, river beds and low-lying areas have been layered with heavy toxic waste destroying the rainforest canopy and villagers' garden plots, killing wildlife and fish. In 1994 Ok Tedi villagers filed a claim against BHP seeking remedial action and A$4 billion in damages. In 2001 the new company BHP-Billiton shifted its controlling interest to a Singapore trust and at the same time the PNG government legislated the Ok Tedi Mine Continuation Act to protect BHP-Billiton from PNG's claims against it in regard to environmental damage. In 2004 the Australian law firm Slater & Gordon seeking compensation on behalf of Ok Tedi villagers and others gave up the case.

Another example of the scale of the problem is the Lihir Gold mine, a highly profitable investment managed by Rio Tinto and partly funded by the Australian government Export Finance credit agency (EFIC). One of its directors, Ross Garnaut, is a former colonial administrator and now a professor at the Australian National University. The mine has been discharging large amounts of waste containing cyanide and other chemicals into the sea (Divecha 2002). The ocean dumping of waste from barges is in breach of international law and locals are increasingly concerned about the impact of the mine on their lives, 'most people on Lihir now oppose it. We think it is the next Bougainville' (Roberts 2002).

Extensive logging taking place in many parts of the country has led to violent protests from villagers affected by the impact of deforestation and the destruction of the environment. Many Asian companies are involved in logging activities. Companies from Malaysia and Singapore which control the logging sector are said to have bribed PNG elites with substantial wealth in order to gain logging licences. Bribing politicians has also enabled foreign companies to manipulate the legislature to advantage such as securing tax exemption on income. An example is the case of Rimbunan Hijau (RH) a Malaysian–Singapore company which has a number of logging camps in the Western Province. The company is the province's de facto government and buys the services of the Port Moresby-based PNG police force to enforce their rule and pressure landowners for access to their trees (SBS 2004). The extent of the damage to PNG's social and natural environment has been so well documented that even the World Bank has had to be critical of logging practices in a country which has the world's second largest tropical rainforest. Nevertheless, destructive logging continues because it is linked to the corruption of the political class and tied up with foreign loans and Australian aid which the government needs to keep afloat.

At the heart of the problem is the corruption of the political elite and a kleptocracy which has impoverished the country and seriously undermined its institutions and viability. Transparency International says that PNG 'has been undermined by wide-range corruption in public and private enterprise. Funds earmarked for social services are siphoned off by unscrupulous politicians and public servants. Schools, hospitals and essential infrastructure are unfunded or non-existent, and the people of PNG suffer' (TI 2004). Former prime minister Julius Chan has accumulated a fortune estimated at more than A$100 million. His family made vast profits through land speculation, government contracts and privileged access and speculation on mining shares. Many ministers have been involved in corrupt dealings involving the allocation of logging licences and mining shares, and payoffs by business interests involved in government contracts. The corruption of the political elite was clearly evident during the Bougainville crisis and the hiring of mercenaries as the final solution to the problem.

At the time substantial public money was illegally diverted to a trust fund to pay for white mercenaries and expensive military hardware from the former USSR. Eventually the South African London-based Sandline company received US$43 million for 'a contract it was never able to fulfil' (O'Callaghan 1999:366). Australian intelligence knew most details of the operation and it must be assumed that the Australian government supported it as long as it 'worked' and solved the Bougainville crisis.

Massive fraud involving PNG's National Provident Fund is further testimony of PNG's problem with the sophisticated thieving of public wealth. The fund which administers a compulsory superannuation levy on PNG's private sector workers and employers and provides superannuation for all private sector employees had by 2002 lost half of all workers' entitlements accumulated since the establishment of the fund in 1980. Money was moved into overpriced investment in Australia and into private hands. The inquiry 'implicated high-profile people inside and outside PNG in what appeared to be systematic and massive fraud, and the report shows that huge sums of money are being siphoned off into the pockets of a few greedy and unscrupulous people' (TI 2003). The report cited 37 people for corrupt conduct including former prime minister Bill Skate and Brisbane resident and former Chairman of the Fund Jimmy Maldina.

Growing discontent with the failings of government has led to a serious breakdown in law and order and the fragmentation of the country. PNG's armed forces have mutinied on several occasions and threatened to take over the reigns of power. Leaders of the 2001 military mutiny called for the IMF, the World Bank and Australia to leave the country, and one of its leaders, Captain Stanley Benny, read a statement signed by his troops accusing Australia of having 'denuded the nation's vast resources under the guise of assistance' (Skehan 2001). Other symptoms of fragmentation have been the presence of warlords and heavily armed gangs in the country's highlands, and rebellious elements in other provinces with close links to northern Australia's Torres Strait region, and Indonesia's West Papua's liberation movement OPM (Organisasi Papua Merdeka). Law and order has broken down in Port Moresby and other cities. Urbanisation without modernisation has created vast shanty towns with no electricity or running water as home to dissatisfied youth faced with a hopeless future turning to violence and crime.

The development model imposed on PNG has promoted the appropriation of the country's wealth for the benefit of a minority in and outside PNG. Australia has been the main party to PNG's modernisation and to the corruption of its political elite by moving the country into a destructive developmental path and dependency. PNG's economic growth model has favoured Australia's economic and political interests. The development of the mining and other sectors has been spearheaded largely by Australian capital. Australian advisers have played leading roles in shaping and implementing PNG's economic plans, often through structural adjustment programmes (SAPs) imposed by international lenders such as the World Bank and the International Monetary Fund.

Aid delivery has been linked to SAPs requiring government sale of public assets and an end to subsidies such as school fees for primary school students. PNG's growth model has also been translated in a brain drain of professionals such as medical doctors moving to Australia's rural hospitals while PNG's health system slowly disintegrates. Under pressure the government in the early 1990s deregulated the Kina, slashed taxes, introduced a Goods and Services Tax (GST) and borrowed more money from overseas. The deregulation of the financial market has led to major losses of the country's reserves and a huge outflow of capital to countries like Australia. After 1994 Australia's financial aid turned to tied aid project which largely benefited Australian consultants and companies. Australian expatriates play an important role in the economy. Former colonials and newcomers have developed lucrative networks with PNG's small elite. In some of the worst instances of corruption some have been involved in selling Australian and Israeli military equipment to the PNG unsuitable to the country's needs. Australia dominates PNG's international trade and runs a healthy current account surplus. While Australia provides the country with most of its imports, in particular food items such as rice, it imposes restrictions on PNG's agricultural exports to Australia.

Australia's Port Moresby High Commission dominates PNG's politics. Its feudal-like role is symbolised by vast compounds and expatriate hilltop living quarters surrounded by razor wire protection and security fences. A reminder of Australia's capacity to interfere in local politics was PNG's acceptance in 2002 of Australia's asylum seekers' Pacific solution. Under an agreement which was linked to Australian aid commitment, PNG agreed to establish a detention camp on Manus Island, a former colonial naval base, to house refugees caught on Australian territory or within its maritime jurisdiction. This affair raises many questions about the role of Australia in PNG and the extent to which the interests that prevail have more to do with Australian capital, power and regional geopolitics than with PNG's people. Australia's intelligence community has been privy to corrupt transactions in PNG's politics for many years. The government has known for years that aid funds were used to buy votes and defraud government, that money laundering to Australian entities had flourished, and that Australian companies had been involved in bribing politicians and conducting their businesses in ways that would be illegal in Australia.

Not unlike the Roman Empire, PNG has been a rebellious province in Australia's arc of instability and on the receiving end of the 'big stick' approach as part of Howard's doctrine of preemptive strike. Australia's intervention in 2003 followed a similar operation in the Solomon Islands months earlier. As part of a A$2.5 billion rescue plan Australia has been sending police teams to regain control of Port Moresby, Lae and Mt Hagen in the highlands. Contingents of bureaucrats, technocrats and judges are scheduled to take over or supervise key ministries. Australia will assume control of PNG's finances, judiciary and the police. An important target is to regain control and reform the military establishment and further build up a military infrastructure along the Indonesian border. Australia's military presence is likely to increase in the years to come with training programmes for the police and military, and other programmes which Hugh White, the Australian government defence publicist and former head of the Australian Strategic Policy Institute (ASPI), says aim to restore PNG to a 'sustainable path to political stability and economic prosperity' (White 2004).

Australia's military intervention is partly in response to concerns about homeland security. There were genuine fears that PNG's disintegration would lead to a military takeover and the country's fragmentation which could threaten Australia's north because of arms smuggling, drug trafficking and terrorist activities. Such events would trigger new waves of refugees from PNG and elsewhere landing on Australia's northern shore. Of particular concern are the thousands of Chinese illegal immigrants in PNG. The Australian economy has much to gain from a military intervention in PNG. Since the landing of the first contingent of Australian police in 2003, new mining projects have been announced and there has been a resurgence of economic activities with mining ventures moving from planning stage to infrastructure work. The gas pipeline between PNG's highlands and Queensland is likely to be a key beneficiary of Australia's military presence. Malaysia's state-owned oil company Petronas has been buying into PNG's gas fields and pipeline to Brisbane through a partnership with Australia's AGL. A growing economic presence is China. Government-owned China Metallurgical Construction Corp has acquired a controlling interest for some A$855 million in the Highland Pacific's massive Ramu River nickel and cobalt project. If the negotiations are successful China will build and operate the mine and refinery and purchase the entire production.

Australia's involvement in PNG should be viewed as part of a larger regional and global power play. Malaysia, Singapore, Taiwan and China's commercial interests are growing along with their political influence in the affairs of PNG and the region. As US sheriff Australia's role is to maintain sufficient political control in the affairs of PNG to contain the influence of regional powers particularly in regard to Indonesia and China. It remains to be seen whether Australia is serious about changing PNG for the better. One test is the extent to which Australia's intervention will lead to the arrest and trial of members of the elite implicated in major financial scams. Another is the extent to which the children of PNG have access to the education and care they need and deserve. Extending Australia's democratic ideals to PNG within some form of common market and political union would be a step in that direction. Such an effort would require far more resources than Australia has been willing to commit so far.

BOUGAINVILLE

Bougainville is the largest island in the Solomons chain with a population of more than 180,000. Named after a French explorer adventurer who never sat foot on the island it was claimed by the British as part of the Solomon Islands protectorate. It was then transferred to Australia with Papua New Guinea after WWI by the League of Nations with the mandate to 'promote to the utmost the material and moral well-being and social progress of the inhabitants' (O'Callaghan 1999:17). In the 1960s CRA, an Australia-based mining company, found rich copper deposit on the island and proceeded with the help of Australia's judiciary to dispossess local inhabitants of their land and houses. The government was warned in 1969 that 'until CRA has entered into occupation of the land that it requires, difficulties with the native people, including in some areas opposition to the acquisition of land or pressure for secession may be expected'. Mine opponents were described in the press as 'collaborators with the Japanese' during WWII (Mining Monitor 2000). CRA's Panguna copper mine was the world's most profitable mine when it started operations in 1972.

Three weeks before PNG gained independence in 1975, Bougainville made its first move to secede by raising the flag of the new country and in 1988 people of central Bougainville forcibly closed the Panguna copper mine after 20 years of protest and failed negotiations. This led to a ten-year civil war between PNG and Bougainville's secessionist movement, the Bougainville Revolutionary Army (BRA). From 1988 to 1999, between 15,000 and 20,000 Bougainvilleans were killed or died from preventable diseases such as malaria, and nearly a third of the population were relocated into detention centres in PNG-controlled areas and put into forced labour. PNG's blockade of Bougainville increased hardships for people in an attempt to turn them against the BRA, and effectively sealed off the island from the outside world depriving the islanders of medicines, fuel and humanitarian aid. Most the casualties resulted from the blockade of Bougainville by PNG forces which prevented medical and other supplies from reaching the island. PNG forces also destroyed medical and other facilities on the island using Australia-supplied incendiary mortar bombs.

During the ten-year war, PNG's armed forces committed mass atrocities. Amnesty International reported on many cases of murder, torture, rape and people disappearing after being taken into custody (AI 1997). Bougainville leader Moses Havini claims that during 1991–92 the PNG's Defence Forces (PNGDF) 'went on an execution spree on Buka, they dug up a big trench line there, where people from all over Buka Island were executed and dumped into mass graves ... most of the young boys who were executed by the PNGDF on Buka Island were thrown into the sea, their bodies never recovered' (Butterworth and Shakespeare 2002:26). PNG forces were trained and equipped by Australia. Australia funded the PNGDF operations in Bougainville and provided ammunition, helicopter gunships and patrol boats which caused much human suffering and destruction. Helicopters were flown by Australian hired mercenaries with the approval and support of the Australian government under special provisions of the Crimes Act. The arms and ammunition used to kill Bougainvilleans came from Australia and Australian forces provided expertise and advisers to direct and advise the PNG forces in their day-to-day operations against the BRA.

Probably around 1995, PNG's government decided to hire the London-based Sandline International – a branch of Executive

Outcomes, a South African white mercenary organisation – to deal with the problem. Mercenaries began arriving in PNG in 1996 as well as heavy military transport from Ukraine carrying arms and helicopters, and ammunition ordered from a Singapore government-owned company. The arrival of mercenaries in PNG caused a scandal and a political crisis between PNG's military and the government. The military took over parliament, deported Sandline's foreign mercenaries, and forced the resignation of Prime Minister Julius Chan, replacing him with another corrupt politician, Bill Skate. Sandline's plan was to cash in on the reopening of the Bougainville mine and in a secret deal acquire CRA shares. This was part of Sandline's growth strategy to move in on poor countries with a peace problem and exchange some of their services for a share of the country's resources. In the process it bribed a number of PNG individuals including PNG's military leader General Singirok who received US$500,000 via Cairns. PNG's government has had to pay the full cost of a contract with Sandline validated in international law – about US$46 million. All in all the Bougainville fiasco cost the country some US$1.2 billion.

Australia played an active role in the Bougainville disaster. Australian intelligence had access to all communications in PNG and the region through the use of telephone-tapping equipment located in Port Moresby's Australian High Commission. Intelligence gained information tapping into international calls, e-mail, faxes and other means via their satellite intercept station located at Kojarena near Geraldton in Western Australia, or via links to another station at Shoal Haven near Darwin. At the time of the crisis, Australia set up a mobile listening post at Cape York 'aimed specifically at intercepting communications on the island and with the neighbouring Solomon Islands, where many of the rebels spent much of their time' (O'Callaghan 1999:131).

Australia eventually organised and funded a peace process which resulted in an accord with the separatists to end hostilities and negotiate terms to bring peace to the island. The Peace Monitoring Group (PMG) which includes troops from Australia, New Zealand, Fiji and Vanuatu, have managed to bring some order on Bougainville and collect some weapons from the insurgents. In 2000 Bougainville entered into a class action in California against the Anglo-Australian mining giant Rio Tinto for the killings and damage to the island, an action opposed by the Australian and US governments. An agreement was signed between Bougainville and PNG in 2002 to set up a Provincial Administration and establish the province's independence process. Joseph Kabui became the first president of an autonomous Bougainville following the internationally monitored elections in June 2005.

THE SOLOMON ISLANDS

To the west of Bougainville is the archipelagic state of the Solomon Islands with some 500,000 people three hours flight time from Brisbane. A British protectorate until granted independence in 1978 when it was known as the 'happy isles'. Some twenty years later the population had nearly doubled and Mary-Louise O'Callaghan, a long time observer of Pacific affairs, wrote about the dramatic decline of the once happy isles, 'make no mistake, it is a nation that's dying – a young foolish, weak and vulnerable nation. And with it, an entire people's chance for a better life' (O'Callaghan 2002).

At the time of independence the British left the new nation-state with little to constitute a sound basis for development. Few islanders had been trained, and the infrastructure needed for the task of building a modern state was almost non-existent. Since independence the economy has been largely based on the exploitation of the country's considerable natural resources by foreign entities. The Australian-owned Golden Ridge gold mine provided some 25 per cent of the country's revenues while it operated. Other major enterprises are the tuna factory operated by Japan-based Taiyo Ltd which once employed about 3,000 workers and the British-registered Commonwealth Development Corporation which owns Solomon Islands Plantation Ltd, the country's largest oil-palm plantation and another major contributor to government revenue before it also closed down with another major loss of employment.

There has been extensive logging of the country's forest particularly by Chinese, Japanese and Malaysian companies. Many of their operations are illegal and involve deals with local chiefs followed by operations to quickly log whole areas and load and ship the timber out. Foreign operators have also been involved in extensive fishing operations within the Solomon Islands maritime jurisdiction. Mining activities have left trails of destruction including Gold Ridge gold mine extensive cyanide and copper pollution of mining sites and surrounding areas. Aid from wealthy donor nations has played a major role in the economy and is linked to structural adjustment programmes to privatise public assets such as the post office and shipping services, and cut back on government services and employment. Equally damaging have been the privatisation of customary land, and the introduction of school and health care fees. Bishop Terry Brown, a long-term resident, wrote that school fees keep children out of school and 'the pool of illiterate, dissatisfied, disappointed youth will simply grow. They form the pool that will produce the "terrorists" that Australia is so afraid of'. The Solomon Islands College of Education has virtually closed because of lack of funding and this 'has produced another pool of disaffected young adults, who turn to crime, alcohol and drug abuse' (Brown 2003).

People have little to show for the great amount of wealth created through the commercialisation of the country's resources and revenues from international aid programmes. Poverty and inequality have increased since independence while the population has doubled. According to economic adviser John Martin, from 1980 to 1995 income growth was negligible and disparity in incomes became 'colossal with the top 1 per cent of households receiving 52 per cent of all income' in the early 1990s. At the time the Solomon islanders had the 'lowest education attainment, life expectancy and income per head than any Pacific islanders except Papua New Guineans' (Callick 2000b). According to John Roughan of the Solomon Islands Development Trust:

the quality of village life, especially for women has been substantially reduced: it was harder, less rewarding, poorer and less and less healthy. The gap between the country's minority elite and the villager grew at an alarming rate. Millionaires, non-existent in the days before independence, steadily became more common in the 1980s and 1990s. (Roughan and Hite 2002:85)

By 1998 the economy had shrunk by more than 25 per cent, and the state had accumulated an external debt of some A$250 million or 55 per cent of GNP; the country was bankrupt, unable to pay salaries and recurrent expenditures. Finance minister Michael Maina said during his 2002 budget speech that decline 'entails a downward spiral of falling incomes, declining exports, declining government revenue, declining external reserves and dwindling donor assistance' (O'Callaghan 2002).

The Solomon Islands economic model has benefited a local elite and many foreigners. It has been built as a cash box for savvy opportunists and international operators. Helen Hughes of the Sydney-based Centre for Independent Studies wrote that 'while teachers, medical workers and police have gone without pay, expatriate carpetbagger advisers have helped to siphon off huge private fortunes abroad' (Hughes 2004). Corruption has been a major feature of the Solomon Islands political life since independence. Foreigners including Malaysian loggers have been corrupting the country's elites paying bribes and buying trips to Australia's Gold Coast brothels in exchange for a share of the country's wealth. Synergies between corruption and economic decline create an opportunity for more destructive interference such as some recent deals with Taiwan. In exchange for diplomatic recognition of Taiwan, the Solomon Islands received more than US$100 million in soft loans. In exchange Taiwan obtained tuna-fishing licences, and the right to ship some 3 million tonnes of industrial waste to be dumped on the swampland of the 3,235 km2 Makira island, home to some 23,000 people. The waste comes from Taiwan's garment factories and is said to be loaded with mercury, lead and arsenic. The Solomon Islands will receive US$35 million per shipment. Taiwan has been investigating the suitability of the Solomon Islands to dump 97,000 barrels of low-radiation waste from its nuclear industry (Field 2002).

A failed state led to violence and fighting between major ethnic groups. Over the years more youth have been pushed out of their villages to towns with no prospects for meaningful employment. Rising frustration fuelled centuries-old tribal rivalries, and eventually led to the formation of militias and armed gangs organised along ethnic lines who began fighting each other. Fighting erupted between the Guadalcanal-based Isatabu Freedom Movement (ISM) and the Malaita-based Malaita Eagle Force in 1998. Escalation of the conflict was triggered by the deportation of more than 10,000 Malaita settlers from Guadalcanal to their home island. Eventually the Malaita Eagle Force responded by gaining control of Guadalcanal's capital Honiara in 2001 and taking over the state's apparatus at gunpoint.

The Solomon Islands asked in 2000 for Australia's help to bring the violence to an end. Shortly after Australia's refusal to send a small police force the government was ousted. Australia lost its chance to save the Solomon Islands when following the coup it sailed a warship into Honiara harbour to evacuate Australians; the event created a situation that further emboldened the militias. Peace negotiations brokered by Australia and New Zealand under the Townsville Peace Agreement led to internationally supervised elections in 2001 and a new government was formed under the leadership of Allan Kemakesa. There were attempts to disarm and disband the militias but these failed because of the deterioration of the economic situation. The peace-monitoring mission was unable to complete its task and spent a lot of time preparing evacuation exercises by helicopter which further destabilised the political situation. At the end of the amnesty period in May 2002 most guns had not been returned and the prime minister and his government were held at ransom by various armed parties including the police. By May 2003 Australian banks on the islands had closed down their operations and evacuated their staff.

The idea of sending troops to help restore order to the Solomon Islands was rejected by Australia's foreign minister Alexander Downer in January 2003 by calling it 'folly in the extreme', that it would be difficult to justify to the taxpayers and would not work. But by June that year Downer's tune had changed dramatically with the prime minister warning the country that 'a failed state on our doorstep will jeopardise our own security'. Within a few months the Australia National Security Council (NSC) declared the Solomon Islands a major security issue and possible breeding grounds for terrorism, and in July 2003 the first Australian troops landed in the country as part of a 10-year intervention plan named Helpem Fren – pidgin for helping friend. Australia's Regional Assistance Mission (RAMSI) has deployed more than 2,500 military and police personnel from Australia, New Zealand, Fiji, Tonga and Samoa. The operation is expected to cost in excess of A$600 million and involves Australian control of the country's courts and administration.

Australia's policy reversal was triggered by information that Indonesia was getting ready to intervene in the Solomon Islands. Australian intelligence had tapped Indonesia's Canberra embassy conversations with the Solomon Islands foreign minister Harry Chan asking for Indonesia's help to bring law and order to the islands. In April 2003 a formal request had been made to Indonesia to intervene. Indonesia appears to have supported the move as an opportunity to get back at Australia for 'liberating' East Timor. More important was the consideration that helping the Solomon Islands would build up Indonesia's regional alliance with the Pacific region in support for its claim on West Papua. In a quick response to Indonesia's challenge the Solomon Islands prime minister was called to Canberra and told that Australia would send troops to his country. Mary-Louise O'Callaghan, an Australian writer who has lived in the region for many years, has written that 'small and black, these countries have been treated by us pretty much as we have our indigenous people ... behind the rhetoric of sovereignty, we have allowed these states to flounder. With our wealth, experience and large resources of expertise, we could have made a difference' (O'Callaghan 2000).

FIJI AND OTHER DEPENDENCIES

Towards the eastern end of Australia's arc of instability is Fiji's archipelago with some 850,000 people. Since independence from Britain in 1970, Fiji's development has seen much of its wealth benefit a small minority. Declining living standards triggered a military coup in 1987 which brought to an end Fiji's experiment with democracy and multiculturalism. Australia has extensive economic interests in Fiji's banking, real estate, mining and tourism. Some of the traditional pillars of Fiji's economy have included well-known Australia-based companies such as Colonial Sugar Refining (CSR), Burns Philip Trading Company and Emperor Gold Mine. More recently the clothing industry has become Fiji's leading export. This sector is largely controlled by Australian interests such as Moontide South Pacific, Mark One Apparel and Consolidated Textiles. Australia is Fiji's biggest source of imports. Betting shops in Fiji are part of the Sydney-based Waterhouse family assets and the Fiji Times is owned by the Murdoch Press.

Australia has played an important role in restructuring Fiji's government finance and implementing structural adjustment programmes to move the economy towards a market model favoured by Canberra's economic rationalists. Aid money has played an important role in the liberalisation of the economy including work by Wolfgang Kasper, former professor of economics at the University of New South Wales, who set up Fiji's economic liberalisation blueprint following the 1987 military coup. More recently Kasper, who now works for Sydney's conservative think-tank Centre for Independent Studies, promoted Fiji's new constitution foreseeing the country's break up into some form of corporate state structure (Kasper 2001).

Living standards for Fiji's majority have not improved. In the past 15 years educational and health services have declined due partly to funding shortages and Fiji's brain drain to Australia and elsewhere. Professionals have been leaving the country, including teachers, doctors and nurses. Many ill people can no longer be treated in the country's hospitals and are left to die at home. Unemployment has been a growing problem generating criminal activities and ethnic tensions. Poverty has increased to possibly 50 per cent and more visibly in the urban slums (ADB 2003:29). International investment has reached its lowest point in years and it has been estimated 'that it could be 25 years before the nation returns to its pre-coup levels of economic activity' (Cohen 2001).

Attempts by popularly elected governments to introduce a policy of equity and long-term growth have been opposed by those who stand to lose from higher taxation and a more egalitarian access to the country's resources such as its timber (mahogany), land and gold. The coup of 1987 against the democratically elected Labor coalition government of Dr. Bavendra was organised by groups linked to Fiji's traditional oligarchy 'hiding behind a front of populist communalism' (Howard 1991:5). Local indigenous interests played on concerns about the USSR, Cuba and Libya's role in the Pacific to stir the anti-communist brew and get the United States and probably Australia involved in backing a military coup led by Lt. Colonel Sitiveni Rabuka and his Australian Special Air Service-trained Fijian troops (Lal 1990; Howard 1991). Another military coup in 2000 was triggered by Mahendra Chaudhry government's attempt at more egalitarian economic policies and its opposition to privatisation programmes (Sutherland and Robertson 2001). The coup was carried out by an Australian resident Fijian businessman George Speight with the country's special forces and soldiers of the Counter Revolutionary Warfare Unit (CRWU).

Australia has a major interest in Fiji's affairs. There are substantial links between both countries bridging economic and religious affairs but the overriding concern is to build Fiji's political and military assets to maintain domestic stability and enable Fiji to play a major regional role within a larger Pacific community. Australia's military role in Fiji has been an indirect one until now. After the 1987 coup, troops from the crack third brigade at the Lavarack Barracks in Townsville were made ready for deployment to land in Fiji in an operation code named 'Morris Dance'. In the future, Australia is likely to send troops to Fiji in the event of a serious threat to Fiji's viability which attracts the attention of India.

There is a broad scheme to shape Australia's Pacific realm into some loose form of confederation controlled from Fiji. There are already regional organisations based in Fiji whose role could be expanded, such as the Australia-led Pacific Islands Forum and the University of the Pacific. Australia wants to build up Fiji's military to play a more active role in regional intervention in addition to its role as a mercenary force in UN and Western coalition military operations. Fiji's location and geopolitical role is important to Australia to destabilise efforts on the part of France to gain a foothold in the country and more importantly to thwart possible attempts by India to intervene. India's growing naval power could respond to a serious crisis involving Indo-Fijians.

There are a number of small island-states between Fiji and the Solomon Islands important to Australia's economic and security interests. Nauru, Tonga, Vanuatu and Kiribati were parts of the British Empire whose interests have been passed on to Australia. One of the smallest island-states in the world is Nauru, at 21 km2, totally dependent for its livelihood on foreign import and aid. The population of some 12,000 people includes 4,000 foreigners with many Australian professional managers, doctors and engineers. The island, laid to waste from years of mining guano by Anglo-Australian mining interests, gained its independence from Australia in 1968, and is largely administered from offices in Melbourne's Nauru House. Nauru's economy has served as a cash box to a small group of local and foreign insiders. The mismanagement of its resources and widespread corruption has bankrupted the country and made it dependent for power and water on Australia's aid funding. Money received as settlement for compensation for years of mining and damage to the environment by the British Phosphate Commission has disappeared into private hands. Fraud and shady deals perpetuated by entities based in Australia have contributed to Nauru's poverty and pathetic state of affairs (McDaniel and Gowdy 2000).

In 2001 Nauru became part of Australia's Pacific solution for refugees who arrive in Australia without papers. Nauru accepted A$20 million to set up a detention camp for asylum seekers including many children arrested by Australian authorities. Australia has put pressure on Nauru to keep journalists out of the country and keep refugees' traumas out of the news. Australia's bribe money has been used to pay hospital bills that Nauruans diabetes-prone people have accumulated in Australia, and to repair the island's generators and purchase fuel for their operation. Nauru's political affairs have been transferred to Australian and US interests. These have closed down Nauru's lucrative sale of passports and laundering activities, and swayed Nauru's UN vote to shore up the Western alliance. Its sovereign status has been used by Australian–NZ–US intelligence services to set up an embassy in China to provide an escape route for North Korean high official defectors to the United States. Australia has considered giving Nauru's 12,000 people Australian citizenship or finding them a new Pacific island and there are plans to turn the island into some form of global corporation. Kiribati may follow Nauru's path and look to Australia to resettle its population because of recent sea level rises which threaten the viability of the community.

Since independence from Britain and France in 1980, Vanuatu's 200,000 people have experienced a series of financial scandals and a decline in living standards. Vanuatu has also been involved in international money laundering linked to interests in gambling, drugs and tax evasion. Some of the country's financial assets have been stolen by international scam operators. Vanuatu's aid dependency has put pressure on the government to accept a Comprehensive Reform Programme (CRP) under the supervision of the Asian Development Bank (ADB). This programme known locally as CRAP has forced the country to cut back on public service employment, sell valuable public assets to foreign investors, and borrow large sums from international institutions. Vanuatu was debt-free for the first ten years of its independence but is now burdened by large debts to international financial institutions such as the IMF, ADB and the foreign private banking sector. Vanuatu's politics continue to be troubled by foreign interference. China has shown intense interest in gaining the country's support. It has increased imports from Vanuatu and offered the country large untied grants as alternative to Western aid. China's activities have followed a similar path in Tonga and Kiribati. Kiribati's political parties are bankrolled by either China or Taiwan which in turn fund the country's budget. China had an ambassador until 2003 when Kiribati recognised Taiwan; China's satellite station, used to track US missile tests in the nearby Marshall islands, was closed and aid to Kiribati's 90,0000 people withdrawn.

Australia nevertheless remains the key player. Australia was prepared to send troops as part of operation 'sailcloth' following the Port Vila riots in 1988. Former prime minister Barak Sope accused Australia and New Zealand of involvement in his removal from office in 2001 because of his friendship with China. There is increasing concern in Vanuatu about Australia's interference and spying activities, and more recently Vanuatu blamed Australian advisers in Vanuatu for almost triggering an armed conflict between the police and army. Australia has been openly critical of Vanuatu's support for West Papua's separatists and for allowing the movement to open an office in Port Vila, and is concerned about Vanuatu's role as a centre for a Melanesian alliance against Indonesia and Australia. Vanuatu's leadership has warned Australia that the country would fight if Australia ever occupied the country.

FORTRESS AUSTRALIA

Australia has been party to the deterioration in the economic and political situation of its northern neighbours. In recent years a new militarism largely driven by innate insecurity and recurring fears of invasion has swayed the country's political affairs. There is a new arrogance in Australia's supposed right and duty to lecture neighbouring countries on their failures at democratic governance and to intervene in the name of some greater truth and vision. This new phase in Australian imperialism has been legitimised by a close alliance with the US and a shared vision for a new world order. Closer to the truth is Australia's culture of greed and selfishness which promises more wealth for all and hence nurtures fears of bogy foreigners and terrorist attacks.

The dynamics of Australia's postmodern militarism focuses on homeland security. This is about protecting near unpopulated but resource-rich northern Australia. A critical outcome is to prevent the arrival of refugees from the arc of instability. The basic premise for the militarisation of the north is the danger of failed states to Australia's security. A failed state, says Australia's neoconservative government funded think-tank the Australian Strategic Policy Institute, is like Liberia or Sierra Leone, and characterised by 'economic deterioration, dramatically falling living standards, declining governance, failing institutions and an incapacity to deliver services for citizens' (Wainwright 2003:28). State failure poses a serious threat to Australia's regional and global security and defence planners compare the situation to a petri dish 'in which transnational and non-state security threats can develop and breed' transnational criminal operations, 'drug smuggling, gun-running, people smuggling and terrorism' (Wainwright 2003:13–14).

A failed state, in government parlance, is a disease that spreads and contaminates others. Hence a failed state, like the domino effect, can affect an entire region and may infect the entire earth. The defence establishment claims that failed states can become rogue states and bases for attacks against Australia putting at risk the north's valuable resources and strategic industrial energy centres. The country's new war on terrorism calls for preemptive strike on countries that fail Australia's test of good governance and threaten its national interests. In essence Australia's response to countries with a failing economy and increased poverty is military action and control over their affairs. Australia's national security elite are realists who are not interested in the search for basic cures to regional problems because they fear the revolutionary potential of more deep-rooted changes. Thus arms sales, doses of humanitarian relief, and repression are more suitable political tools than a foreign policy and programmes that would implement human rights and justice for all.

The region is likely to experience climatic change and rising sea levels will force many to leave their homes. Sea levels are likely to rise by 20 cm in the coming decades flooding many islands and affecting their economies and capacity to produce food. Rises in water temperature will cause extensive coral bleaching and depress the tourist industry. Greenpeace's *Pacific in Peril* forecasts a decline in Pacific islands economies by up to 20 per cent by 2020 (Hoegh-Guldberg 2000). Pacific nations unable to afford mitigating the effects of rising sea levels will face severe social disruption and experience mass migration to higher grounds or as asylum seekers to countries like Australia. Norman Myers of Oxford University estimates that global warming will have a dramatic impact on countries such as China, India, Bangladesh, Indonesia and all of the Pacific islands, and generate 150 million environmental refugees in the Asia-Pacific region in the next 50 years.

Australia's militarisation of the north is partly driven by fear of invasion by refugees. Past waves of asylum seekers have been unwelcome because of their ethnicity, religion or 'Middle Eastern' appearance. At the same time the government has been running a campaign to demonise refugees and instill fear about public safety. Australian officials including federal ministers and high-ranking officers have described refugees as wicked people who throw their children overboard. In one such instance Liberal Senator George Brandis accused asylum seekers of trying to strangle a child. As with other cases these allegations have been proven to be lies and were part of a ploy by the Liberal coalition to manipulate the electorate at the time of 2001 federal election. Nevertheless, there is increasing popular support to stop the flow of asylum seekers coming by boat from Indonesia and elsewhere. The electorate has supported the detention of large numbers of refugees including many women and children in concentration camp conditions.

Australian authorities and intelligence services in Indonesia have been involved in passing on information about the movement of refugees and sabotaging boats leaving Indonesia. Such actions may have caused the intentional death of hundreds of refugees seeking safety to Australia. In recent years Australia's defence forces have turned boats around before reaching Australian waters. The legal ploy of excising off-shore islands from Australia has enabled the government to ship refugees to detention centres on Nauru and PNG's Manus Island. The Pacific solution to Australia's refugee problem has become part of Australia's aid programme to Nauru, PNG and other Pacific countries.

Australia has much to gain by projecting power because of its considerable investment and trade with the region. There are substantial opportunities for Australia's economic expansion, including aid projects by private contractors, and the government is keen to put into place mechanisms to help this process. Support for Indonesia's military assures political stability and growing opportunities for Australian investors in that country. There is a possibility that Australia will support the excision of West Papua from Indonesia as a means to reduce Indonesia's regional threat to Western economic interests. There is a plan to rearrange Pacific affairs to promote the economic and political viability of individual member states by creating a form of regional confederation under Australian auspices. Countries like East Timor, PNG, Bougainville, the Solomon Islands, Vanuatu and Fiji would be joined into a form of pooled regional governance. New Zealand, which has considerable economic interests in the Pacific, would be brought into the scheme as joint administrator.

A newly formed Pacific Economic and Political Community would use the Australian dollar as a single currency. The newly formed community would be policed by a force based and trained in Fiji and probably headed by an Australian foreign affairs retiree or other government crony. In the words of Prime Minister Howard, this would be the equivalent of the European Union of the South Pacific and presumably open to potential new applicants such as West Papua and Ambon. Under this scheme Australia would not allow free entry to Pacific people into Australia as with New Zealand's former Pacific dependencies. Australia would nevertheless contemplate some arrangement to allow some movement of labour to meet the need for temporary workers particularly in sectors which require seasonal workers such as fruit picking and cannery work. Behind this plan are major Australian industry group lobbies such as the Queensland Fruit and Vegetable Growers.

Huntington's clash of civilisations scenario has found widespread support among Australians (Huntington 1997). A number of programmes have appeared on the theme including an Australian

Broadcasting Corporation (ABC) major presentation featuring Australian Owen Harries, the former editor of a leading neoconservative US journal the *National Interest* (Harries 2004). Harries was the first person to publicise Huntington thesis in Australia in 1993 (Harries 1993). Mass media coverage has been extensive and picked up by Christian fundamentalist groups. The Bali service in memory of many Australians killed in the nightclub bombing was turned by the press into a new Gallipoli. Howard's campaign against 'terrorism' has been meshed into the clash of civilisation scenario as a fight between Islam and the Christian West, with Australia on the fault line between the two civilisations. Indonesia is the new battlefield between the West and the rest and Australia must be prepared to intervene in the affairs of its neighbours.

Australia's new militarism is dominated by a view of the world closely akin to that of the US. At the core is a belief that Eurasia's control by an Anglo-American alliance is the key to world peace and prosperity. Australia's role as US regional sheriff is to enforce US imperial directives within its geographical sphere of influence. Of particular concern is Indonesia's future. The country has become a major problem for Australia's policy makers amplified by mass media voices which portray Indonesia as a dangerous country for Australians to travel to and work in, and as a major exporter of 'terrorism'. Reports accuse Indonesians of fishing in Australian waters, stealing Australian resources, sending refugees to Australia, and not being like 'us'. Prime Minister Howard's call to put the Bali bombers to death found widespread public support. Yet there is no call to put to death the many serial killers languishing in Australian jails. The same electorate which for many years supported Indonesia's terrorising East Timorese now demonises Indonesians for sponsoring terrorism. Turning against Indonesia externalises domestic guilt about the abominable treatment handed out to refugees in Australia. Indonesia is now perceived as the enemy among middle and junior ranks in the Australian armed forces. Former prime minister Malcolm Frazer claims that only the United Nations action prevented a war between Indonesia and Australia during the 1999 East Timor debacle.

After twenty-five years supporting Indonesia's invasion and colonisation of East Timor Australia's policy underwent a remarkable change of direction. From one year to the next Australia under Howard became a major force pushing for East Timor's referendum and independence. With East Timor's independence fully established in 2002, Australia's colonial sphere has expanded considerably.

The region bordering on the Arafura Sea has gained considerable importance in relation to national security and economic growth. It is an area rich in natural resources which Australia needs to sustain its high living standards. In the near future Australia's intervention in 'liberating' East Timor could well extend to other parts of the region and put further pressure on the country to expand its military forces and budget.

Australia's powerful neoconservative elite believe that China is the main threat to US hegemony and to the Anglo-American plan for a new world order. Defence planners talk about a possible Chinese attack on Australia's northern energy infrastructure using cruise missiles or missile-firing bombers, and of the linkage between China and Islamic countries in an alliance against Western interests. China's political and economic weight in Australia's zone of security has been gaining strength. Investment and trading links have been growing with the Pacific region and China has been offering large amounts of aid in the form of untied grants to Vanuatu, Kiribati and Tonga, and other countries. Some of these activities are linked to the externalisation of the China–Taiwan conflict. Closer to Australia, China has been courting PNG politicians and military senior officers and claims that its aid to PNG amounted to more than A$300 million in 2000, not including military assistance to the PNG defence force. China's role in PNG and the Pacific may explain why Australia decided to recolonise PNG and the Solomon Islands in 2003.

6
Engagement with Asia

In the absence of reform, the world economy will fragment as its imbalances become insupportable. Trade wars will make international cooperation more difficult. The world economy will fracture into blocs, each riven by struggles for regional hegemony.

John Gray (1999:218)

Australia is a very wealthy society, perhaps the country with the highest living standards in the world if we include the amount of space, coastland and sunshine enjoyed by its 20 million people. The good life in Australia is based on the consumption of vast amounts of goods and services, and Australians consume more energy, water and other essential resources per capita than any other country on earth. According to the World Wildlife Fund *Planet Report 2004,* Australia needs 7.7 hectares per capita to sustain each person and has the third biggest ecological footprint in the world after the United Arab Emirates and the US (WWF 2004).

Australia's neoliberal wealth enterprise and politics of greed can only be sustained by exporting more, attracting more foreign capital and increasing the size of the population. The country's model of political economy creates growing inequality and high social and environmental costs, a situation which is only politically viable by pushing for more growth combined with the propagation of powerful myths that people, particularly the losers, will benefit in time from the politics of economic rationalism. For the good life to continue, and given the nature of the global economy and Australia's location, it needs to develop close commercial ties with Asia and enmesh its economy with the growing markets of the region. In other words, Australia needs a substantial share of Asia's growing wealth to maintain its high living standards, and an increasingly inegalitarian system of income and wealth distribution. Australia's economic engagement with Asia in turn requires the protection of the US and abidance to its global political agenda.

ENMESHMENT WITH ASIA

Australia's modern economic engagement with Asia began with the inclusion of the continent into the British Empire's trading network. Sydney's early dealings with China and India's colonial outposts provided New South Wales with enough capital to start the wool trade. Australia's economy became increasingly linked to the needs of Britain for resources and food while developing important ties with other colonies such as Singapore. In the early decades of the twentieth century, commercial activities expanded with Japan and the United States. Wool was a commodity increasingly traded with Japan while the United States was beginning to build up its market share for cars on the Australian continent. By the early 1930s Japan was embroiled in a trade dispute about Australia's discrimination against Japanese imports.

The US–Russia conflict shaped Australia's economic engagement with Asia following WWII. The Korean war boosted demands for resources and the Cold War opened up Australia to Japan's need for resources and gave the US more opportunities to gain a greater foothold in Australia's economy. Britain's accession to the European common market was a major event which helped Australia focus on the opportunities arising in Asia's emerging economies. This was accompanied with a shift away from Keynesian economics to a type of market fundamentalism which sought to minimise state capitalism and the state's role in the economy. New-right economics was gaining strength in Britain and the US and influenced economic reforms in Mikhail Gorbachev's USSR and Deng Xiaoping's China.

A new laissez-faire capitalism found strong support in Australia's academic, government and business circles and became the mainstay of post-Cold War politics. Neoliberalism in domestic and foreign economic policy came to the forefront of Australia's politics with the election of a Labor government in 1983. The deregulation of the labour and financial market, and advancing business welfare, became the mainstay of Labor's response to an economic crisis, and to the danger, according to former prime minister Paul Keating, of Australia becoming a 'banana republic' and another Argentina. The strategy to mesh Australia's future with Asia's growing economies became incorporated in countless reports and documents such as the 1989 Garnaut report (Garnaut 1989).

Ross Garnaut, Professor of Economics at the Australian National University, businessman and former ambassador to China under the Hawke government, wrote a detailed prescription for Australia's engagement with the economies of Northeast Asia – especially China, South Korea and Taiwan. Australia's economic viability was tied up, according to Garnaut, with its capacity and determination to take advantage of the opportunities presented by the rapid economic development of the region. Particularly important were the potential for Australia to meet Northeast Asia's need for resources, especially in regard to food and aluminium metals and semi-processed iron and steel. Others areas offering growth in trade potential for Australia were educational services and tourism.

Garnaut joined many leading opinion makers who saw China's export market as Australia's cash box to sustain the country's living standards. China was to become another Japan and compensate for Japan's maturing relations with Australia. Stephen FitzGerald, Australia's first ambassador to China, recalled the period marked by 'official intoxication with the China market' (Rees 1989). Australia's leaders' slavering attitudes towards China began with former prime minister Bob Hawke's adulation of Chinese leaders. During his 1986 visit to Deng Xiaoping, who later became known as the butcher of Beijing, Hawke declared in the Great Hall off Tiananmen Square that he had 'unqualified respect for all of China's leaders'. Kowtowing to China reached its nadir with Chinese President Hu Jintao's official visit to Australia in 2003. Before he addressed Federal parliament the Howard government obliged the Chinese leader's entourage by closing parliament's public gallery, excluding two Greens senators from the chamber, and keeping protesters well away from Australia's centre of political life.

The Asianisation of Australia's economic relations has been part of a national strategy involving government, business and universities. All have been involved in joint efforts to push Australia's exports to Asia. The Australian government has been particularly generous using various subsidies to promote Australian exports. One such channel is through the Australian aid programme. Australian aid is largely controlled by the Department of Foreign Affairs and Trade (DFAT) which runs the Australian Agency for International Development (AusAid), the Australian Trade Commission (Austrade), the Australian Centre for International Agricultural Research (ACIAR) and the Export Finance Insurance Corporation (EFIC). All are engaged in boosting Australia's economic growth through commercial activities involving Australian goods, services and finances.

Aid is above all a form of business welfare to boost Australia's economic growth. It is a means by which private companies gain access to public revenues. Most of Australia's aid contracts under AusAid are directed at the Asia-Pacific region and awarded to private Australian companies to purchase goods and services in Australia. Among the ten leading companies specialising in aid delivery which received some A$1.2 billion worth of contracts from AusAid in 2000 was Kerry Packer's company GRM International. The largest recipient of aid in 2000 was Melbourne-based ACIL Australia with A$354 million worth of contracts. Other big players were South Australian firm SAGRIC International, Coffey MPW and SMEC International. These companies in turn subcontract and engage the services of a small army of highly paid consultants and experts.

Under the 1980s and 1990s AusAid programme the government's Development Import Finance Facility (DIFF) granted Australian companies funds to undertake construction projects in many Asian countries such as China, the Philippines, Indonesia, Vietnam, Laos and Thailand. Most of the money was given to a small number of companies, in particular Transfield Holdings, one of Australia's biggest construction companies and a major contributor of the Liberal Party. Projects of this nature are geared to buy favours from the recipient country which is expected to grant Australian companies major civilian or military contracts. This was the case with Transfield Holdings expectations to build a defence system for the Indonesian military, and naval units for the Philippines military. Large government grants have also been used to cajole the Chinese government, such as the cement plant in Fujian Province and a wool warehouse in Nanjing built in the 1980s.

AusAid money buys compliance on the part of small or poorer countries. In recent years Australia's aid budget has included substantial funding in defence cooperation programmes and for the 'Pacific solution' to its refugees problem. Under this scheme, as mentioned earlier, countries such as PNG and Nauru are paid to detain and process refugees arrested by Australian authorities. Because PNG and Nauru are totally dependent on Australian aid for their survival, acceptance of the Pacific solution is not an issue over which they have a choice. Most AusAid and other aid projects financed by the Australian government are geared to create commercial conditions favourable to Australian exports and investments. This is the case with all projects on governance focusing on market reforms and market accessibility of recipient countries. Australia has had a vigorous programme to encourage market reforms in the Asia-Pacific region often tying up aid and financial assistance to economic reforms in the recipient countries. Poor countries have to cut back on subsidies for food and energy, privatise their public assets and deregulate their trading regime.

Structural reform programmes provide Australia with many opportunities to export food, technology and services. ACIAR programmes are linked to potential Australian exports such as projects to improve China's pasture which have led to the import of 40,000 cattle a year as part of China's effort to build a dairy industry. Structural adjustment programmes which are part of Australia's aid package also shape new investment opportunities for Australia-based companies. This often leads to financial obligation on that country for intellectual property payment as part of the adoption of a package of new technology and technique. Governance projects on financial reform in Indonesia and many Pacific countries have increased their indebtness to and food dependency on Australia.

Austrade spends some A\$200 million a year to help Australian companies 'win overseas business for their products and services by reducing the time, cost and risk involved in selecting, entering and developing international markets' (Austrade 2003). It also hands out market grants under Austrade for Australian exporters to develop overseas markets. Austrade has been busy developing food and beverage markets in the Middle East particularly in Libya and Iran, and India. Austrade's annual report focuses on the important role it plays in China in 'supporting the ALNG consortium to secure Australia's single biggest export transaction valued at A\$25 billion over 25 years ... to supply liquefied natural gas to the Guangdong Phase 1 LNG project' (Austrade 2003). Another important government agency advancing special interests is EFIC, which makes loans to countries to enable them to buy Australian goods and services, and provides insurance for Australian investments overseas. In recent years EFIC has helped finance exports of arms to Indonesia, the supply of components for nuclear power plants in China, and some environmentally disastrous mining investments in Bougainville and PNG (AidWatch 1999). EFIC loans are repayable at commercial rates and the debt is added to a country's official debt. Poor countries of the Asia-Pacific region owe considerable sums to Australia-EFIC related activities including Indonesia's A\$1.6 billion debt.

Less obvious has been the role of intelligence in expanding Australia's economic reach in Asia. While intelligence is something that is gathered by all entities looking for a market or a profitable venture, less known is the role of espionage carried out by private and public entities. Australia's intelligence agencies have accessed valuable commercial information and passed it on to interested business parties. Intelligence is also coming from Australia's participation in the US–UK intelligence grid of supercomputers known as Echelon, which taps into all forms of transmission. It is widely alleged that commercial communication on bids, tenders and investment offers is used by the United States, Britain and Australia to further their economic interests. The European Union parliament has found overwhelming evidence that Echelon has been used to steal valuable information on big tenders to supply communications and transport equipment to Asia. It also claims that Australia's Defence Signals Directorate and the Office of National Assessment have had access to information on trade negotiations with Japan on coal and iron ore, among other dealings, which was probably passed on to commercial entities.

ECONOMIC RELATIONS

Australia's strategy to Asianise its economy has met with a high level of success. By the beginning of the twenty-first century the Asia-Pacific region accounted for about 64 per cent of Australia's total merchandise exports and more than 43 per cent of all Australian merchandise imports (ABS/DFAT). The region accounted for more than 30 per cent of Australia's total trade in services. Among Australia's top ten trading partners in 2001 were Japan, China/Hong Kong, South Korea, Singapore, Indonesia and Taiwan. In 2003 Australian exports to China had reached new heights and came second to Japan's market.

Australian exports to the region have been dominated by resources from Australia's mines, energy fields and farms, particularly iron ore, aluminium, gold and other metals, coal and gas, and wheat and dairy products. In the case of China, for example, Australia's main exports in 2003 were iron ore, wool, crude petroleum and coal; while the main imports from China consisted of computers, toys, games and sporting goods, and textiles and clothing. Exports to Asia generally reflect Australia's global position as a key exporter of primary products with a declining share in the exports of manufactures and services. In 1996 total shares in primary products, manufactures and services were 51.0, 25.4 and 23.5 per cent respectively; by 2001 these had changed to 54.8, 24.9 and 20.3 per cent (DFAT 2001). The value of manufactured exports has fallen by more than A$7.8 billion between 2001 and 2003.

Australia's major trading gains have been in East Asia and mainly in the export of resources. There are indications that markets may have plateaued in the case of Japan, Taiwan and South Korea. Overall, exports declined three years in a row after 2000, but great expectations are placed on China's economic expansion to deliver major growth increments to Australia's export trade and economy. China-led Asian growth is widely expected to play an even bigger role for Australia than Japan did decades earlier. Rio Tinto, BHP Billiton, Mitsui Iron Ore and other mining companies and their Chinese partners are investing some A$4 billion into iron ore development in the Pilbara region of Western Australia. China is also increasing its imports of steel, other metals, and energy from Australia. BHP Billiton in 2004 signed a long-term contract to feed four large Chinese steel mills in a contract said to be worth A$11.6 billion over twenty-five years.

The most important commercial tie up with China was recently signed to supply 3 million tonnes of liquefied natural gas (LNG) yearly for the next 25 years starting in 2005 and worth about A$700 million annually. The gas will be shipped to a terminal at Shenghen near Hong Kong to feed six new power stations and converted oil-fired plants. The contract is worth an estimated A$25 billion to the Australian consortium with Woodside Energy, BHP Billiton, BP, Chevron Texaco, Japan Australia LNG and Shell, and China Offshore Oil Corp (CNOOC). The gas comes from the Northwest Shelf project off Western Australia's coast. In addition, there are ongoing negotiations for a possible A$30 billion gas deal with a Chevron Texaco consortium based on the development of the Gorgon gas field located south of the Northwest Shelf.

The increased number of full-fee paying students from the region has been a major boost to Australia's exports of services and a major source of revenues for Australia's tertiary system. Overseas students enrolled in schools, TAFE (Technical and Further Education) and universities increased from 147,000 students in 1996 to more than 303,000 in 2003. The top five sources for tertiary students were China/Hong Kong (57,579), South Korea (22,159), Indonesia (20,336), Malaysia (19,779), Japan (18,987), Thailand (17,025) and India (14,386). While more than 20,000 Indonesian students were studying in Australia, less than 50 Australian students were studying at Indonesian universities. Foreign students generate substantial additional revenue linked to living expenses and visiting families, and the sale of real estate particularly in city apartments.

Commercial activities with other parts of Asia have been on the increase, including South Asia and the Middle East. The Middle East has been a major market for food particularly in regard to live animals and wheat. The Australian live animal trade is worth in excess of A$1 billion yearly. Most cattle trade goes to Southeast Asia but the sheep trade goes almost exclusively to ten Middle Eastern countries. Australia exports more than 6 million sheep a year under difficult conditions for the animals. The trade in live animals has caused major domestic dissent and a call by animal liberation movements for a total ban on the trade. Australia is the world's third largest exporter of wheat and has exported an average of 15 million tonnes per year in the last five years. Until recently about 3 million tonnes were exported to the Middle East. One of the key markets has been Iraq where Australia had the lion's share under Saddam Hussein's oil-for-food programme. Since the 2003 US war on Iraq, US farmers have mounted an attack against Australia to capture the country's wheat market.

The Middle East has also been a growing market for Australia's manufactures, in particular the export of more automobiles. In 2003, Saudi Arabia, Kuwait and the United Arab Emirates were taking more than 55 per cent of Australia's car exports. Australia's exports to the region are likely to increase with Australian partnership in the US–UK coalition occupation of Afghanistan and Iraq. Australian companies have been working with the Department of Foreign Affairs and Trade to sell Australian goods and services in both countries. The occupation of Iraq has led to a number of contracts given to Australian companies including the Worley Group, SAGRIC International and the CSIRO, SMEC, ANZ, Multimedia, GRM International, and Patrick Group and AWA Ltd, worth more than A$500 million.

Deepening trade ties with the region brings with it the expansion of illegal activities such as substantial drug shipments from Asia in a widening trade that has been estimated to exceed A$4 billion yearly. Southeast Asia's golden triangle and South Asia have been the main sources of opium-based products. Southeast Asia could also be a new source of cocaine coming into the market. New chemicals such as methyl-amphetamine, also called ice, are new drugs imported in large quantities from countries such as Thailand and Burma. China has become a major supplier of drugs like pseudophedrine to Australian drug syndicates in major cities and on the Gold Coast.

The expansion of money laundering activities is part of an extensive drug trade that uses various means including Australian casinos to legitimise income.

Investment from East Asia, shown in Table 6.1, increased from some A$69 billion in 1990 to more than A$111 billion in 2003. In contrast, Australian investment in the region increased from A$13.57 billion to A$15.2 billion in the same period. Japan's role has declined while China's investments have surged ahead in recent years. Japan and China's investments need to be viewed in the light of the dominant role of UK and US investment in the Australian economy. Australia has become a major destination for investors from Asia. Mining has traditionally been controlled by US and UK interests but in recent years Asian companies have become major players, first from Japan and more recently China and South Korea. China's investment arm CITIC has been buying Australian assets such as the Portland aluminium smelter. China has joint ventures with Rio Tinto and BHP- Billiton in iron ore development in the Pilbara region of Western Australia. Other ventures include partnership in the Northwest Shelf gas fields by China National Offshore Oil Corporation (CNOOC). South Korea has been moving in downstream of the energy sector by investing into the chemical industry. Korea's chemical group LG Chem plans to bring its total investment in Queensland's chemical industry to more than A$1 billion in the coming years.

Table 6.1   **Foreign investment in Australia, 1990 and 2003 (A$ million)**

	1990	2003
ASEAN	7,952	30,715
China/Hong Kong	11,547	35,547
Japan	49,839	44,771
South Korea/Taiwan	538	778
Total East Asia	69,876	111,811
UK	65,682	258,792
US	64,110	297,311
Total all countries	325,980	978,135

Source: Australian Bureau of Statistics: 5352. 0.

Considerable money has been flowing into the food sector as part of a strategy by Asian investors to meet the region's increasing demand for food. Indonesian investors in Australia are important cattle producers and exporters. Indonesia's Bakrie group is one of the largest foreign landowners in Australia, and exports live cattle from their Australian operations to their feedlots in Indonesia. The Sultan of Brunei and interests linked to the Sabah government run similar operations in northern Australia and own cattle stations and other properties in excess of 6,000 km2. Japan, China and South Korea are major meat producers and exporters. Japan controls cattle farms feedlots and meat processing plants. Their products are exported through large Japanese trading companies which serve the Japanese and other overseas markets. Korean and Chinese operations in Australia compete with American companies such as Australian Meat Holdings, which is Australia's largest meat processor and owned by US agribusiness giant ConAgra. China has several plants including Australia's second largest meat processor, Metro Meat International, owned by CITIC, the Chinese government investment company. South Korean investment includes cattle farms near Wagga and Tamworth in New South Wales. Companies such as Lucky Gold Star have extensive food distribution facilities and networks of department stores and supermarkets. Southeast Asia and China-based companies are also major investors in Australia's food industry and are building vertically integrated food empires based on Australian farm resources and stretching to the Asian supermarket.

Hong Kong and Singapore have become dominant players in the country's hotel industry and central business district (CBD) office blocks. In the late 1990s Japanese investors were moving out of the property market, forced to sell off some of their assets under pressure from the banking sector, and many of their properties were being sold at huge losses to other foreign buyers, particularly to China and US-based investors. Demand for land and real estate by Asian investors has risen sharply over the years. Wealthy Asians are attracted by the space, cheapness of land, and Australia's safe environment. Among the largest investing countries have been the United States, New Zealand, United Kingdom, Japan and Singapore. US investors in the late 1990s owned more than 700,000 hectares of Queensland compared to Japan's stake of 100,000 hectares (Strutt 2000). Hong Kong's takeover by China in 1997 was preceded by massive capital outflows into Australia's urban residential market. Increasing levels of corruption in Indonesia and the fall of Suharto also triggered large-scale residential investments in Western Australia and elsewhere. China is now a major source of investment in urban office blocks, land and housing, particularly high rise apartments in Australia's largest cities.

Asian investors gained a strong presence in the tourist, banking and insurance industries, and in other areas of the service industry, such as Singapore Telecommunication's purchase of Australia's telecom operator Optus in 2001. Energy production and distribution in Australia is in the process of being privatised and sold to a large number of foreign companies. Japan's Mitsui and Tokyo Electric Power have been investing in Australia's power plants while US companies have been pulling out. China and Hong Kong investors have been moving into the energy market. Some of China's recent acquisitions include China Light and Power's acquisition of Yallourn power station in Victoria in 2003 and the China's Huaneng Power Group's purchase of half of Queensland's Millmerran power station for more than A$300 million. Singapore Power owns Victoria's high-voltage transmission network GPU PowerNet and is expanding its acquisition of Australia's energy market.

GEOPOLITICS OF TRADE

The geopolitics of capitalism pushes countries in close proximity to develop closer relations. Proximity, economic development and transport efficiencies present potential for further integration as well as conflict. Trade plays a significant role in advancing Australia's national interests with Asia in terms of growth and maintaining the country's affluent lifestyle. An equally important role however, is to advance an Anglo-American, and to some extent G7-based, globalisation agenda. This is the cornerstone of US policy to bind the world into a US-style global market and maintain its hegemony. Free trade deals and other regional schemes are part of Australia's regional game plan to promote US globalisation and a US-controlled regional balance of power.

One aspect is Australia's scheme to create a Pacific Economic Community. The project would join PNG, the Solomon Islands, Bougainville, Fiji, other Pacific island states and possibly Timor Leste into some form of Pacific Community. Donald Denoon, Professor of Pacific History at Australia's National University, has argued that the project revitalises the nineteenth century concept of Australasia when it was used as a collective term 'for all British colonies and dependencies south of the Equator and west of Samoa. By 1900 it included New Zealand, British New Guinea, Solomon Islands, Cook Islands, Fiji and Tonga as well as the colonies which were forming the Australian federation' (Denoon 2003). Australia's northward neo-colonial expansion is partly a reaction to the economic deterioration of small Pacific states. More important is the fear that failed states will threaten Australia's security. In response to failed states in the region, Australia has activated a new doctrine of regional engagement in conjunction with the US alliance and war on terrorism to respond to perceived threats to its national security. A free trade reaching across Australia's arc of instability under Australia's economic and political control has merit only as part of a wider development plan to provide educational opportunities for all and the free movement of people into Australia. If the plan falls short of such expectations an Australia-led Pacific Economic Community will be seen in the context of Australia's geopolitical interests as a form of neo-colonialism.

Australia's main engagement pathway involves trade deals with individual Asian countries in the hope of substantial economic gains. A free trade agreement (FTA) with Thailand in 2003 should increase the level of commercial exchanges between both countries. Keeping in mind that the reduction of tariffs extends over a period of some 20 years, Australia is likely to export more cars, mining resources and food while Thailand will send more light trucks and other manufactured goods such as textiles and clothing to Australia. Thailand will also be able to export agricultural products such as tropical fruits and vegetables which will compete with northern Australia's agricultural industries. It has been suggested that the Thai–Australia FTA (TAFTA) was largely driven by the dairy industry's desire to access the Thai market in exchange for a deal with Thailand's Prime Minister Thaksin Shinawatra telecommunication company to invest in Australia's communication sector. This would involve the construction of satellite and relay stations in Australia to service Singapore's satellite to be launched in French Guyana. Already the FTA with Thailand has had severe repercussions on Australia's economy with the announcement in 2004 of the closure of Mitsubishi Motors' Adelaide engine plant with the loss of more than 700 jobs. Mitsubishi no longer sees a future as a manufacturer in Australia and has decided to move some of its operations to Thailand where it will be able to make money exporting more cars to Australia.

A free trade agreement with Singapore was relatively simple to conclude considering the city-state's small size and low or no tariff regime. Australia's trade deal signed in 2002 favours mainly service suppliers and gives bankers, engineers and lawyers freedom to practise. The agreement frees these professions from Singapore's restrictive foreign investment, licensing and residency requirements. Australia's exports to Singapore are likely to increase to the extent that they become part of Singapore's re-export economy and smuggling activities to the immediate region, particularly Indonesia. From Singapore's perspective the FTA represents a major territorial expansion for the island-state particularly for the export of surplus capital and population. Already Singapore has gained access to military training facilities in northern Australia and controls a major share of the country's telecommunication sector with the acquisition of Optus and its military satellite by the Singapore government's telecommunication company, SingTel.

Australia is considering other bilateral trade deals with the region and has entered into negotiations with China, Malaysia, South Korea and Japan. The signing of bilateral trade deals, however, carries with it a number of costs and complications. Among them is the cost of administration which tends to be high because the process of determining how much of the product or service originates in the country concerned is complex and prone to conflict. Bilateral trade agreements discriminate against third parties and therefore often invite retaliation on the part of excluded countries. Such agreements make a statement against multilateralism in trade negotiations and weaken the entire process of global trade liberalisation. Bilateral deals are therefore often motivated by geostrategic needs and great-power rivalry. The trend towards bilateral trade agreements will reinforce the division of the world into three major regional trading blocs and increase the level of conflict among major powers. Australia's economic dependency divided between East Asia and the US is likely to generate sufficient leverage to greatly influence the nature of its domestic politics.

Australian trade deals need to be viewed in the context of a global game involving the world's biggest powers and economies. The shape of the global economic order is being dictated by the world's economic cores. At the forefront is the US, the world's largest economy, with Canada and Mexico as members of the North American Free Trade Area (NAFTA). The US is in the process of negotiating NAFTA's expansion to the whole of Central and South America. The European Union (EU) is also expanding its membership and the creation of the Euro has introduced a new global currency to challenge the dominance of the US dollar in international trade and as a reserve currency. In Asia, China's 1.3 billion people and growing economy is moving the country to challenge and possibly displace US dominance in the next 20 years. China's economic pull has been integrating neighbouring countries, and trade deals with the region are shaping the possibility of a China-centred economic bloc. A number of free trade agreements are being signed or negotiated involving China, Japan, South Korea, India and member countries of the Association of Southeast Asian Nations (ASEAN). A regional bloc could link China with Japan, South Korea and the ASEAN Free Trade Area (AFTA) in a proposal that has become known as ASEAN +3. The dynamics of this process have already moved China to sign an agreement in 2002 with the ASEAN founding members – Malaysia, Indonesia, Philippines, Singapore and Thailand – to create a free trade area in the coming decade.

The formation of an East Asia trading bloc of 1.8 billion people or more depends on the capacity of the players to overcome many problems and obstacles. Some are based on historical antagonisms while more modern issues have to do with different levels of economic development and capacity to open up economies which could harm some member countries and threaten their political stability. One major obstacle is the entry of agricultural goods. However, China announced in 2004 that it will allow duty-free agricultural imports from ASEAN nations. Its recent deal to allow Thai exports of fresh fruits and vegetables demonstrates China's willingness and desire to build strong commercial ties with the region. Stephen Fitzgerald, the director of the Asia Institute at the University of New South Wales, argues that the formation of an embryonic type of confederation around China is taking place and that Australia should become part of that process (Fitzgerald 1997). He warns that Australia faces the possibility of becoming subsumed by those events. What happens will be significant for the future welfare of Australia. Nevertheless, the emergence of an East Asia economic bloc should be viewed as a reaction to the growing strength of the US-NAFTA and EU global economic cores. China's regional economic agenda is also driven by the challenge of US hegemony and the potential threat of US capitalism to China's political regime.

Australia's politics of trade have become interweaved with US national interests and gained momentum with the ascendancy of neoconservatives to power. Australia's military intervention in East Timor, Howard's doctrine of preemptive strike against its northern neighbours, and the widespread perception that Australia is regional sheriff to the US have affected its efforts to participate effectively in the economic integrative process taking place in that part of the world.

In recent years Australia has made several attempts to join ASEAN and the ASEAN Free Trade Area (AFTA) without success. Malaysia and other countries have opposed Australia's membership on the grounds that Australia is not an Asian country. In 2004, Singapore's prime Minister Goh Chok Tong felt the need to say what had been on the minds of many Asian leaders – that Australia would be kept out of a possible Asia-based free trade area because 'Australians are not regarded as indigenous Asians. Over time when there are more Asians going to Australia and the population is over 50 per cent non-white and the rest white, then maybe you will be regarded as Asians' (Dobell 2003a). Even Thailand, thought to be Australia's greater supporter in ASEAN, has opposed Australia's participation in an emerging regional trade architecture. Behind such statements is a new climate which combines growing Asian nationalism and resentment against a US-led West.

In 1989 Australia attempted to shape regional development by sponsoring the formation of the Asia Pacific Economic Co-operation (APEC) forum. This scheme, which eventually brought 18 countries together, was a vehicle to diffuse economic rationalism and pressure Asian participants to liberalise their economies and facilitate foreign investments and trading opportunities. Another aim of APEC was to advance Australia's plan to enmesh its economy with the rising tigers of East Asia. By 1992 the US had taken the lead and turned APEC into a political vehicle to propagate US-style neoliberalism and deregulate Asian financial markets. Another objective was to develop the organisation as a counterweight to the European Community and divert momentum away from some regional formation around China or Japan. Under US leadership, 'APEC became the leading organisation promoting globalisation in East Asia' (Johnson 2000:208). This was the Trojan horse to force East Asia and the tiger economies to deregulate their financial sectors and open up their economies to US investment flows. What brought APEC down was the Asian financial crisis of 1997 which Johnson suggests was a US 'rollback operation in East Asia to maintain its global hegemony'. The Asian financial crisis killed APEC because it proved to be a political machination to advance the interests of the West and left the organisation as a gravy train for a network of retired diplomats, technocrats and academics.

There is a strong view in the region that Australia is a legacy of the West's colonial empire and a reminder that Western interests could again clash with Asian social and political aspirations. Australia's track record has not been a source of confidence and inspiration given its role in the Vietnam war and the country's support for Suharto and other corrupt and authoritarian regimes. The dominance of US interests in Australia's domestic politics has become a source of regional concern. This was exemplified by Australia's collusion with the US in the Asian financial crisis of 1997 when it helped derail Japan's proposal for an Asian fund to stabilise the financial situation in Southeast Asia. Japan's offer of US$30 billion in aid to the region was vetoed by the US and Japan's foreign ministry responded by saying that the 'US government was possessed by an evil spirit' (Johnson 1999). More recently Australia has become integrated in the US geostrategic mission and strategy as regional sheriff and member of the tripartite Anglo-American alliance. Howard's doctrine of military preemptive strike and the recently signed free trade agreement with the US cement what is already a close economic and political union between Australia and the US, and move Australia a step closer towards inclusion into the US North American Free Trade Area (NAFTA).

Australia's aggressive push into the global market has increased the country's economic dependence on Western Europe, North America and East Asia. In turn this makes Australia a bigger pawn in emerging conflicts among the three major players for economic and geostrategic advantage. Australia has lost what independence it had by becoming an adjunct to the US empire and signing a free trade agreement (FTA) with the US in 2004. The FTA further advances US economic interests in Australia while Australia gains minor concessions to the US market for its agricultural products with promises of more to come in ten to twenty years time. In contrast the US has gained more access for its manufactured goods, investments and intellectual property rights. The FTA is likely to increase health costs for Australians, particularly in regard to their pharmaceuticals needs, and further empower US national interests as Australia's prime investor with extensive control in many sectors such as energy resources and information technology. Under the FTA the US will exercise a right of access to essential services in health and education, and maximise the privatisation of what is left of Australia's public assets. Australia's major current account deficit with the US will increase because of the massive US economic presence and substantial income outflow for intellectual property rights.

Globalisation and bilateral trade deals increase the level of conflict among states and open up the possibility of economic warfare. Ross Garnaut has argued that from 2004 onwards Australia will start feeling 'the effects of discrimination against them in the Chinese market as the early harvest for the China-ASEAN FTA has its effect' (Garnaut 2004). Australia's food exports in beef, dairy products and even energy and resource markets could all be targeted for retaliation as a result of the alliance with the US. Australia recently proposed to curb Chinese imports of manufactures by introducing changes to Customs legislation on anti-dumping provisions which would specifically penalise imports of chemicals, steel and plastics from China. There is an active US–Australian lobby against an FTA with China and China has accused Australia of anti-Chinese feelings for not recognising China as a full market economy.

One of Japan's most powerful lobbies, the Central Union of Agricultural Co-operatives, has been lobbying the government to buy Asian food. Any move in that direction would threaten Australia's food exports to Japan which absorbs a third of all Australian food exports. Japan increased its tariffs on beef imports in late 2003 from 38.5 per cent to 50 per cent and has rejected pleas to reconsider the decision. Japan's deputy director of the Ministry of Economy, Trade and Industry (MITI) complained about the concentration of coal production among Rio Tinto, Xstrate, BHP Billiton and Anglo Coal and suggested that Japan should look to China and Indonesia as sources for Japan's coal imports. South Korea has also expressed problems with its trading deficit with Australia and accused Australia of keeping Korean products out of the market through the use of anti-dumping tariffs.

POPULATE OR PERISH

Populate or perish has been an integral part of Australia's relations with Asia since the occupation of the continent by British forces. Convicts and white settlers had to be shipped in large numbers to take the land from indigenous people and prevent Chinese and other Asians from dominating the new settlements. The British Empire's military bastions in the East, particularly Singapore, provided some sense of security until the beginning of WWII when Japan's bombings of Darwin and Broome in 1942 brought home the vulnerability of white Australia and challenged the legitimacy of British rule over the continent of Australasia. With the fall of Singapore it became clear that geographical isolation was no longer sufficient protection and the political reaction was to propagate the image that Australia was too weak and underpopulated to stand on its own against the yellow peril from the north.

A nationalist agenda after the war successfully implemented policies to rapidly build up population numbers as part of an effort to enlarge the economy. Since the end of WWII, migration has been an important factor in Australia's population growth. More than 1 million new settlers were admitted to Australia for each decade following the war with the exception of the 1990s when the intake reached a low of around 770,000 people. Australia's population reached 20 million in 2003. In recent years intake of settlers has increased substantially and was in excess of 133,000 in 2004. In addition the government has added another intake stream based on the recruitment of long-term residents who are issued temporary residence visas which allow them to work in Australia. The scheme targets young skilled and professional people preferably with financial assets, as well as unskilled temporary workers to meet market needs such as fruit picking and construction work. In 1999 more than 135,000 people were issued temporary resident visas.

Australia's population policy is to increase numbers by adding migrants and permanent residents who can contribute to its economic growth and competitiveness in the global market, particularly in regard to the need for Australia to enmesh its economy with Asia. Australia competes for brains and capital with many other rich countries which all offer similar incentives to attract the highly skilled young. Australia's 'populate or perish' lobby consists of powerful organisations such as the Australian Chamber of Commerce and Industry, the Property Council of Australia, the Committee for Economic Development of Australia, the Business Council of Australia, and the Housing Industry Association. The Master Builders Association has argued that an increase of 50,000 migrants a year adds 7.5 per cent to real GDP. Business Committees for Sydney and Melbourne have come together to wage campaigns to boost migrant intake. Former prime minister Malcolm Fraser says that Australia should aim at a population of 60 million by the middle of this century while other prominent citizens are bolder in their vision of 200 million by the year 2100.

Since the end of the white Australia policy in the 1970s, Asia has become a major source of migrant settlers and long-term residents. Following Australia's economic engagement with Asia and its assimilation policy of multiculturalism, society has been significantly strengthened by the intake of large numbers of migrants from Asia, as shown in Table 6.2. From 1992 to 1999 the number of new settlers arriving in Australia averaged more than 80,000 yearly. There has been a steady increase since 2000 with an expected intake in 2005 of more than 140,000. The percentage of new residents from the region progressed from 5.4 per cent of all migrant intake in 1970 to more than 31 per cent by 1979. A peak was reached in 1990 as a result of Bob Hawke's decision to allow all Chinese students in Australia to stay permanently in the wake of the 1989 Tiananmen massacre. From 1986 to 1997 some 1.24 million migrants arrived in Australia of whom 46 per cent were born in Asian countries.

Table 6.2   **Permanent settlers born in Asia, 1961 to 2003**

Year	1961	1970	1980	1990	2003
Intake	85,808	170,011	80,748	121,227	127,000
%Asia-born	3.0	5.4	30.4	41.7	43.4

Source: Goldworthy (ed. 2003). For 2003 based on Australian Bureau of Statistics and government Department of Immigration.

Australia's policies towards Asian migrants has changed dramatically over time. In the early days of settlement Asians were enticed to work in the colonies because of the shortage of labour. When the inflow of Asians became a threat to white settlers' wage and land claims the British establishment quickly legislated for the exclusion of Asians and encouraged their deportation. A hundred years later Asian migrants have been made welcome to join a society which prides itself as egalitarian, free and multicultural. Northern towns and cities which once deported Asians now pride themselves on their Asian links and dependency on trade with the region.

While there has been a substantial change in mentality towards the constitution of a new Australian society the country is also constructing a fortress mentality to keep out refugees from the region. Asian refugees who are arrested by Australian authorities are badly treated, incarcerated in concentration camp conditions, and shipped to remote Pacific detention camps for processing and deportation. Pressure from refugees seeking to settle in Australia is likely to increase in the coming decades because of population growth, poverty and instability in the Asia-Pacific. These processes will put more pressure on Australia to secure its borders and develop negative views about countries which encourage the export of their surplus population.

Countries in the region are likely to press Australia to take more migrants and point to the emptiness of the continent, particularly northern Australia.

COST OF ECONOMIC RATIONALISM

Economic dependency on the region accentuates Australia's domestic problems and questions the viability of the country's neoliberal economic regime. An important insight into these issues is the deterioration of Australia's balance of payment current accounts. While Australia's exports have grown, regional industrialisation has created vast export flows to the world market adding further pressure on Australia's growing current account deficit. That deficit increased from A$13 billion in 1990 to more than A$46 billion in 2003. Most of this is linked to a growing deficit with the United States and the European Union.

Table 6.3   Australia's current account with East Asia, US and EU, 1994 and 2003 (A$ million)

	1994	2003
East Asia	12,546	–7,001
EU	–16,921	–23,568
US	–17,289	–15,648
Total all countries	–28,849	–46,633

Source: Australian Bureau of Statistics (ABS): Balance of Payments and International Accounts: 5363.0 and 5338.0, various years.

East Asia however, has been making consistent gains in Australia's market as shown in Table 6.3. Exports of manufactures to Australia from Southeast Asia and China are gaining ground because of their low labour cost and economies of scale. Steady inroads in Australia's economy are not compensated by Australia's gains in the region. Investments from the region have also increased the income outflow and further damaged Australia's balance of payments. The case of China should be of particular concern with major gains in Australia's trade account from minus A$809 million in 1994 to minus A$5.1 billion in 2003. China has become a major player and substantially increased its political leverage in Australia's domestic economy and politics.

Australia's deficits are translated into higher foreign debt levels and the selling of what is left of Australian-owned companies, and of land and real estate. Selling the farm has been an important factor in shifting the control of Australia's economy into foreign hands. Deterioration of Australia's terms of trade and a foreign dominated economy in turn pressures government to increase the competitiveness of Australia's economy and further deregulate the labour market and increase business welfare incentives. All this is consistent with more losses in Australia's sovereignty, the disempowerment of its electorate, and the weakening of the country's democratic ideals.

The Asianisation of Australia's economy has put more pressure on the country's fragile ecosystem. Australia has become a major food supplier to the region and the demand is likely to require the intensification of agricultural production in the coming decade. Projections for food exports show that demand for Australian wheat and other grains is likely to rise by some 60 per cent by 2015 (Duncan 2004). Such increases must be seen in the context of existing problems with soil erosion, dry-land salinity and irrigation salinity, declining soil fertility and widespread land clearing. Land clearing and grazing have caused major soil losses through wash-outs and huge dust storms. Water resources in the southern agricultural regions are becoming more saline and affecting rural production. Salinity has expanded and affects some 2.5 million hectares of agricultural land, and scientists project the damage to extend to more than 15 million hectares in the coming years. In Western Australia in excess of 30 per cent of the wheat belt could be lost within two decades. Costs to mitigate environmental degradation have been rising and paid through public revenues. Food exports to Asia are already subsidised to the extent that farmers have had access to cheap water, generous tax incentives, transport and diesel fuel subsidies, legal protection from Aboriginal land claims, and other public benefits.

Pressure to export has caused problems in other sectors of the economy. The expansion of the cotton industry which has been a main supplier to the Asian market has put pressure on scarce water resources. Demand for cotton has encouraged the industry in Queensland to build the country's largest private dam fed by extracting water from surrounding water courses. As a result, flows to nearby lakes and wetlands further downstream in New South Wales have dropped considerably, causing water shortages in the Murray-Darling basin. Moreover, the cotton industry has been linked to the contamination of drinking water and food supplies due to the widespread use of dangerous chemicals. Increases in minerals and aluminium exports will add to greenhouse gas emissions. The aluminium industry consumes almost 15 per cent of all electricity generated in Australia and in 1999 it was estimated that it contributed around 5.9 per cent of Australia's total greenhouse gas emission (Turton 2002). Australia's greenhouse gas emission affects climatic change and drought episodes. Drought conditions in the early years of this century were particularly severe and affected unprocessed food exports which dropped by some 29 per cent in 2002.

Migrant intake has been a major component in Australia's annual population growth and most new residents want to emulate Australian lifestyle and seek the good life in the consumption of a broad range of expensive goods and services. Research by the Australia Institute on greenhouse gases shows that Australians have the highest greenhouse gas emissions per capita in the world at 26.7 tonnes per annum. Their research suggests that migrants become mass consumers, particularly in their use of fuel and power and 'alter their lifestyle to that of Australians'. Their report concludes that 'immigrants to Australia do adopt Australian consumption patterns over time so that their greenhouse gas emissions rise from the levels in their countries of origin to higher Australian levels' (Turton and Hamilton 1999:25).

Australia's neoliberal economic regime is based on a vast inflow of migrants required to sustain economic growth and the expansion of an export economy largely geared to the needs of Asia's industrialisation. Population growth and the politics of economic rationalism generate more domestic competition for resources such as employment, housing and education. Migration in recent years has been part of a major social transformation which has increased inequality in the distribution of wealth and income, and led to the formation of a substantial underclass and strata of working poor. The coming of large numbers of migrants and other permanent residents has created considerable pressure on the country's major cities. Most migrants have settled in Australia's largest cities of Sydney, Melbourne, Brisbane and Perth. Sydney has grown rapidly and is home to some 40 per cent of the new residents. The Sydney greater metropolitan area covers more ground than Tokyo and stretches from Newcastle to Wollongong with a total population of some 5 million, or 27 per cent of the country's population. Problems of urban sprawl, traffic congestion and pollution have worsened leading to a decline in the quality of life for many residents.

Australia's political economy encourages the population growth of southern cities while regional Australia and the north continue to be relatively empty of people. This situation reflects the capture of the political process by developers, financiers and others who greatly benefit from the accelerated growth of cities like Sydney, Melbourne and Perth. Networks of urban growth promoters have become the main source of funding for both the Liberal and Labor parties and have gained control over an important slate of Australia's political agenda. Capital allocation by a neoliberal regime has promoted a surge in real-estate speculation by domestic and foreign buyers. This has been largely engineered by the expansion of liquidity and the availability of cheap credit, and the privatisation of the money supply by the major banks. One outcome has been a dramatic rise in housing prices, and the exclusion of many who can no longer afford to rent or buy in large cities. Australia's poor have been moving to regional centres and smaller cities such as Hobart and Adelaide. A national policy to sustain economic growth by expanding the urban sprawl of southern primate cities has been at the expense of many Australian regions and towns.

CHALLENGE TO DEMOCRACY

A neoliberal economic agenda has eroded Australia's sovereignty by removing controls over currency, interest rates and taxation. Asianisation of the economy has further compromised Australia's sovereignty by accentuating the country's current account deficit and increasing the level of foreign ownership of its capital assets. The country's dependency on Asia for the exports of farm and mine products exposes the vulnerability of Australia's small economy to external controls and changes in global economic conditions.

Foreign control of the economy has implications for Australia's industrial policy and future welfare. The country's economic structure has been largely dictated by the interests of foreign investors. Because of their size and control over various sectors of the economy, Australia's foreign investors have been in a position to dictate terms to government and shape the nature of state–society relations. It was largely as a result of pressure from business and related lobbies that government initiated a major reform slate beginning in the late 1970s and implemented programmes to deregulate the labour market, privatise public assets and further unburden transnational companies of their tax liabilities and other obligations to society.

The Asianisation of Australia's economy has encouraged more manufacturing activities to relocate in the Asia-Pacific region and ship some of their exports to Australia. It is likely that this trend will increase in the coming decade. Economic growth and competition in the region will accentuate the loss of Australia's competitiveness for a range of sectors, further depress the current account deficit and erode Australia's industrial capacity.

Pressure is increasing on Australia to become more competitive and offer lower labour costs, offer more incentives to foreign investors, and sell off more of the farm. The Business Council of Australia and other major lobby groups exert a controlling influence on both major political parties through their twin leverage of economic power and political party funding thus assuring that their agenda prevails whichever party wins the election. The business community's main leverage is the threat to shift their business to Asia where labour and operating costs are so much lower than in Australia. Australian manufacturing operations in China do not have to worry about factors such as minimum wage, industrial safety, pollution or the impact of their operations on the community. Already a number of Australia-based companies have taken advantage of big profit potential and moved their operations to China.

The promotion of commercial ties with Asia under a neoliberal market regime threatens Australia's democratic ethos. The country's exports growth policy and dependency on Asian markets for economic growth have been conducted in disregard of the region's human rights. Australia's cargo-cult foreign policy calls for the primacy of commerce in foreign relations over the protection and the empowerment of individuals. This policy has empowered corrupt regimes – power elites that have captured power without free and fair elections and therefore without the consent of their people. Until his downfall in 1998, Australia supported Suharto's dictatorship and to this day continues to provide legitimacy to Burma's military clique with its widespread abuse of human rights.

Australia's subservience to China's dictatorship was sealed when Howard's government greeted China's President Hu Jintao in Canberra in 2003 and gave him the privilege to address both houses while prohibiting members of the public from entering parliament. On that day the unelected leader of the world's most populous nation whose party denies the right of free speech to its people had been given the right to oust two Australian Senators from the house and to warn Australia not to interfere in Taiwan. Journalist Mike Seccombe wrote that it was the 'first time the leader of a totalitarian state had addressed the Australian Parliament and the first time an Australian government had the running of its parliament dictated to it by a foreign power. It was a disturbing day' (Seccombe 2003). Appeasement of authoritarian regimes to promote commercial interests legitimises corrupt governance and encourages power elites to abuse the civil and political rights of their fellow citizens.

Singapore and Malaysia deny their citizens freedom to express their opinions and dissent from government policies. Control of the judiciary and other means of repression have given their ruling parties power to punish and jail dissenters. Australia's policy towards authoritarian regimes legitimises their abuse of human rights and allows corrupt regimes to challenge Australia's democracy by contesting the universality of human rights. Singapore's Lee Kuan Yew and other Asian leaders have lectured Australia on the right to be different and the need for Australia to respect cultural differences and Asian values. Australia's politics of greed and commercial considerations have promoted the use of cultural relativism to manipulate public opinion and shape the curricula of many Australian schools and universities. This propaganda has been an effective magnet to strengthen anti-democratic forces in Australia and propel to power organisations such as Pauline Hanson's One Nation Party and Christian fundamentalist groups.

Support of corrupt regimes weakens Australia's own democracy because such a policy denies the humanity of people in countries outside Australia. Support for Burma's military regime and China's dictatorship carries with it the message that people who live in those countries are not worthy of the protection and freedom which are deemed essential to Australia's civil society. A society that denies humanity in others is in danger of fermenting within its own society doubts about its own legitimacy, and these are eventually reflected in how people are treated. In other words, in denying others the rights which legitimise one's own society, Australia risks further disenfranchising its own citizens. A foreign policy based on commercial considerations and the denial of human rights to others is a dangerous pathway which can only reinforce a similar process at home. There is evidence of this situation in the deprivation of many Aboriginal communities and the recruitment and enlargement of Australia's underclass. Boris Frankel argues that Australia is witnessing the reinvigoration of sadism in the workplace which thrives on a new form of citizenship based on widespread political apathy (Frankel 2004).

Australia's commercial ties have no direct bearing on the region's sustainable development and the provision of basic economic rights of employment, education and health care for the population. There are many instances where commercial relations can be shown to have impoverished a country by wasting its natural resources and polluting its environment, and corrupting the national elite. This has largely been the story of Papua New Guinea, the Solomon Islands and other small and vulnerable island-states in Australia's north. Australia's market diplomacy with Indonesia did not contribute to the country's welfare under the Suharto regime. In more recent years, trade relations have made Indonesia more dependent on food imports, particularly rice and other grains from the highly-subsidised US farming sector and on Australia's subsidised environmental degradation. This policy has further destabilised and impoverished Indonesia's rural communities, increased the country's food prices and foreign debt, and encouraged migration to already overcrowded cities.

AUSTRALIA IN THE EMPIRE

Support for neoliberal globalisation is faltering because it exacerbates predatory capitalism and transfers wealth from the poor to the rich. Globalisation, writes Susan George, has 'increased inequalities both within and between nations. It has remunerated capital to the detriment of labour. It has created far more losers than winners' (George 2003:18). Billionaire financier George Soros also warns that globalisation is destructive of society because it does not address 'collective needs and social justice' and has 'favoured the pursuit of profit and the accumulation of private wealth over the provision of public goods' (Soros 2003).

The economist and Nobel Prize winner Joseph Stiglitz has implicated the International Monetary Fund, the World Bank, and the World Trade Organisation in a number of economic and social crises in the developing world, and argued that these institutions have worked largely for the benefit and protection of bankers and Wall Street and not for the advancement of societies they were meant to protect and empower (Stiglitz 2002). Ha-Joon Chang's economic history (2003a) shows that the rules of globalisation were not meant to help poor countries but to advantage the rich nations (2003b). Chang quotes from the 1841 work of German political economist

Friedrich List who argued that 'it is a very common clever device that when anyone has attained the summit of greatness, he kicks away the ladder by which he has climbed up, in order to deprive others of the means of climbing up after him' (Chang 2003b). Under globalisation, trading rules have effectively kicked away the ladder which was used to industrialise and enrich countries which are now powerful and in control of global governance.

John Gray describes globalisation and free trade as a destructive US project that European and Asian culture will not tolerate and that the world will not converge on the basis of that model (Gray 1999:216). What he calls a US version of market fundamentalism 'engenders new varieties of nationalism and fundamentalism ... it imposes massive instability on developing countries' (210). Gray concludes that the US brand of capitalism is 'endangering liberal civilisation' and 'setting sovereign states against each other in geo-political struggles for dwindling natural resources' (20). Philosopher John Saul makes the case for the demise of another grand ideology and the rebirth of nationalism and suggests that people will reclaim their sovereignty and bring back the state to re-establish a social agenda which globalisation has destroyed (Saul 2004).

The 1997 Asian financial crisis, symptomatic of globalisation's destructive role, damaged the social and political fabric of the region's weaker societies such as Indonesia. The role of the West in triggering the crisis has thrown a shadow over Western economic ideology and managerial practices. Many countries are regaining control over their economies and pressing ahead with regional economic cooperation schemes. The failure of the 2003 talks in Caucun Mexico heralded a new phase in the dynamics of the global economic order with the formation of an anti-G7 bloc headed by the largest developing countries. Caucun failed largely because of a Brazil–India–China alliance which rallied many developing countries in their demands that the EU, the US and Japan open up their markets to agricultural imports and end generous subsidies to their producers. There has been a worldwide frenzy in bilateral trade deals overshadowed by the gravitational pull of the US, EU and China in their efforts to shape three major regional trading blocs. .

Australia will become increasingly confronted by the region's problems dominated by the pressures of modernisation and economic growth. Growth without social justice is creating conditions for future conflicts, and poverty and inequality are becoming major political issues and sources of tensions. The United Nations report on the habitat suggests that these problems are manifesting themselves in the high rate of Third World urbanisation and the prevalence of megacities and urban slums (UN-Habitat 2003). Close to 1 billion people lived in slums in 2001 and their numbers are projected to rise to 2 billion in the next thirty years. About 60 per cent of the world's slum dwellers in 2000 lived in Asia, or 554 million in 2001. Globalisation is a triage mechanism to warehouse surplus population in slums. The formation of large slums in the region is the outcome of a neoliberal global economic order and the dominant role of markets and free trade in developing economies. United Nations research on the global habitat reports that 'neoliberalism has found its major expression through Structural Adjustment Programmes (SAPs) which have weakened the economic role of cities throughout most of the developing world' (UN-Habitat 2003:3).

Rural poverty will continue to be a major obstacle to peace particularly in countries with a high birth rate. Much of the increase of the poorer population in the coming decades will be in Asia. Insufficient employment opportunities, political instability over human rights abuse and conflict over resources will add considerable pressure to migrate to rich countries. Climatic change and sea-level rises in the Asia-Pacific are likely to displace millions of people. Former World Bank president James Wolfensohn has warned Australia to prepare itself for the prospect of large numbers of people coming to the continent. He said 'rich countries such as Australia failed to understand the dangers to their own security of the explosion of the world's poor' (Eccleston 2004). China and India may one day put pressure on Australia to let millions of their refugees settle in Australia's empty north.

This highly insecure environment will further draw Australia into the US orbit. Australia's sense of insecurity, its great wealth and high living standards, its location and small population, together combined with the politics of greed will force the country to make further concessions to the US for the sake of more protection.

7
Confrontation with Asia

What freedom can the new world order offer if it is not prepared to free the vast majority of the human race from hunger, disease and ignorance?

Chandra Muzaffar, 1992

US HEGEMONY

Modern history is the Western construction of US hegemony. The defeat of Napoleon's army heralded the dominance of the British as the ruler of the first global empire. This was followed by Germany's challenge to Britain in two world wars. At the end of WWII Britain was bankrupt, the British Empire finished, and Germany destroyed. The next round was between the US and Russia, and at the end of the Cold War the communist challenge had collapsed and the Soviet Union had disintegrated. At the beginning of the twenty-first century the United States was the world's hegemon with the most powerful military machine ever seen in the world's history.

With 5 per cent of the world's population the US accounts for 20 per cent of the world's economy and more than 50 per cent of global spending on defence, and consumes about 23 per cent of the world's oil production. The nature of its empire is defined by the large number of military bases and establishments dispersed throughout the world. Chalmers Johnson says that the United States acknowledges 725 military bases in about 130 countries, and many more under various forms of agreements or under various disguises; more than half a million people are employed by the military to operate the US military empire (Johnson 2004a:1). The US also controls international waters with large fleets plying the world's seas and oceans. Military power extends into outer space where the US has been rapidly expanding its military might. US military bases are the modern equivalent of colonies and protectorates, and map the extent of the US imperium. By studying the changing politics of global basing 'one can learn much about our [the US] ever larger imperial stance and the militarism that grows with it. Militarism and imperialism are Siamese twins, joined at the hip' (Johnson 2004b).

US military might is essentially an instrument of political change and military power provides the leverage needed to manage the world's economy and political affairs. The US defence budget in 2003 was around US$500 billion but closer to US$600 billion if it includes linked military expenditures of the National Aeronautics and Space Administration (US$85 billion), and the country's intelligence agencies (in excess of US$45 billion) such as the Central Intelligence Agency. The Pentagon and Department of Defense officials have more power and political influence than members of other government institutions such the Department of State. Generals and their civilian equivalents shape US foreign policy and bring directives to foreign governments. Australia's prime ministers, for example, often negotiate directly with visiting US generals and Department of Defense officials. Among the most powerful individuals in the US are the Commander-in-Chiefs of the US central command which include the five regional commands (Priest 2003; Bacevich 2001). General Anthony Zini, former commander of the Central Command, an area that includes the Middle East, described himself as a 'modern-day proconsul, descendant of the warrior-statesmen who ruled the Roman Empire's outlying territory, bringing orders and ideals from Rome' (Powers 2003:20).

The military-industrial complex has been growing over the years as a dominant component of the US economy. The military operates some 1,600 bases in the United States and its territories. Government defence expenditures subsidise many sectors of the US economy including food, metals, automotive products, aircrafts, clothing and a whole range of high technology products and services. The military-industrial complex employs a substantial share of the US workforce and supports many more millions with military service related pension checks. Universities are major recipients of military funding and depend on military expenditures to support their budget and research activities. Foreign sales of military equipment represents a large share of US exports and in 2001 totalled more than US$100 billion. Many members of the political elite benefit financially from their links with the military-industrial complex and also rely on contributions from civilian contractors to fund their election campaigns. The US military machine links together corporations, universities and government and forms an elite which reproduces itself and grows with every generation.

At the core of the US political regime is a national security elite influenced by military values and traditions with too much power over matters of peace and war. This situation did not start with President Bush but has been a progressive manifestation of the capture of government by conservative forces. The Vietnam war demonstrated how a small group of largely non-elected officials were in control of the executive seat of power, lied to the electorate, and took the country on a path to a catastrophic war. Daniel Ellsberg's Pentagon Papers gave a vivid account of the rise of the military mindset in government and the routine lying of the executive to Congress and the electorate (Ellsberg 1972). Historian Christopher Lasch wrote that in the formulation of foreign policy in Southeast Asia 'no conflicting claim had to be accommodated. Pluralism and countervailing power were non-existent. Congress was silent and the public was without effective representation of any kind. Working largely in secrecy, the policy-makers found themselves unopposed and virtually unaccountable' (Lasch 1971:1–2). The Vietnam war was the product of a system where power was 'exercised at the higher levels of the American government by the group variously described in the past as the power elite, the foreign policy establishment, or the representatives of the military-industrial complex' (2).

Since the fall of the Soviet Union the US has expanded its military might out of Western Europe enlarging NATO with the inclusion of Russia's former satellites. Poland and Hungary's inclusion was followed in 2001 by Estonia, Latvia, Lithuania, Slovenia, Slovakia, Romania and Bulgaria. At the same time the US has emplaced new bases in the Balkans, the Caucasus and Central Asia. Military bases are now operating in Afghanistan, Iraq and Pakistan as well as in the former Soviet territories of Georgia, Uzbekistan, Turkmenistan, Tajikistan, Kyrgyzstan and Kazakhstan. New military colonies advance US power in a resource-rich region. In Uzbekistan, for example, the US has built a permanent base at Khanabad near the capital of Bishkek to house some 3,000 troops as part of a major transport and surveillance hub in the region. US military expansion is also taking place on the African continent with a focus on the control of West Africa's oil resources (Abramovici 2004). Countries that sign up with US military expansion receive an economic aid package and trade benefits which includes arms, training and equipment for their military and police, as well as access to the US armoury through the US Export-Import Bank credit scheme.

US global military intervention has been the more obvious aspect of US imperial rule. The US is a martial nation, of its 43 presidents eleven have been former generals or military leaders, more to the point is the long US tradition of military intervention in the affairs of other countries. In its less than 250-year history the US has carried out more than 200 military interventions in the affairs of other countries (Grimmett 1999; Hippel 2000; Elias 2002). Between 1945 and 2000 the US attempted to overthrow more than 40 foreign governments and 'crushed more than 30 populist movements struggling against dictatorships, killing several million in the process, and condemning millions more to a life of misery' (Elias 2002:45). Since the disintegration of the Soviet Union the US has intensified its overseas intervention beginning with Yugoslavia where its policies were instrumental in the destruction of the federation.

Since 2001 the US has invaded Afghanistan and Iraq and plans to reshape the geopolitical map of West and Central Asia. The US war on terrorism, on rogue states and members of the 'axis of evil' is shifting the focus towards regime change in Iran and North Korea. At the same time the US continues to expand its military might in space. Hegemonic military strategy in recent times has evolved from the command of the seas and airspace to that of outer space. US Space Command is the agency implementing the US strategy to control space. This involves the militarisation of outer space 'to dominate the globe from orbiting battle stations armed with an array of weapons' such as high energy lasers 'that could be directed towards any target on earth or against other nations' satellites' (Johnson 2004:81). The control of outer space and the Missile Defense System are both US tools for global dominance whose role is mainly to contain China's possible hegemonic aspiration.

US military intervention in global affairs is driven by two coexisting cosmologies that have dominated US foreign policy since the formation of the country. One is a realist view that the world is a nasty place and the US needs to defend itself against many enemies. It is a social Darwinian position about competition, the survival of the fittest, and the need to have power to survive and prosper. There is an element of paranoia in this discourse which is about the question of control, about who is controlling whom, because 'the aim of all paranoid thought and action is to get a firm grip on that which controls the world ... and all activity, mental and actual is directed toward obtaining a certain kind of controlling power' (Sagan 1991:16). The question of control is a key element in US realist foreign policy and its spatial analysis of geopolitical forces in Eurasia – Russia, the Middle East, China and India. US hegemony according to this position depends on the control of Eurasia because only in Eurasia can a power emerge to contest US hegemony.

Henry Kissinger makes the case when he writes that 'the domination by a single power of either of Eurasia's two principal spheres – Europe or Asia – remains a good definition of strategic danger for America, Cold War or no Cold War. For such a grouping would have the capacity to outstrip America economically and, in the end, militarily' (Kissinger 1994:813). The US realist approach to world politics is put more forcefully by Zbigniew Brzezinski, former national security adviser to US presidents, that 'America's global primacy is directly dependent on how long and how effectively its preponderance on the Eurasian continent is sustained ... Eurasia is thus the chessboard on which the struggle for global primacy continues to be played ... it is imperative that no Eurasian challenger emerges, capable of dominating Eurasia and thus also of challenging America'. The imperatives of US imperial geostrategy 'are to prevent collusion and maintain security dependence among the vassals, to keep tributaries pliant and protected, and to keep the barbarians from coming together' (Brzezinski 1997: xiv, xvi, 30, 31, 40).

What sustains the operations and budget of the US Department of Defense and the Pentagon are the never ending threats emanating from Eurasia. In recent years the focus has been on radical Islam and the axis of evil, and there are new scenarios in the making such as the operations of the US Space Command in preparing to wage wars against groups or countries likely to use weapons of mass destruction against the US. Other military contingencies are linked to secret Pentagon studies on climatic change which predict major European cities sunk beneath rising seas by 2020. According to Randall and Schwartz, global warming 'could bring the planet to the edge of anarchy as countries develop a nuclear threat to defend and secure dwindling food, water and energy supplies' (Townsend and Harris 2004).

The utopian side of US policy is ensconced in its belief in its own manifest destiny – that it is an exceptional nation chosen to bring justice to the world. Some years before the American revolution, its leader John Adams wrote that 'I always consider the settlement of America as the opening of a grand scheme and design in Providence for the illumination of the ignorant and the emancipation of the slavish part of mankind all over the earth' (Arendt 1970:15). Herman Melville in 1850 wrote that 'we are the peculiar chosen people, the

Israel of our time. We bear the ark of the liberties of the world'. This notion of America's special and divinely inspired mission played a key role in the US policy of expansionism from its early days to president Harry Truman's doctrine of bringing freedom to the people of the world, and onwards to US boasts about the New Economy and market fundamentalism's power to solve world poverty. Under President George Bush the new US global mission is a war against terrorism and the enemies of liberty. In 2002 Bush declared that 'the United States welcomes the great mission to secure the freedom and human dignity which is the birthright of every person everywhere from all the foes which threaten these human rights. We will champion the cause of human dignity and oppose those who resist it' (Bush 2002).

Realism and utopianism are two sides of the same religious coin that underlies US political culture and colonial history. Christianity plays a powerful role in US politics. Foreign relations are influenced by the vote of nearly 40 per cent of the population who are white evangelical Christians (Borger 2004). What the evangelicals have in common is that they all believe in the infallibility of the bible and that humans can be 'born again' through faith and the power of Jesus. They believe in the personification of Satan in human affairs and the role of the devil in manifestations such as communism, Islam and 'terrorism'. The Christian fundamentalist's cosmology is built around global conflict between the forces of evil and the role of the US in bringing eternal life to all those who are true believers. Christian fundamentalism sustains the US military global enterprise and empire. Gore Vidal writes that '39 per cent of the American people believe in the death of the earth by nuclear fire; and Rapture [when God's chosen will be lifted into the clouds]' (Vidal 1987:104).

In Amarillo Texas where nuclear weapons are made, munition workers believe that their work is part of a divine mission and that god will save them when the time comes (Vallely 1987). Rapture is part of the catastrophic event which fundamentalists believe will accompany the second coming of Christ and the defeat of the anti-Christ at Armageddon, north of Tel Aviv. Polls show that most Americans believe in the second coming of Christ, and many millions are premillennialists who believe that the foundation of Israel in 1948 and the coming destruction of Jerusalem's al-Asqsa mosque is part of God's final plan for the world (Ruthven 2002:33, 271). Christian fundamentalists are ardent supporters of Israel's policy to occupy Palestinian land. General William Boykin, who was given the job of hunting down Bin Laden and other Pentagon-named evil men, told the press that the war on terrorism is a clash between Judeo-Christian values and Satan, and that God put George Bush in the White House to fight satanic forces in the world. Boykin, who headed US forces in Somalia in 1993, declared at the time: 'I knew my God was bigger than his. I knew that my God was a real God and his was an idol' (Cooper 2003).

The US empire's ideology is based on a combination of utopianism and radical Christianity. This dangerous chemical mixture fuels US hegemony in a new phase that historian Claes Ryn calls the neo-Jacobin ideology of 'democratism', to bring democracy to the world. Evil, in other words, is found where democracy is missing. Ryn maintains that the US doctrine of American armed hegemony to 'promote freedom, democracy, and free trade' preached by the US new Jacobins is dangerous for a number of reasons but not least because this movement is 'within reach of controlling the military might of the United States' and that its continued ascendancy 'would have disastrous consequences for the United States' (Ryn 2003:397).

THE AMERICAN DREAM

The American dream is the belief in human progress and that everyone can find happiness on earth. Hannah Arendt reminds us of America becoming a symbol of a society without poverty and the 'conviction that life on earth might be blessed with abundance instead of being cursed by scarcity'. This idea was 'prerevolutionary and American in origin; it grew directly out of the American colonial experience symbolically speaking' (Arendt 1970:15). The migration of tens of millions of people over the years yearning to improve their lives has been part of that dream which continues to this day with millions of people in the world wanting to migrate to the United States or another wealthy part of the world. In Third World countries one hears the voices of those who say 'we want to be Americans but America will not let us'.

The US policy to bring democracy and freedom to all is essentially a reflection of that American dream. But if the US wants a world safe for democracy it will need to force governments to provide their population with the means to join the ranks of the middle class and participate in a global society as equal citizens. All must receive a living wage and have the opportunities and rights which their richer human kindred in the G7 enjoy. The social inclusion of the world's population requires large-scale transfer of resources, a reorganisation of the instruments of global change to ensure that people in Indonesia or Zambia, for example, receive the same level of protection and rights as their US counterparts. Bringing democracy to the world requires fundamental changes in the ways the market operates, and of the use of capital and political power on the part of the US and the other capitalist cores of Japan and the European Union.

Trying to impose democracy by force is not likely to work. Iranian Nobel Prize winner Shirin Ebadi, the first Iranian female lawyer to become a judge, has argued that 'democracy is not an event that can happen overnight. Democracy is not a gift that can be delivered on a golden platter'. For democracy to take hold requires above all a huge injection of capital and knowledge which can only come from rich countries and particularly the US. Democracy evolves together with political equality, and these conditions are sustained by the creation of wealth distributed equitably among the majority of the people. The viability of democracy is based on the existence of a middle class sufficiently large to legitimise the system and promote and defend human rights. Unfortunately the G7 are not willing to reform and introduce the economic and political changes necessary for democracy to flourish elsewhere because it would undermine the sustainability of their own societies which are based on mass consumption and the accumulation of more wealth. This system is based on the exploitation of people and resources and growing inequality.

US aid has fallen over the years – despite having the largest economy the US devotes only 0.1 per cent of GDP to international aid. Other forms of aid such as the lending practices of the IMF and the World Bank have not been sufficiently generous or well-intentioned to address the issues. Former World Bank chief economist Joseph Stiglitz and many other experts have criticised these institutions for failing to promote human development. Stiglitz claims that the world financial markets have engineered major financial crises in poor countries that have increased world poverty and inequality (Stiglitz 2002). The US and other rich democracies would need to change the role of global financial institutions, regulate global financial markets and increase levels of saving and taxation in their own societies if they were serious about improving the living standards for the rest of humanity. Such changes, however, would likely be opposed by their electorate and endanger the democratic workings of the G7.

Instead the US has opted for a military solution to what are essentially economic and social problems. President Bush's doctrine of preemptive strike does not address the conditions which give rise to violence. The US war on terrorism and the inability of the rich to address the problems of inequality and social injustice will lead to increasing conflict in poorer countries and escalate the level of violence directed at rich countries. The war on terrorism supports and legitimates authoritarian regimes to suppress voices demanding more open and egalitarian societies. Other countries are following the US and Australia's declared right to preemptive strikes. Russia has announced its intention to strike against perceived threats and said that it will use its nuclear arsenal to deter terrorism and instability along the former Soviet states borders. Thailand has followed suit by declaring war on its southern Muslim minority.

Chalmers Johnson argues that US imperialism and militarism will bring the world into 'a state of perpetual war, leading to more terrorism against Americans wherever they may be and a growing reliance on weapons of mass destruction among smaller nations as they try to ward off the imperial juggernaut' (Johnson 2004:285). Violence begets violence and leads to blowbacks against the US and other rich countries. The military solution approach to global inequality strengthens the US military-industrial complex and builds military might and a culture of militarism which undermine US democracy. The danger is that the size of the US military establishment and its overseas expansion will take on a life of its own where US generals influence on US political leaders is such that the military agenda becomes the determining issue in US politics moving the US further along a pathway towards some form of fascism.

Greed and a climate of fear undermines support for the American idea of human progress and questions the sincerity of the US elite in their declared mission to bring freedom and liberty to humanity. The ascendancy to power of neoconservatives indicates growing support for the ideas of social Darwinism and the survival of the fittest among the electorate. Market fundamentalism is one major instrument to promote inequality and shift the blame on the losers or victims. Another instrument is to ignore the plight of people who are surplus or even a threat to the continued comforts of the G7. This new racism explains the US tendency to let Africa die rather than make the necessary effort to build the economies of the continent and save millions of children from deaths. The US refused to act in Rwanda in 1994 and succeeded in removing most of the UN peacekeepers, thus triggering the killing of some 800,000 Tutsi and politically moderate Hutu. Writer Samantha Power described the 1994 Rwanda genocide as the 'fastest, most efficient killing spree of the twentieth-century' (Power 2001). US actions during the crisis and its explicit policy of staying out of Rwanda and denying UN help made it an accomplice in the massacres during which US officials were forbidden to use the term 'genocide' 'for fear of being obliged to act' (Power 2001:86).

Legitimacy is essential to US hegemony and its mission to make the world safe for democracy. But there are signs that credibility and respect for what the US says it is trying to achieve is wavering. To some extent the US vision for the world is being undermined by US domestic problems about widespread corporate corruption and scandals and growing inequality among its citizens. US attempts to propagate market fundamentalism have raised serious concerns in many countries about US motives when farming subsidies are at an all-time high. John Gray argues that the claim that the US is a model for the world is 'accepted by no other country'. The social costs of American economic success for US society are such that 'no European or Asian culture will tolerate' (Gray 1998:216). The legitimacy of the US democratic model is also a stake in the US–China conflict and China has questioned the authenticity of US claims of a superior brand of civilisation with attacks on US domestic problems such as family breakdown, corporate crime, drug and crime problems, and the failure of most US citizens to vote in federal elections.

Equally problematic is the rise of anti-Americanism in the world fuelled by widely publicised events which expose major contradictions between what the US preaches and what it does. What is unfolding today is a repetition of the past. US massacres of civilians and the use of torture were a major problem during the Vietnam war and Christopher Lasch wrote at the time that 'already the war has made us the most hated nation in the world' (Lasch 1971). At the beginning of the twenty-first century the situation has been exacerbated by new but similar dramas. The invasion of Iraq and the torture of prisoners in Afghanistan, Iraq and elsewhere by US forces and their civilian contractors has seriously undermined US claims to moral leadership in the fight against evil. In the eyes of many it has blurred the distinction between terrorist acts and the US abuse of human rights throughout the world.

US unilateral action in world affairs is causing widespread discontent among world leaders and a loss of faith in US integrity and its capacity to lead the world. The US has been walking away from international treaties such as the Geneva Convention on Prisoners of War. It has refused to renew the Antiballistic Missile Treaty, or sign the Anti-Biological Weapons Convention, the Convention Against the Use of Land Mines, and the UN Covenant on Economic and Social Rights. The US has refused to sign the Kyoto Treaty on global warming hence undermining global efforts to reduce greenhouse gas emissions and avert or minimise major natural catastrophes. The US invaded Iraq in 2003 without UN support on grounds that proved to be lies. By reneging on the Antiballistic Missile Treaty the US has started another armament race and moved the world towards a new Cold War. Wallerstein and others argue that the hawkish US position and its unilateral actions have 'undermined very fundamentally the US claim to legitimacy' and that the US is a lone superpower 'that lacks true power, a world leader nobody follows and few respect, and a nation drifting dangerously amidst a global chaos it cannot control' (Wallerstein 2002a; 2003a:307).

DECLINING US POWER

Historian Paul Kennedy's study of 'imperial overstretch' raises the problem the US faces in maintaining its status as the world's superpower. The US cannot preserve its existing position 'for it simply has not been given to any one society to remain permanently ahead of all the others because that would imply a freezing of the differentiated pattern of growth rates, technological advance, and military developments which has existed since time immemorial' (Kennedy 1989: 533). US power relies on strong economic growth and access to a critical range of overseas resources to meet its military commitments. Immanuel Wallerstein argues that the US has already entered a period of decline which 'while it can be managed intelligently', which the US is not doing now, 'it cannot be reversed' (Wallerstein 2003a:306).

US decline is an integral part of the capitalist world system where the US is faced with structural decline from two main sources. One is competition from the other core economies of the European Union and Japan. An aspect of this development is a decline in the weight of the dollar in the global economy in favour of other strong currencies such as the Yen, the Euro and possibly China's Yuan. Considerable US investments in defence is diverting capital from innovation and productive enterprise. The other source of decline is its loss of legitimacy as the world's leader. The moral basis for the US role as the world's hegemon has been seriously weakened in recent years and increasingly opened to new challenges by those with claims to more wisdom or higher moral grounds.

US economic overstretch puts pressure on the US to restructure its economy, become more efficient, save and increase taxes to pay for its military enterprise. Given the nature of the electorate the US is more likely to exploit its allies and other countries. There is the danger of the empire becoming more repressive and exploitative. Already foreign exporters are forced to fund their sales and buy overvalued treasury bonds. The US is also attempting to extract considerable wealth based on extraordinary claims to a wide range of intellectual property rights and patents. Mining the world for young and well-trained professionals is another form of exploitation. Selling security brings more wealth to the US. The first Iraq war was paid for by Saudi Arabia, Kuwait, Japan and other countries and made a small profit for the US. The second Iraq war will benefit the US economy with war contracts and control of the world's second largest oil reserves. Arms sales to other countries have been increasing over the years as well as the demand for training and private security; all these products contribute to the maintenance and growth of the US military-industrial complex.

The dynamics of the world capitalist system raise the question of hegemonic transition. Eventually new powers will challenge the US position as world leader. The European Union is likely to become a global superpower in the coming decades with the decision to integrate and modernise its armed forces. Challenges to the US could come about with new alliances such as a Paris–Berlin–Moscow axis. What is more likely is the emergence of China as the potential successor to the US. Hegemonic transition is a period of instability in world politics, particularly 'when one great power begins to lose its preeminence and slip into mere equality, a warlike resolution of the international pecking order become exceptionally likely' (Doyle 1983:233). How far will the US adjust to and accommodate the rising economic and political power of a China-centred East Asia? The US National Missile Defense plan and the militarisation of outer space indicate the US resolve to maintain dominance over Eurasia and confront attempts by China to dominate the region.

What happens to the US empire will be determined to a large extent by domestic politics and changes in the health of US democracy. Is democracy in the US a passing phase in its history as the political system metamorphoses into something less democratic and increasingly more authoritarian? US imperial policy and its associated militarism could well bring democracy to an end. John Hobson noted long ago that imperialism and imperial wars promote the growth of non-liberal forces at home and concentrate power in the hands of conservative coalitions (Hobson 1938:147). There are grave concerns that the US could be on a pathway to some form of constitutional dictatorship. Paul Krugman described the current Bush administration as the outcome of a radical right-wing political movement against the government which has been evolving in the past century. US neoconservatives he claims have gained control of both houses and the country's administration (Krugman 2003). Gore Vidal said that the country has only one party, a conservative party, and that people cannot trust the supreme court after its 'mysterious' decision which voted in favour of Bush in the 2000 presidential election, and a mass media in the hands of few owners with close interests in wars and oil (Vidal 2003).

Since the attack on New York's World Trade Center there has been a further decline in human rights protection in the US. The new Homeland Defense Agency and the Patriot Act and other legislation restrict the rights of US citizens and residents, and provide authorities with considerable powers to arrest, detain and spy on people. To help protect the homelands the US plans to recruit and organise millions of spies into an East German Statsi-type organisation. The Bush administration's Terrorism Information and Prevention System (TIPS) will recruit millions of Americans to act as spies on their fellow citizens. The programme, managed by the Federal Emergency Management Agency (FEMA), started in 2002 in the ten largest US cities with 1 million informants participating in the trials. In earlier years, FEMA had plans drawn to put millions of black Americans in 'assembly centres or relocation camps' in the event of a 'national uprising by black militants' (Goldstein 2002). FEMA's broad powers could now be used to arrest and detain American-Arabs or members of other ethnic groups declared to constitute a threat to the internal security of the US. The powers of FEMA need to be viewed in the context of existing high levels of incarceration. In 2002 some 6.7 million people were on probation, in jail or prison, or on parole, that is 3.1 per cent of all US adult residents. In 1997, 32 per cent of 'black American males between the ages of 20 and 29 were under some type of correctional control, incarceration, probation or parole' (Lapido 2001:110).

Power and politics in the US is the domain of the wealthy. Lewis Lapham of *Harpers Magazine* argues that the US is a plutocracy and compares modern, moneyed America 'to the excesses of imperial

Rome'. He writes that 'the nation's corporate overlords don't associate the phrase national security with the health and well-being of the American public; they define the terms as means of acquiring wealth and as a reason for directing the country's diplomacy towards policies that return a handsome profit – the bombing of caves in the Hindu Kush preferred to the building of houses in St Louis or Detroit' (Lapham 2002). Journalist Robert Kaplan believes that 'democracy in the US is at greater risk than ever before, and from obscure sources' and that in the future the US regime could resemble 'the oligarchies of ancient Athens and Sparta more than they do the current government in Washington' (Kaplan 1997:56).

Kaplan focuses on the power of corporations to transform the political landscape of the US, particularly in their role in structuring and defining new social spaces. He maps the corporation footprint in gated communities, shopping malls, tourist bubbles and other private spaces such as sports and health clubs. US cities are undergoing a reconfiguration of space into corporations, and a macro fragmentation of space to enable the well-off to secede from the public sphere. This is a process of secession on the part of the wealthy from their social contract with the rest of society. In essence, corporations are becoming states because they are reshaping the meaning of life and power. Many American cities are re-emerging as little Singapores with 'corporate enclaves that are dedicated to global business and defended by private security firms' (Kaplan 1997:72).

A similar process affects other important social areas such as the corporatisation of universities. Along with these changes is the widespread use of mind- and behaviour-altering chemicals which encourages political apathy and a voyeurist escapist culture of mass entertainment and gladiator-type games. Kaplan argues that the US is sliding into a system of corporate power 'to the advantage of the well-off and satisfying the twenty-first century servile populace with the equivalent of bread and circuses'. Norman Mailer believes that US democracy is at risk with power increasingly in the hands of the military and corporations. This combined with mass-spectator-flag-waving sport spectaculars suggests the possibility that the United States is moving towards some form of fascism (Mailer 2003). Chalmers Johnson who has written extensively on the US empire writes that US militarism and imperialism will doom democracy 'as the presidency fully eclipses Congress and is itself transformed from an executive branch of government into something more like a Pentagonized presidency' (Johnson 2004:285).

CONFRONTATION WITH ASIA

Australia's continent was invaded and its indigenous people dispossessed of their land and culture as part of the expansion of British capitalism in Asia. Australia's state formation was an extension and consolidation of the British Empire in South and Southeast Asia and China. Nation-building was an early expression of confrontation with Asia as the country shaped a sense of social cohesion and nationalism built on racial hatred. Keeping Australia white formed the basis for nationhood and the 1902 act of federation. An outcome was to keep northern Australia empty of people and strengthen the obsession of an Asian threat. Fear of China and Japan became a major force in Australia's search for protection leading Alfred Deakin to invite the US to send its 'Great White Fleet' to visit Australia in 1908. Australia eventually became embroiled in the imperial ambitions of Europe, Japan and the United States. During the last clash of empires Australia became a major platform for the US war against Japan for the control of the region.

In the wake of WWII, Australia collaborated with Britain's attempts to consolidate Anglo-American economic and military power in the region against rising nationalist and anti-colonial movements, and the growing influence and aspirations of the Soviet Union and China. The Cold War was essentially a Western civil war between the United States and Russia which became global when it projected the geopolitics of its conflict onto the aspirations of the Third World for liberation and a better life. An early development in the Cold War was Australia's military expedition to Korea as part of a major commitment to the Anglo-American effort to fight communist movements in Asia. Korea was partitioned into Soviet and US zones following Japan's defeat thus preparing the grounds for a civil war which has yet to end. Fighting between the two sides began in 1950 when North Korean troops crossed the 38th parallel. Australia committed troops the same year and participated in a US-led military intervention. The decision to go to war did not have the concurring vote of the Soviet Union and therefore Australia's action was illegal because it breached the United Nations Charter. The war, which killed more than 4.5 million people, kept the country partitioned and prepared the grounds for the emergence of a North Korean nuclear state.

At the time Australia was seeking US protection against the possibility of the resurgence of Japanese aggression. Another issue which haunted politicians was China's yellow peril and expansion into Southeast Asia. Australia's foreign minister Richard Casey believed that Australia was China's ultimate target. One outcome was Australia's partnership in the US–UK agreement which integrated their intelligence agencies. The image of falling dominoes which was widely propagated by Australia's media was used to condition the public to an addictive dependency on the US for the safety and protection of the continent from invasion from the north. Australia's response was to support Britain's efforts to protect their investment in Southeast Asia and to use Australian troops to fight off anti-British insurrections. As part of this policy the country engaged in military expeditions between 1948 and 1960 to protect British interests in Singapore and on the Malayan Peninsula and Borneo to fight left-dominated independence movements. Britain was keen to maintain economic power over the territories particularly since tin, rubber and other investments earned substantial dollar revenues to guarantee the stability of sterling in world markets.

After the formation of the Federation of Malaya in 1957 the British put together a plan to withdraw from their last colonial outposts in the region, and link Singapore and the Borneo territories of Sabah and Sarawak into an expanded Federation of Malaysia, while keeping control over the small sultanate of Brunei because of its oil wealth. This proposal was firmly opposed by Sukarno as a neo-colonial scheme to maintain British control and interests in Southeast Asia and a threat to Indonesia's independence. Sukarno opted to confront the British, and Australia sent troops to help the British fight off Indonesian military units and help secure the viability of the 1965 Federation of Malaysia. At the time Indonesia had the largest Communist Party in the region and the US wanted to remove Sukarno and engineer a regime change. Early plots to overthrow Sukarno included funding secessionist movements in Sumatra and Kalimantan. The situation was resolved with a 1965 military coup which removed Sukarno and replaced him with General Suharto. In the aftermath there were widespread massacres of Communist Party members and other dissidents. More than 500,000 people were killed and hundreds of thousands were taken prisoner and moved to concentration camps in remote parts of Indonesia where many were to die or spend the best part of their lives in captivity.

Australia's Cold War engagement in Southeast Asia expanded with the Anglo-American emplacement of a security system linking together Southeast Asia's pro-Western regimes. The US Southeast Asia Treaty Organisation (SEATO) was replaced with the Association of

Southeast Asian Nations Treaty (ASEAN) in 1967 linking together the Philippines, Thailand, Malaysia and Singapore. All these countries were to play a crucial role in the US war on Vietnam; Singapore sold fuel and other military supplies and Thailand and the Philippines provided troops and military bases for US warplanes to bomb Cambodia, Laos and Vietnam. Another anchor to the security scheme was the 1971 five-power agreement, a British-led consortium linking Australia and New Zealand to protect Malaysia and Singapore from Indonesia and other regional threats.

Australia's confrontation with Asia reached its height in the war against Vietnam. Following WWII the dynamics of the Cold War repeated the Korean situation and partitioned Vietnam. The Ho Chi Minh independence movement's defeat of the French at Dien Bien Phu in 1954 led to further Western intervention in Vietnam, bisecting the country along the 17th parallel. US intervention in the civil war that ensued escalated in the early 1960s and by late 1965 the US had more than 500,000 troops in the region. In the early days of US involvement in South Vietnam the Menzies government lobbied Washington to escalate the conflict and invite Australia to send troops. Australia's conservative regime built up the myth that Vietnam's communists were proxies of China. According to former politician Don Chipp, China was 'fanatical' and 'dedicated to the domination of the world' and Australia was 'undeniably in the sights for conquest by this nation at a relatively early date' (Sexton 1988:118).

The Menzies government 1965 military intervention in Vietnam's civil war destroyed the credibility of Australia as an independent country in the Asia-Pacific. Australia's next prime minister, Harold Holt (1966–67), told US president Lyndon Johnson that Australia 'was an admiring friend, a staunch friend that will be all the way with LBJ'. John Gorton (1968–71) followed with an oath of fealty when he assured Richard Nixon that Australia 'will go Waltzing Matilda with you'. In the end the US was defeated and Australian troops returned home unwelcomed and unfêted with many veterans subsequently prone to debilitating depression. Between 1960 and 1975 some 2.8 million Vietnamese were killed, most were northern Vietnamese. The country was devastated by US chemical aerial attacks which to this day inflict death and suffering on the civilian population. Some sixty million litres of Agent Orange containing dioxin, one of the deadliest poisons known, were used by the US to strip away the jungle and kill food crops, but they also caused genetic mutation and a variety of cancers in the population. Between 1965 to 1971 the country was bombarded with about 'twice the tonnage used by the US in all theaters of WWII' (Westing and Pfeiffer 1972:20) and the cratering of the landscape by bombing and shelling caused unquantifiable damage to Vietnam's environment and people.

Secret US carpet bombing of Cambodia and Laos was directly responsible for the rise of the Pol Pot regime and the mass killings that followed. The Khmer Rouge regime is estimated to have killed more than 1.5 million people. The legacy of the West's war on mainland Indo-China can be readily observed in the extent of poverty and human suffering in the region. In recent years, Robert McNamara, former US defense secretary and key Vietnam war architect-planner, declared to the world that the war had been a big mistake and should have been avoided. He admitted that the people in charge did not understand the situation, exaggerated the threat to the United States, and deceived the press and the American public about the war. Before the US coalition attacked Iraq in 2003, Australia's then chief of the Defence Force General Peter Cosgrove declared that Australia's role in Vietnam had been a mistake.

Australia's obsessive support for Suharto's dictatorship enabled Indonesia to invade and gain control of East Timor following the departure of the Portuguese in 1974. The incorporation of East Timor into Indonesia was encouraged by Australia's Labor government. Suharto's discussion with Australia assured him of a green light for the invasion plan. Australia's national security establishment decided that East Timor was not viable as a sovereign entity and if independent would fall under the influence of the Soviet Union and threaten Australia's security. Government records show that 'secret briefings by the Indonesians kept the Australian government closely informed of Indonesian intentions and operations at every step' of their invasion and annexation of East Timor in 1975 (Monk 2001). For over two decades thereafter Australia under Hawke and Keating legitimised a government in Indonesia which killed more than 200,000 East Timorese.

NEW WORLD ORDER

With the end of the Cold War Australia's partnership with the United States broadened to support the consolidation of US hegemony in Eurasia and the expansion of a capitalist world system. In the aftermath of the disintegration of the Soviet Union the Yugoslav federation broke apart and erupted in violent ethnic wars. This led to the occupation of the region by NATO forces, with the help of Australia, to maintain peace and order in the Balkans. The main arena of action however, has been in West Asia where the United States was intent on restructuring the region's political order.

Iraq had been a useful ally to the US in its strategy against Iran, and fought the latter in a costly war between 1980 and 1988. Iraq's military might was built using oil money to buy all the instruments of mass destruction from Western regimes. US and European companies provided Iraq with all the necessary ingredients to build its war machine including germ and chemical weapons, and some components to put together nuclear weapons. Iraq used chemical weapons against Iran and in 1989 used nerve and mustard agents to kill tens of thousands of Kurdish villagers in attacks that went uncondemned by the US and the world community. At the time, Colin Powell, US national security adviser to the Reagan administration, declared that calls for sanctions against Iraq were 'premature' (Galbraith 2004). Recent evidence by a former CIA agent suggests that Iran was behind the killing at Hlabja in 1988 when the villagers got caught in a gas-battle between Iran and Iraq (Pelletiere 2004).

By the late 1980s Iraq had become a liability to the US and its allies Israel and Saudi Arabia, and plans were made for a regime change. The opportunity came when Saddam Hussein decided to invade Kuwait, a small oil enclave ruled by another dictator. Iraq may have received a green light from the US for the invasion of Kuwait. Saddam Hussein discussed his plan with the US ambassador April Glaspie. Her response was that this was an entirely local problem and that the US had no interest intervening over this issue. Glaspie is reputed to have said 'I know you need funds. We understand that, and our opinion is that you should have the opportunity to rebuild your country. But we have no opinion on the Arab-Arab conflicts, like your border disagreement with Kuwait' (Caldicott 2002a:145). Following the invasion of Kuwait a US-led military coalition with a large Australian contingent invaded part of Iraq and forced Saddam Hussein to withdraw from Kuwait but left him in power.

More than 220,000 Iraqis died and the coalition lost less than two hundred troops during the first Gulf war. The war caused extensive destruction to the built landscape and infrastructure. The widespread use of explosives including highly toxic and radioactive munitions detonated during the war caused great environmental destruction and pollution. Damage to the 'earth, water, air, sea and the upper atmosphere cannot avoid, in both the short and the long run, causing further severe damage to human, plant and animal life not only in terms of the regional ecosystem but also on a wider planetary level' (Zolo 1997:25). The widespread use of depleted uranium (DU) munitions caused enormous damage to the health of all involved. US health physicist Dough Rokke, who was once US Army director for the Army's Depleted Uranium Project and had first-hand experience with DU contamination in Iraq, said that the use of depleted uranium and the US cover up about its casualties was a war crime. Depleted uranium is toxic, radioactive and pollutes, and according to Rokke causes lymphoma, neuro-psychotic disorders and short-term memory damage. Affecting semen, it causes birth defects and trashes the immune system. Ramsey Clark, former US attorney general, said that the US use of conventional weapons in the Gulf war 'exceeded the bounds of war crimes and crimes against humanity established by the international conventions and by the rules of the Nuremberg Tribunal' (Zolo 1997:25).

The war left Saddam Hussein in power and marked the beginning of UN-managed economic sanctions which took a heavy toll on the civilian population. A United Nations Children's Fund (UNICEF) study found that some 500,000 Iraqi children died between 1991 and 1998 because of United Nations imposed economic sanctions on the country (Pilger 2002:62). Some Australian military units stayed to join an Anglo-American Iraq watch to control Iraq's southern and northern regions. There were also weapons inspectors headed by an Australian diplomat who compromised the UN by collaborating with the CIA. Former senior intelligence officer Andrew Wilkie said that the UN was full of spies and that the Special Commission on Iraq (UNSCOM) and its Monitoring Verification Commission (UNMOVIC) were 'a key part of the intelligence operation against Iraq' and added that the Anglo-American alliance including Australia had been spying on the United Nations (Wilkie 2004). Australian special forces with their US and UK allies operated in Iraq after the Gulf war preparing the grounds for the March 2003 invasion. The Gulf war was good for business and paid for by the European Union, Japan, Saudi Arabia and Kuwait. While the United States made a profit out of the war Saudi Arabia came out with its first national deficit and a foreign debt in excess of US$40 billion.

Despite strong public opposition the Australian government was a key supporter for the US-led military expedition in the Gulf to force Iraq out of Kuwait. Australia's decision to go to war was to a large extent based on racist campaigns against Muslims and Middle Eastern communities in Australia. Some sections of the mass media generated hatred against those who opposed the war. English lobbyist Pryce-Jones toured Australia in 1990 as a guest of Australia/Israel publications and during his meetings presented a negative stereotype of Arabs and Muslims as 'depraved, opportunist, cruel, violent and corrupt, and inaccessible to the Western mind' (UTS 1991). Don Chipp, founder of the Australian Democrats Party, added his voice to vilify Arab-Muslims, calling for an all-out attack on Iraq and for the US and its Western allies to fight 'the Islamic enemy on Middle Eastern territory' (UTS 2002). There were some tangible economic benefits such as the sale of Australian wheat. During the UN-managed oil-for-food programme between 1991 and 2003 Australia became a prime provider of wheat and other foods to Iraq. An unintended effect, however, was the beginning of a racist campaign in Australia against Muslims and Middle-Eastern people.

With the end of the Cold War, Australia re-emerged as a regional actor in the economic and political development of the region. In 1989 the Hawke government launched the Asia-Pacific Economic Forum (APEC) to promote a neoliberal economic agenda but also as a security building scheme. Soon after Australia took control of the UN-mandated military intervention in Cambodia. In 1991 nineteen countries and the four Cambodian factions fighting for power signed the Paris Peace agreement giving the UN the task of setting up a transitional authority in the country, disarming the various armies and preparing the country for electing a new government. The Australian-led United Nations Transitional Authority in Cambodia (UNTAC) mission was to lay the foundation for peace and democracy in the country. UNTAC came under the authority of Australian general John Sanderson who commanded more than 16,000 international troops. In Australia UNTAC was widely praised as part of Australia's regional engagement to cleanse a collective guilt over its disastrous involvement in the Vietnam war. Despite spending more than US$3 billion the UN was unable to disarm and demobilise the four main factions and allowed the Khmer Rouge to keep control over part of the country along the border with Thailand.

The 1993 elections failed to break the former Khmer Rouge commander Hun Sen's Cambodia People's Party (CPP) control over the military and state apparatus. Despite some positive achievements the UN mission has been described as 'amazingly wasteful and incompetent and marred by internal conflict', and general Sanderson was described as 'incapable of taking crucial decisions' (Murdoch 1993). In 1997 the Hun Sen government took over complete power in a bloody military coup and organised the destruction of opposition forces including the killing of many political figures. In 1998 Cambodia held a fraudulent general election which was validated by the international community and hence legitimised the CPP military coup a year earlier. In recent years Australia has made a concerted effort to influence the cultural development of Cambodia by funding large-scale English language and other cultural programmes. Other projects involve communication networks and staffing various ministries with consultants in an effort to displace French influence in the country. Many such programmes were directed by a former Australian diplomat who subsequently left the country accused of paedophilia while ambassador to Cambodia.

US SHERIFF

The election of President George Bush emboldened the country's national security neoconservative elite plan to restructure West Asia's geopolitical configuration. Former Treasury secretary Paul O'Neill said that George Bush planned to attack Iraq within days of becoming president and long before 9/11. Part of that scheme was to change Iraq's regime and position US military forces in the region. The opportunity for direct military intervention came with the destruction of New York's World Trade Center on 11 September 2001 by members of the Saudi Arabia-based Al Qaeda movement headed by Bin Laden, the wealthy son of a Saudi Arabia billionaire. Australia's Prime Minister John Howard was in Washington DC during the attack on the Pentagon and quickly pledged Australia's military support for the US invasion of Afghanistan and Iraq. According to Bob Woodward's *Plan of Attack* Howard gave Bush his total support on an attack on Iraq as far back as September 2002 (Woodward 2004). Within weeks of 9/11 Australia's Special Air Service (SAS) units were operating in Afghanistan alongside their British and US counterparts before the main attack on the country. In 2002 Anglo-American forces with Australian units invaded Afghanistan after intensive bombing in various parts of the country. Three years later the situation in Afghanistan had not improved for the majority of its people and the reconstruction of the country was falling behind because of lack of funding and the resurgence of ethnic separatism (Rashid 2004; Khosrokhavar 2004).

The cost of the war has been high. Many civilians were killed during the early days of the country's occupation by Anglo-American bombings. According to a US officer, referring to the use of 2,000 lb cluster bombs dropped by B-52 bombers: 'no matter where you drop it, it is a significant event for anyone within a square mile' (Herold 2002). More than 3,700 civilians and 8,000 troops were killed, and 30,000 wounded, in the first two years of the Anglo-American war. Hundreds of Taliban fighters captured by the US–UK–Australian forces were subsequently killed by warlords. During the Anglo-American campaign the US began a secret programme of widespread arrest and torture. The torture of prisoners was carried out by US allies in Saudi Arabia, Jordan, Israel, Lebanon and Egypt, and also by US military and mercenaries at various locations including Diego Garcia in the Indian Ocean, Kabul's Bagram Air Base, and Cuba's Guantánamo Bay to obtain information about insurgent groups in the region. This policy was pursued in Iraq until the scandal of Baghdad's Abu Ghraib prison was exposed by the mass media in May 2004.

Seymour Hersh told the world that the Pentagon's Secretary of Defense Donald Rumsfeld was running a highly secret operation, unreported to Congress, to snatch people and process them for interrogation and torture in various locations. The operation began with the invasion of Afghanistan in 2002 and was extended to Iraq in 2003 (Hersh 2004). Abu Ghraib was a predictable consequence of the US administration's war on terrorism and the creation by the US of a global network of extra-legal and secret US prisons with thousands of prisoners. The US gulag 'stretches from prisons in Afghanistan to Iraq, from Guantánamo to secret CIA prisons around the world' (Blumenthal 2004). By subcontracting torture to private companies the US can evade the law and the US military code of justice. Several Australians have testified that Australians have been involved in these interrogation processes.

In defiance of the United Nations an Anglo-American coalition invaded Iraq in 2003 with the help of some 1,000 Australian troops including special forces. While the country was quickly occupied and Saddam Hussein deposed and captured, the coalition's incompetence contributed to the rise of a major insurgency against US occupation. Humanitarian group Medact estimates that casualties in Iraq until the end of 2003 were somewhere between 13,500 and 45,000. Towards the end of 2004 a study by the British medical journal *The Lancet* suggested that an estimated 100,000 had died since the 2003 invasion and that 'most individuals reportedly killed by coalition forces were women and children' (Roberts 2004). By June 2005 the war had cost the US economy and treasury more than US$182 billion (Cost 2005). The use of torture by the Anglo-American coalition and an inability to meet expectations for services and employment has created a severe crisis in governance reminiscent of the situation that existed in South Vietnam before the defeat of the United States in 1975. This human tragedy could have been prevented had the US been willing to buy the loyalty of the Iraqi military for about US$300 million, according to Prince Bandar the Saudi Arabian ambassador in the US.

Australia's involvement in the war against Iraq was opposed by many Australians. Prior to the Anglo-American invasion, polls showed that some 94 per cent of urban Australians were against a war without a UN mandate. On the weekend of 14 February 2003 more than 500,000 Australians rallied around the country in a national anti-war protest, including some 250,000 in Sydney. Australia's Returned Servicemen League (RSL) opposed the involvement of Australian troops without UN backing. Many other organisations demonstrated against the war, such as the Australia Council for Overseas Aid and the Catholic church which condemned Howard's unconditional support of the US war plans. Support for Australia's attack on Iraq came from the bush and regional Australia and Australia's new governor-general, a former army general and Vietnam veteran. The war was declared illegal by a large number of legal experts who stated that a preemptive strike on Iraq would be a fundamental violation of international law and a crime against humanity.

Australian special forces were operating in Iraq in early 2002 along with their US and British counterparts in preparation for the main attack. In a speech to the country two months before the invasion, Prime Minister Howard urged quick action on Iraq or face a 'Pearl Harbor terrorist catastrophe because of Saddam Hussein's resolve to arm terrorists with weapons of mass destruction', and that Hussein was a 'direct, undeniable and lethal threat to Australia and its people. That's the reason above all why I passionately believe that action must be taken to disarm Iraq' (Riley 2003b). In another address to the nation on 20 March 2003 the prime minister said that 'we believe it is right, it is lawful and it's in Australia's national interest' and added that 'it is critical that we maintain the involvement of the US in our own region where at present there are real concerns about the dangerous behaviour of North Korea ... a key element of our close friendship with the US and indeed with the British is our full and intimate sharing of intelligence material' (Tingle 2003).

Prime Minister Howard lied to the electorate about why Australia was going to war. Claims about weapons of mass destruction and information regarding intercepted centrifuge aluminum tubing, reports of Iraq's direct links to the 2001 terrorist attack on New York and of Iraq's import of uranium from Niger, all proved to be false. All these stories were widely diffused by the mass media to generate fear and hatred among the electorate. Australian intelligence agencies were fed information by the British and the US and the intelligence dossier was reconfigured to meet political demands to make a case for war against Iraq. In other words, the national security establishment fabricated a case for war because the decision had already been made on grounds other that those presented for public consumption.

Australia's intelligence agencies fiddled with poor or unreliable intelligence provided to them by British and US agencies. Andrew Wilkie, a senior intelligence officer who resigned his position, said that after September 2003 the Office of National Assessment, Australia's main intelligence agency under the prime minister's control, 'hardened its description of the threat posed by Iraq after the Bush administration directly called for Australia to help make the case for action against Saddam Hussein' (Forbes 2004). The entire affair was reminiscent of the Johnson administration's lies to the public about North Vietnamese attacks on US naval units to initiate a full-scale war on Vietnam. In October 2003 the Senate censured the prime minister for misleading the Australian public over his justification for going to war in Iraq. This was the first time in 102 years that the Senate had withdrawn support for a sitting prime minister.

The Iraq affair demonstrated the power of government to manipulate intelligence and, with the support of the mass media, lie to the public. It showed the widespread power of intelligence agencies in Australia to influence and direct the decision making process above that of parliament. Furthermore, it pointed out that Australia's bedding down with US and UK intelligence agencies is a liability in relation to the national interest. There is clear warning in this experience about the danger that intelligence agencies and a culture of secrecy present to Australia's democracy. It exemplifies the growth of a militarist culture carefully grafted and nurtured by the country's national security elite. It should be a reminder to the electorate that secrecy corrupts government and public institutions and is the enemy of a free and democratic society.

The torture of prisoners in Iraq has compromised Australia's involvement with the United States. Some Afghan and other fighters who were taken prisoners at the time of the invasion by Australian troops were tortured in US facilities. Australia's foreign affairs and defence departments, and the attorney-general's department, knew of the torture of prisoners but failed to take action or inform the public about the issue. The mass media collaborated with these practices by not investigating the issue until US-based journalists exposed the scandals in 2004. At the Canberra Senate hearings in June 2004, military leaders, the defence minister and other members of Australia's national security elite lied to the Senate inquiry about what they knew and what the government knew about the torture of prisoners in Iraq and elsewhere and brought 'discredit upon themselves and the armed services' (Allard 2004).

Anglo-American intervention in Afghanistan and Iraq will not likely bring democracy to the region. Afghanistan's elections in 2004 cannot assure the unity of the country. This will be particularly so if the large amount of foreign aid needed to reconstruct the country is not forthcoming. NATO's involvement in the security of the country may not be enough to stop Afghanistan's future break up with peripheral regions moving out of Kabul's orbit towards other centres of power in Pakistan and Iran. Democracy in Iraq is another flawed vision. Intense religious and ethnic division in a country plagued by poverty and unemployment are grounds for continuing unrest and civil war. The US occupation of Iraq will increase the economic and social polarisation of the population and the resentment of the losers. Regional anti-Western movements will use Iraq to pursue their deadly struggle and generate political instability in Iraq's neighbours. Iran and other countries like Israel will play realpolitik and advance their agendas which may well include the partition of Iraq into Kurdish, Shiite and Sunni regions. Iraq's general election held in 2005 was neither free nor fair and began the process of Kurdish secession from Iraq with powerful Kurdish factions demanding their right to bring Kurdish minorities in Iran, Iraq, Syria and Turkey into a new nation-state of Kurdistan.

AUSTRALIA IN THE EMPIRE

Soon after Prime Minister Howard's 1999 declaration that East Timor had been liberated he announced that as the leader of the multinational security force in East Timor Australia was now playing a new role in Asia's security. The country would upgrade its military, he further added, boost defence spending, and become Washington's deputy sheriff in the region. At the time, the chief of the armed forces Admiral Chris Barrie declared that after Australia's success in East Timor Australia was expected to lead similar forces in the future as part of the US-led coalition or on its own initiative. Howard's intervention doctrine was given a serious boost by the Bali nightclub bombing in October 2002. Later that year Howard made his announcement that Australia would launch preemptive strikes against countries in the region to protect its security and national interests. Defense Minister Senator Robert Hill argued that a unilateral action on the part of Australia was redefining the doctrine of self-defence 'for a new and distinct doctrine of preemptive action to avert a threat' (Reus-Smit 2002). Australia was the first country to publicly endorse the US preemptive strike policy and in July 2002 Foreign Minister Alexander Downer came out in support for a strike against Iraq citing Iraq weapons of mass destruction as a clear threat to world peace. Senator Hill endorsed a first strike against Iraq 'rather than waiting to be attacked' and said that Australia's security responsibilities were no longer confined to the immediate region. Australia's Howard doctrine has been incorporated in a paper by the Australian Strategic Policy Institute (ASPI) entitled *Beyond Bali* (ASPI 2002). The institute is a government-funded neoconservative think-tank headed by former defence personnel whose main task is to publicise and make palatable Australia's military intervention in the region.

Following the Bali bombing Australia launched a number of covert and overt operations to its north as part of the war against terrorism. Some expeditions took place in Indonesia where the Australian Security Intelligence Organisation (ASIO), the Australian Secret Intelligence Service (ASIS), the Australian Federal Police (AFP) and military went searching for those responsible for the Bali bombing and gather information on Islamic groups. These developments have been part of a broader plan to secure the political stability of the country by backing the Indonesian military, the Tentara Nasional Indonesia (TNI), and helping in the training and expansion of special forces and elite troops (Kopassus) into an effective force which can collaborate closely with the US and Australian military. Close cooperation with paramilitary organisations such as the police is also seen as a priority to stop refugee boats leaving for Australia. Australia's alliance with the TNI underlines Australia's current support for Indonesia's repression of secessionist movements in West Papua and Aceh.

Australia's war on terrorism has been integrated into the 1971 Five Power Defence Arrangements (FPDA) – the British-initiated security scheme joining Australia and New Zealand to protect Malaysia and Singapore from attempts to destabilise the former British colonies, particularly from Indonesia. The FPDA has now been reconfigured to wage war on terrorism and meet threats to shipping along the strategic Malacca Straits. The US wants to deploy military units along this strategic sea transport lane which links the South China Sea to the Indian Ocean, and to control the security of the region's main export ports. Australia's FPDA is part of a US deployment in the pro-Western ASEAN countries to build the equivalent of a NATO organisation anchored around Australia and Japan. Thailand is a major player in this emerging security scheme and a formal agreement will soon secure Thailand's access to US military hardware. Another key country is the Philippines where the US is keen to support President Gloria Arroyo's regime. In 2002 the US moved some 1,000 troops including some Australian units in the southern part of the country to fight Islamic independence movements such as the Moro Liberation Front.

Australia's proactive role in Malaysia, Singapore, the Philippines and Indonesia has been widely interpreted as an Anglo-American campaign against Islam, and Howard's preemptive strike doctrine has generated a great deal of hostility in the region against Australia. There has also been a campaign against Muslims in Australia where government intelligence agencies and paramilitary units have increased their level of intervention against Islamic groups in various cities targeting Sydney's western suburbs. Indonesia's former president Megawati Sukarnoputri warned Australia to lay off Muslims and accused the US and its allies of exceptional injustice against Muslim countries. Other Asian leaders have expressed the view that this was part of Australia's anti-Asian national psyche, while some Asian academics suggested that rising anti-Australian sentiments were tied to rising anti-Americanism in the region and that Australia's role as US regional sheriff and its pro-Israel policy would increase animosity towards Australia.

Howard's preemptive strike doctrine has targeted 'failed states on our doorstep' [which] are threats to Australia's national security because they lead to gun smuggling, drug running, money laundering and are 'breeding grounds for terrorists'. Underlying these issues is Australia's reaction to outside powers gaining political and military influence in island-states such as PNG, the Solomon Islands and Vanuatu. In June 2003 Australia's new governor-general, Major-General Mike Jeffery, declared that 'in PNG and the Solomons, I fear we are breeding future terrorists' and made a case for Australia's need for a bigger army (O'Callaghan 2003). Six months after Australia's Foreign Minister Alexander Downer said that sending troops to the Solomon Islands 'would be foolish in the extreme' Australia was occupying the country and running the Regional Assistance Mission to Solomon Islands (RAMSI) headed by Australia's first Ambassador for Counter-Terrorism Nick Warner, and backed by more than two thousand personnel including police and bureaucrats to administer the country. With it came a large number of aid contracts to Australian companies such as GRM International, owned by Australia's richest man Kerry Packer, to run the country's prisons. The cost of the operation in its first year has been around A$800 million, making the Solomon Islands the third largest recipient of Australian funds after PNG and Indonesia. Australia's decision to effectively take control of the Solomon Islands came only after Canberra was warned by Australian intelligence that Indonesia was getting ready to intervene in the Solomon Islands to help restore law and order.

While Australia's intervention has brought relative peace it was clear that the problem of the Solomon Islands could not be resolved under the existing mandate. What the country needed was a massive injection of funds to reconstruct and develop the infrastructure and provide educational and employment opportunities for all its young people. A better option is to invite the Solomon Islanders to join Australia or New Zealand as fully fledged members of either community. Unfortunately it was clear in 2004 that Australia and other rich countries were not willing to deal with the Solomon Islands fundamental problems and therefore it was likely that there would be some future crisis to again endanger the viability of the small, isolated and poor nation-state.

A year later Australia began sending another contingent to take over the affairs of its former colony of PNG. The decline in the nation-state's integrity in the last ten years has been highlighted by the Howard government as a threat to Australia's national security and investment. Australia has plans to resume control of the armed forces and the police and staff all key ministries with their own officials under the Enhanced Co-Operation Programme (ECP). Intervention will be accompanied with a substantial amount of aid, most of it contracted to Australian businesses through AusAid and other government institutions. One of the prime motivations for intervention in PNG, the Solomons Islands and elsewhere in the Pacific is to counter the increasing role of China, Taiwan, also known as the Republic of China (ROC), and other countries in the affairs of island-states whose control by Australia is seen as vital to Australia's national security and economic growth.

The new world order outlined in President Bush's National Security Strategy sends a powerful message to humanity about US intentions to reshape and control the world (White House 2002). Washington's strategy to wage war against terrorists, rogue states and the axis of evil is part of a broader plan to manage the economic and political development of Eurasia and advance US military hegemony through aerospace power. The US will not allow any power to challenge it and will use its military might to defeat any adversary. In this grand geopolitical game Australia has chosen to play an important role. At the October 2003 APEC meeting President Bush described Australia as sheriff of the Asia-Pacific. He said 'we don't see Australia as a deputy sheriff. We see it as a sheriff. There's a difference ... equal partners, friends and allies. There's nothing deputy about this relationship' (Riley 2003a). Bush's mating call to Australia was a serious reminder of Australia's increasing involvement in US hegemony and imperialistic ideology.

Australia will become further involved in West Asia's affairs in efforts to showcase Iraq's regime change as a model for the region and to assure a steady supply of cheap oil. There are many questions about the wisdom of a strategy to privatise the economy, including its oil resources, and open the country to market forces and foreign investors. Iraqi oil revenues will be used to pay for US war expenses and finance US companies to reconstruct the country and help US economic recovery. Underlying the economic recovery of Iraq is the question of political stability and viability in the light of increasing resistance and demands by the Kurds for independence. US intervention to shape Iraq's future is part of a strategy towards changing Iran's political regime and neutralising its nuclear programme. Iran is building a nuclear capability and the US and Israel clearly intend to bring an end to this.

Israel has threatened preemptive strikes and to use US-supplied submarines to strike at Iran's nuclear facilities. The US military has encircled Iran with bases in West Asia, the Caucasus and Central Asia. The US and its allies have positioned their military in Turkey, along the western shores of the Persian Gulf from Iraq, Kuwait, Bahrain, Saudi Arabia, and Qatar to the United Arab Emirates and Oman. On the northern and eastern sides are US bases in Georgia, Uzbekistan, Kyrgyzstan, Tajikistan and further south in Afghanistan and Pakistan.

The US is said to be conducting secret reconnaissance missions inside Iran (Hersh 2005). A large number of naval units have been deployed in the surrounding waters including aircraft carriers from the US, Italy, France and the UK. These are more vital signs that the third world war may have already started.

Australia's foreign minister warned Iran in 2003 that the country had a last chance to crack down on Al Qaeda and other terrorist groups in the country and about the dire consequences of not providing unfettered access to inspectors from the International Atomic Energy Agency (IAEA). Downer's message contained threats of Australia's military action against Iran including special forces working closely with the British and the US to control international shipping and intercept and search ships carrying nuclear material, missiles, drugs and other illicit cargo. Australia's role in the control of nuclear proliferation comes under the US implementation of the US Proliferation Security Initiative. The implications of Australia's collaboration with the US should be understood in the context of the Pentagon's *Nuclear Posture Review* to revise US nuclear strategy in the coming years to use low-yield precision-guided nuclear weapons such as earth penetrating bunker bombs against China, Russia, Iraq, North Korea, Iran, Libya and Syria (CLW 2001). Nuclear strikes are also planned in the event that sudden regime change in Pakistan or India endangered US national interests.

As part of its missile defence plan the US is developing the capacity to destroy missiles at launch stage or in flight, and to destroy military, industrial, and political resources on the ground using fast, accurate and global reach weapons. The militarisation of the Australian continent is part of the US global strategic mission and clear evidence of Australia's deepening commitment to US imperialism. US policy is to contain China because its emergence as a powerful economic and military power will threaten US hegemony. The US national missile defence system and other Star War projects will position large numbers of missiles, intelligence satellites, and weaponry in outer space to manage China's ambitions. Australia's contribution to this scheme is to emplace new generation radars and missiles aimed at ground targets in China and other countries in the region. The US military presence in Australia is likely to increase with new facilities such as another major US military training base and military equipment depot probably in Australia's Northern Territory on a 8,700 km2 former cattle station southwest of Darwin. The Australian Strategic Policy Institute, a public front for the government's military strategy, argues that Australia must collaborate with the United States to ensure the security of the Asia-Pacific (ASPI 2002) and accept the need to go to war against China if the US and China became embroiled in a deadly conflict triggered by a crisis. In the event of a conflict over Taiwan or the Korean peninsula, Australia's military have plans to send forces as part of a US-led coalition or as peacekeepers. Australia's sheriff fealty to the world's hegemon could become the main pathway for Australia's confrontation with China.

8
Conflict with China

The international system breaks down not only because unbalanced and aggressive new powers seek to dominate their neighbors, but also because declining powers, rather than adjusting and accommodating, try to cement their slipping preeminence into an exploitative hegemony.

David Calleo (1987:142)

China's ambition and legitimate right to bring 1.3 billion Chinese into the First World raises important issues about peace, conflict and the environment. Projecting recent levels of economic growth and given the dynamism of its civilisation, China should become the world's second most powerful military power by 2020 and the world's dominant economy by 2040.

The modernisation of China and the rise of East Asia as a new and powerful core in the capitalist world system is likely to challenge the West's control of the global economy. Asia's past contestation of Western control led to human disasters. Japan's resistance and competition with Western imperialism ended with the destruction of Hiroshima and Nagasaki by nuclear weapons in 1945. Communist China's front against Western colonialism in Asia ended with mass killings in Korea, Vietnam, Cambodia and Laos. The rise of East Asia's tiger economies suffered a major setback when the West mounted an attack on East Asia's economies which triggered the Asian financial crisis of 1997. China's rise as a superpower in the twenty-first century and the need for its accommodation in the G7-dominated world raises important issues. China's likely emergence as global hegemon will test the relationship with the US during the transition period. Another issue is the possibility of a changing balance of power between Western and non-Western civilisations and the re-emergence of a powerful China-centred civilisation. What lies ahead of us, write Arrighi and Silver, 'are the difficulties involved in transforming the modern world into a commonwealth of civilisations that reflects the changing balance of power between Western and non-Western civilisations' (Arrighi and Silver 1999:286).

A SUPERPOWER IN THE MAKING

Mao Tse Tung's original revolutionary project of transforming an agrarian society into a modern nation is now well advanced. China's vast undertaking to transform peasants into an urban middle class of more than 1 billion people began in earnest with the market reforms introduced by Mao's successor, Deng Xiaoping, intended to open China to the outside world and deliver modernisation in four areas: agriculture, industry, science and technology, and national defence. Market oriented economic growth was initiated by the rural reforms of the 1970s, freeing the sale of food and encouraging local production for private consumption. Collective farms were abolished during this period and peasants were allowed to grow individual crops and start small businesses. This marked the beginning of personal freedom for domestic travel, personal consumption and pursuit of career paths.

Another reform wave began in the early 1980s with the creation of coastal growth centres (Wang 2002). Under leader Deng Xiaoping, China set up four Special Economic Zones (SEZ) along the coastal south as models to work out market reforms with the meshing of foreign capital, technology and Western management practices into the Chinese economy. These privileges were extended to interior provinces in the early 1990s in the aftermath of the Tiananmen events to boost the country's economic growth and reward the interior for their military assistance to Beijing in May 1989. A more recent phase in market capitalism has reduced the influence of government, and encouraged private business and entrepreneurship, and the role of foreign investors in buying public assets. Many state companies have been closed or privatised in a programme of popular capitalism to share wealth around, but insiders have taken advantage of the process to grab the best deals in a process best dubbed as crony privatisation. In the early years of the twenty-first century it was estimated that some 60 per cent of China's economy was in private hands.

China's political economy has relied heavily on the transfer of foreign capital and knowledge. Capital from Hong Kong, technically part of China, Taiwan and Southeast Asia's overseas Chinese network has played a significant role in the development of southern cities. Japan, the US and the EU have been major players in sectors such as the automobile industry. By 2003 China was the top recipient of foreign direct investment in the world. Foreign investors have been attracted by China's endless supply of cheap labour, a quickly educated workforce, and the profit in supplying a growing domestic and export market. China has become a major exporter of manufactured goods and exports a large percentage of the cameras, washing machines, microwaves, refrigerators and other goods sold on the global market. Exports of high-tech items such as DVD players, computers, and other more sophisticated goods are also increasing.

China's economic power is being translated into military power through the formation and expansion of a military-industrial complex to build China's military machine. This new industrial giant builds the weapons and military infrastructure, exports weapons and military services, and provides research for China's military development such as the country's extensive space programme. China's military complex is involved in a range of civilian activities which contribute substantial amounts to its large military budget. The People's Liberation Army (PLA) business networks run airlines and hotels, and make a range of products from airliners and refrigerators to sports bicycles. A major earner for the PLA is the sale of weapons to other countries. One of the PLA's main arms-trading companies is the Poly Group Corporation which sells military hardware ranging from small arms to sophisticated weapons such as the M11 missiles sold to Pakistan and CSS-2 intermediate-range ballistic missiles sold to Saudi Arabia (Cheung 1993).

Construction has been a key feature in China's economic growth with the building of cities, highways and railways, bridges, airports, dams and energy infrastructure. Rapid urbanisation has propelled China's modernisation programme and transformation into a market economy. This trend began under Mao's leadership and between 1949 and 1990 China's '300 million people were provided and re-provided with housing without slum formation and without inequality' (UNHS 2003:126). Since then the movement of population to urban areas has been accelerated and by 2003 China's level of urbanisation had reached 41 per cent of the population, albeit not without the formation of new class structures and growing inequality. Another 300 million people are expected to shift in the coming decades from rural regions to China's growing cities. At the beginning of the twenty-first century China had the world's largest municipality, Chongping, with 31 million people, and by 2020 China's level of urbanisation was expected to be close to 60 per cent of the population.

China's entry into the age of mass consumption can be readily seen in the growing number of vehicles crowding the roads. In the late 1990s the motor vehicle industry was producing more than

1.5 million vehicles a year, mostly trucks, in addition to more than 100,000 units imported yearly and the many more used cars imported illegally. In 2003 more than 2 million new cars were sold and car sales are expected to reach more than 5 million yearly by 2010 and 20 million by 2020. Domestic production is increasing rapidly and expected to reach more than 6 million units by the year 2005. A recent survey shows that more than 20 per cent of China's urban households intend to buy a car soon (PD 2001). Assuming that China is moving towards Germany's car population per head of population China will need to produce or import 650 million vehicles in the coming years.

Road transport and other demands for energy has put pressure on China's energy supply. China was the largest user of petroleum in 2003 after the United States. Oil consumption is likely to increase from more than 5.6 million barrels a day (bbl/d) in 2003 to more than 10.5 million bbl/d by 2020. Imports are now about 2 million barrels a day and expected to reach 4 million barrels a day by 2010 or about what the US imported a day in 2003. Japan and South Korea's oil consumption rose from 1 to 17 barrels/year per capita during their phase of industrialisation and China's consumption of around 1.3 barrels in 2000 was expected to follow the same incline in the coming decades putting substantial pressure on the global oil market (Bannister and Mason 2004). Projecting current growth would see China's consumption of energy exceed that of the US before 2030.

The project to urbanise more than 1.3 billion Chinese and provide them with the means to join the ranks of the world's middle class requires annual growth rates of more than 9 per cent. Whether the level of economic growth of past decades can be sustained remains to be seen. China's capitalist pathway must eventually face severe crises which are built into capitalism's business cycles and world competition, and include unexpected developments such as natural catastrophes. Such crises can be amplified in their consequences given the level of secrecy and repression in China. China's membership of the World Trade Organisation will increase the pressure to further open up of the economy to market forces and foreign competition, which may disadvantage the country in the short term. However, the size of the domestic economy is such that demand is more likely to be affected by other pressures emanating from the global environment and security situation.

DEMOCRATIC VISTAS

World history suggests that modernisation and urbanisation have been accompanied by the liberalisation of politics and the formation of a more open and democratic society. The transition to a liberal democracy, however, is not certain and another pathway could be some form of fascism. Barrington Moore's history of the transition of several European countries from pre-industrial to modern societies outlined the different pathways from agrarian societies to parliamentary democracy, fascism or communism (Moore 1984). China has already had a great peasant revolution and civil war which culminated in the rule of the Communist Party. China's new modern phase focuses on the urbanisation of its people, and the major issues in China's political development have to do with the transformation of the Communist Party, the viability of a one-party state, and the possibility of opening the country up to party politics.

Recent changes indicate that China is developing the structure of a corporate state. This is reflected in the transition of the ruling party, the China Communist Party (CCP), towards another political formation more akin to a fascist movement. The CCP cannot survive in its present form because it is losing mass support and is increasingly perceived as ideologically outmoded. The need to regain legitimacy is transforming the system into a more progressive one-party state along Singapore's lines. Deng's successors have changed the charter of the Communist Party. Mao's revolutionary terminology has been abandoned and key items such as class warfare and socialism with Chinese characteristics are no longer political issues. China's former president Jiang Zemin closed the Party's main theoretical journals, and the Party ranks of some 52 million have undergone dramatic change to bring in younger and better educated members. The Party has opened its doors to the new economic elite and rich entrepreneurs. Power is increasingly in the hands of a Central Committee dominated by military, technocrats and other professionals which in 2003 dropped plans to introduce democratic reforms in the southern city of Shenzhen which would have been a test case for the country's democratisation pathway.

China is moving away from communism towards a new nationalism to maintain national cohesion and the power of a one-party system. The CCP is retooling Confucianism as part of a programme to reshape the political ideology for a new China. This is particularly important to counteract powerful centrifugal currents unleashed by market reforms which have bankrupted communist ideology and undermined China's social cohesion. Deng's exhortation that greed is glorious is moving China towards a more competitive society which encourages individualism and inequality. Liu Binyan a former Communist Party member said that 'nationalism and Han chauvinism are now the only effective instruments in the ideological arsenal of the CCP' (Chanda 1995).

Confucius, once rejected by Mao's revolutionaries as decadent, is now a cornerstone for a new brand of nationalism which teaches loyalty to the country, obligations to the common good, and obedience to one's masters. The imperial tradition is being resurrected with teachings of a natural order and hierarchy where everyone has a place and a role to play. Confucianism is a useful vehicle to promote a Chinese form of social Darwinism legitimising the elite's authority and obligation to maintain the stability of the country for the well-being of all. Confucian ethnocentrism is the new social cement which expresses Chinese pride and self-confidence; it is used by the Party to ascertain China's cultural differences and manifest destiny in regional and world affairs.

The state is pursuing a policy of patriotic education 'under the slogan of renewing China'. This campaign to build the nation-state lays 'special emphasis on arousing what is called "consciousness of suffering" about foreigners' intention to cause disorder, disunity and humiliate China' (Chanda 1995). As part of constructing a siege mentality, children are taught in primary school about China's past humiliations at the hands of foreigners, the British policy of addicting the Chinese to opium, and that 'their country can never be threatened again' (Mirsky 2001:47). China's many grievances have been encoded in an encyclopedia of abuses by foreign powers since the 1800s, used to promote shared feelings that China has many scores to settle with foreign countries. Among these are the irredentist claims which range from claims to the Spratlys islands in the South China Sea, which the Chinese call Nansha, to Taiwan and areas of Russia's Far East.

China's political elite is pushing a form of resentful nationalism as a unifying ideology to replace a morally bankrupt communist doctrine. The party is nurturing anti-Japanese feelings particularly among young people and encourages a large number of Internet nationalist sites which run material on Japan's atrocities during WWII and sovereign claims to volcanic islands in the East China Sea (Senkaku Islands), and savage the bullying attitudes of the US towards

China. Perceived attempts to humiliate China are manipulated to advantage to externalise domestic aggression. The bombing of Belgrade's Chinese embassy in May 1999 led to an outpouring of anti-US feelings particularly among young Chinese. Another form of humiliation which caused a great deal of anger and boosted national pride and prejudice was the International Olympic Committee's decision to deny Beijing the 2000 Olympics. Soon after the decision was made China exploded a nuclear weapon in its western province. Rejecting Beijing's bid was interpreted as part of the West's policy to keep China down. Singapore's Lee Kuan Yew told the world that giving the games to Sydney was intended to punish China for being overambitious and to remind China that the West was in charge.

Bruce Dickson suggests that China's society is shaping into corporatist structures which become 'substitutes for coercion, propaganda and central planning to maintain party hegemony' (Dickson 1997, 2003). At the core of the corporatist state is the party system (CCP), the People's Liberation Army (PLA), the Ministry of State Security, the Propaganda Department, and other key ministries which plan and manage the corporate state. China is learning from Singapore the essentials of corporatism and gradually developing and shaping civil society by incorporating associations of businesses, workers, religions, artists, cultures, technocrats and professionals into the state's ruling party structure. In essence the government is extending its power by integrating civil society into the state's command structure which manages economic growth, national cohesion and political stability. As with Singapore's model the state is particularly interested in co-opting cultural formations such as churches, writers and theatrical groups. Both communist and corporatist regimes are about control, the main difference is that in the corporatist model control is enmeshed in a capitalist framework of a market economy and culture of mass consumption. Both however, rely on the widespread repression of dissent and of anti-systemic movements.

China's growth under a neoliberal economic regime is creating new inequalities, discontent among the have-nots, and demands for a more democratic and egalitarian society. A market economy is also creating tensions among regions, and demands for self-determination by major ethnic minorities. Among the losers are the majority of the rural population whose incomes have declined in recent years – many are unemployed and have joined the ranks of a vast population surplus to agricultural and rural production (Chen and Wu 2004).

In the early 1990s between 22 to 25 per cent of the 450 million rural workers were redundant and available as migrant labourers (Kaye 1994:33). Some years later a survey of Chinese peasants described the plight of hundreds of millions of impoverished and angry peasants (Chen and Wu 2004). The floating population of workers estimated at more than 150 million is part of a mendicant agricultural labour force looking for work in various cities. Labourers in townships and village enterprises mostly funded by capital from Hong Kong, Taiwan and South Korea are working in appalling conditions. Regional inequality between cities and rural areas are wide and getting wider (Yang 1998). This is particularly so between the coastal provinces and the 700 million people of the central and western provinces.

Mass discontent arises from rampant corruption among the country's elite. Members of the ruling party and their families benefit from a vast range of illegal privileges in keeping with the 'getting rich is glorious' mentality. Economist He Qinglian writes about the 'carving up' of public assets among the power elite and the use of public funds from state banks to do business and speculate in real estate. The CCP is emerging as a regime closely allied with a criminal underworld (Qinglian 1998). Julia Kwong's study shows that corruption has increased as China has become richer and where power can easily be exchanged for personal benefits, and that with the reform period of the 1980s corruption became universal (Kwong 1997). Dissident former party leader Bao Tong claims that the party has become 'a party for the rich and powerful which will entrench the privileges of the ruling elite' (Bao Tong 2002).

During Deng's rule, electrician Wei Jingsheng led a movement for a more open society and with other political activists in 1978 plastered pro-democracy essays on a wall close to the nation's elite Zhongnanhai compound in Beijing's Forbidden City. The Democracy Wall movement was crushed in 1979 and Wei Jingsheng was jailed for many years. Demands for human rights, equality and social justice came to an end with the Tiananmen Square massacre of 1989 when hundreds of protesters were killed by the military acting on the order of the CCP. James Miles estimates that between three and five thousand people were killed in Beijing (Mirsky 1997:33). Most of those killed were not students but workers and ordinary people. During the month of June 1989 hundreds of People's Liberation Army (PLA) soldiers were jailed or executed.

Repression of dissent has been on the rise throughout the country. There have been a large number of illegal strikes and the party has been stamping down on attempts to form independent unions which are illegal in China with the exception of China's state sponsored body, the All-China Federation of Trade Unions (ACFTU). The state's security apparatus has attacked unauthorised religious groups such as underground Catholic churches and other banned groups including the Falun Gong. The Communist Party has been waging a war against the Falun Gong, a millenarian movement which has attracted large numbers of jobless and retired workers who are dissatisfied with the political regime. The regime uses torture to break the bodies and minds of leading dissidents. Ian Buruma writes that Wei Jingsheng, the founder of China's tiny Democracy Party, 'was locked up in stinking death cells, interrogated day and night for months, had his teeth smashed and his health wrecked, and when he staged a hunger strike in desperation, he was hung upside down, his mouth wrenched open with a steel clamp and hot gruel pumped into his stomach through a plastic hose' (Mirsky 2001:46). Dissidents such as Harry Wu have been sent to China's gulag in remote areas where armies of political prisoners are held without trial and forced to work making goods for export. Others end up in psychiatric detention as in the case of Wang Wanxing, one of China's longest serving political prisoners who has been held in an asylum for the criminally insane for the past decade.

Hong Kong's movement for democracy has grown since the British colony's reintegration with the mainland in 1997. Residents of this large and wealthy urban centre fear that their relative freedom will soon dissipate. In 2003 China introduced a new security law which outlaws a wide range of activities regarded as subversive of communist rule or promoting separatism, and gives power to local authorities to deregister organisations which are banned in the rest of China. The new security measures threaten academics and others with arrest and jail for divulging Chinese 'state secrets'. Equally problematic is the situation among an estimated 100 million people who represent China's minorities and live in some of the country's poorest regions. The Xinjiang Uighur Autonomous Region (XUAR), which covers one-sixth of China's territory with 19.2 million people in 2002, is the home of 8.6 million Uighurs who are Turkic-speaking Muslims with close religious, ethnic and cultural ties with their independent neighbours in Central Asia. Lop Nor in Xinjiang is where China tests its nuclear weapons, and the region is rich in natural resources and oil and gas potential. Most of the region's Muslims are Sunni with the exception of a small minority of Shiite Tajiks who are Iranian linguistically.

Chinese authorities are fighting nationalist and Muslim separatist groups pressing for an independent East Turkistan in Xinjiang province. Violence has been sporadic and fuelled by major riots due to the settlement of large numbers of Han Chinese coming from poorer regions in China (Sala 2002). In response to the 1997 riots the authorities executed more than 100 Muslim separatists after summary trials. Another source of confrontation in the northwest region is Tibet where harsh political repression has been the response to demands for human rights and Tibetan autonomy. Animosity towards the Chinese has increased and there is a growing desire among a younger generation of Tibetans to use violent means against what they see as the illegal occupation of their country since 1951.

What are the prospects for China's regime change towards party politics and a more democratic society? Chinese-American corporate lawyer Gordon Chang hypothesises that China is on the brink of a financial crisis (Chang 2001). He argues that the economy is largely fuelled by state financial subsidies and has reached a critical threshold in the expansion of state credit. China's accession to the World Trade Organisation is the trigger that will cause a crisis in domestic confidence and a financial meltdown because 'it will expose the incompetence, insolvency and institutional corruption behind China's façade of miraculous economic success' (Chang 2001). While there is a problem with the country's finances, the regime is likely to introduce reforms to avoid a catastrophic crisis. There will be challenges from other directions such as a possible repeat of the severe acute respiratory syndrome (SARS) crisis of 2003 which threatened China's trading relations with the world.

Whatever crisis China faces there will be great pressure on the regime to maintain social cohesion and the territorial integrity of the state. Threats to China's national pride and drive to modernise are more likely to cause a shift to the right and strengthen one-party rule than open up the country to democratic politics. Among the supporters for a tough reaction will be China's middle class because they will fear for the security of their newly acquired wealth. Bernstein and Munro, in their book *The Coming Conflict with China*, view a China evolving towards some kind of 'corporatist, militarized, nationalist state, a state with some similarity to the fascism of Mussolini or Franco … moving towards some of the characteristics that were important in early twenty-century fascism' (Bernstein and Munro 1998:61–2). Their analysis outlines key features of a corporatist state which duplicates Singapore's micro-model of Asian fascism. Among them is the role of the political elite and the networks which tie up economic and political power to financial interests in state corporations, foreign banking and corporations. Other aspects of the syndrome include the country's military-industrial complex which is associated with promoting a popular culture of siege and fear, and a sophisticated security apparatus to repress any attempt at free elections and freedom of speech.

RE-ENTER THE DRAGON

China's rise to superpower status has led to an expansion of its economic and military role in the Asia-Pacific region. The region is becoming increasingly tied to China's expanding market and demand for resources, and security challenges. The process of integration of the Asia-Pacific with China is largely defined by the nature of the conflicts that emerge and how these conflicts are settled among states which view each other not as partners but as competitors. There is a belief in the West that China wants to resume control of Taiwan, neutralise Japan, win control of the South China Sea and get the US out of Asia altogether (Bernstein and Munro 1998). Such actions would be opposed by the US and the set the stage for another Cold War.

Among many problems is the high level of mistrust that exists among northeast Asian countries. Japan, the Koreas, Mongolia and Taiwan have relatively low levels of empathy for each other and for China generally. All are concerned about Japan's possible re-emergence as a militarist power armed with nuclear weapons. There is a reciprocal fear in the region about China's regional hegemony. China's firing missiles across the Taiwan Straits in the 1990s was a deliberate message to Taiwan's politicians and population. North Korea's recent firing of a missile across Japan's northern island is another symptom of the tensions that exist in the region. These are reminders that there is no Pacific community but only countries that see themselves as competitors and potential enemies. The dynamics of the relationship is therefore based on power calculations and projections.

Taiwan's 23 million people are a core issue for Beijing. China maintains that Taiwan is a breakaway province that must be reunited by force if necessary with the mainland. The 1979 US agreement with

China acknowledges that all Chinese on either side of the Taiwan Strait are part of China. Since the occupation by nationalist forces in 1949, Taiwan has become a wealthy middle class society and in 1986 president Chiang Ching-kuo, head of the ruling party Kuomintang (KMT), unexpectedly opened the country to democratic politics. Taiwan had its first free and fair election in 1996 when Lee Teng-hui was elected as the island's president. There is now a strong nationalist movement to carry out a plebiscite on independence in the first decade of the twenty-first century. Taiwan is well-armed and has a large quantity of missiles. Some years ago it was developing nuclear weapons and had tested a nuclear device in the southern Atlantic in a joint venture with South Africa and possibly Israel. Taiwan has also been accused of developing biochemical weapons.

On many occasions China has warned Taiwan that it would be attacked if it declared independence. Tensions over the issue have escalated the conflict. When the US sold F-16s to Taiwan, Beijing sold missiles and nuclear blueprints to Pakistan. At the time of the 1996 Taiwan election China test-fired missiles in the Taiwan Straits and the US sent a carrier-led fleet as a deterrent. China has more than 400 missiles (SRBM) targeted at the island and has embarked on war preparations to attack and invade the country. China warned the US in 2003 that it was willing to pay the price, cancel the 2008 Beijing Olympics and rupture relations with the US to stop the island's formal separation from the mainland. The tension has not stopped economic integration between Taiwan and the mainland. At the beginning of the new century Taiwan was China's biggest investor with more than US$150 billion tied up in the economy, more than 1 million Taiwanese were living in China with many more millions visiting each year (Callick 2003). China's resolve about its demand will be tested when Taiwan's leadership formally arranges a referendum for the electorate to decide on its future, possibly in 2006.

China's subversive role in Southeast Asia gave way in the 1980s to a new strategy towards greater use of diplomatic and economic relations. China's economic influence in the region is growing rapidly, and networking with the overseas Chinese business community plays an important role in the economies of Southeast Asia. The 25 million Overseas Chinese in Southeast Asia have become a bridge in the integration of the region with southern China. The commercial influence is readily seen in the northern corridor through Yunnan and across the road network to Burma and Northern Laos bringing in large inflows of goods, migrants and traders. China has become a financial investor in Southeast Asia matching Japan's generous aid programme. In recent years China has moved to integrate the region's economies with free trade agreements with ASEAN members.

China's market economy and rising inequalities generate substantial immigration to other parts of the world. The influx of Chinese workers in Southeast Asia is already considerable and growing as many search for a better life elsewhere. There are more than 100,000 Chinese workers in Thailand and larger numbers in Burma and elsewhere in the region. Migration networks are extensive and essentially global in nature. Movement of people to Southeast Asia is often part of a series of migrations onwards to places such as Australia, the United States, or the European Union. Many Chinese migrants and traders are moving to the Pacific region causing considerable friction with local populations. The role of Chinese migrants coming to Papua New Guinea has generated considerable political anxiety in the country. Similar problems have arisen in other areas of the Pacific such as the Solomon Islands.

Southeast Asia has a long history of interaction with China and it can be assumed that China will gradually exert a new form of regional hegemony to reflect its growing economic and military power. One dimension in the equation is the competition between Japan and China's capitalism in the region. Japan's economic growth relies increasingly on the expansion of its overseas interests in Asia. Japan has a firm hold in various sectors of ASEAN economies with substantial investments in commercial banking, real estate, resorts and hotels, and manufacturing and construction. Southeast Asia is an area where Japan, China and the US will compete for market share and dominance. China's success in modernisation is likely to translate in the contestation of the role of transnational corporations in the region in advancing a US free trade agenda. There exists a strong cultural empathy among Southeast Asian Chinese for Confucian ethnocentrism, particularly in places such as Singapore where it forms the core of the city-state's ruling ideology. A more powerful China competing with the West, according to Professor Jamie Mackie of the Australian National University, would lead to the re-Sinification of the Chinese population and become a pressing issue in the political integrity of several Southeast Asian countries (Mackie 1998).

China will challenge the integrity of ASEAN and test whether or not the organisation is more than a set of hollow drums – hollow drums make the most noise according to a Chinese proverb. The association is plagued with enmity but one element which keeps it together is that most members fear Chinese hegemonism. The extent of China's power will be reflected in the process of settling many territorial and maritime disputes in the region. China claims sovereignty over the Spratly (Nansha) Archipelago which occupies about 180,000 km2 in the southern region of the South China Sea. Vietnam, Taiwan, Malaysia, Brunei and the Philippines have claims to various islands, islets or reefs. In 1988 China seized a number of islets in the Spratly Archipelago from the Vietnamese and set up a garrison on Mischief Reef claimed by the Philippines. China took control of the Paracel Islands claimed by Vietnam in 1974 while the North Vietnamese were busy with their final offensive in the south.

China has become a close ally and supporter of Burma's military dictatorship. It is the main provider of weapons and other military aid and Burma's economy has come under the influence of China's expanding capitalism; the country's north is virtually under Chinese economic domination. Burma's military regime has provided China with land and sea military bases. China's intelligence agencies are operating in Burma monitoring signals from the region, and its naval presence in the Bay of Bengal and the Andaman Sea gives it access to the Malacca Straits, one of the region's most important maritime routes. China has become the main backer of the Heng Seng regime in Cambodia and played an important role in the coup mounted by the former Khmer Rouge leader in nullifying the United Nations intervention in 1991 to bring democracy to the country.

China has important strategic interests in other parts of Asia. As the world's second largest user of oil it is increasingly reliant on imports of crude oil. The country is making major investments to secure its energy needs both in gas and oil in countries such as Australia, Venezuela, Peru, Iran, Iraq, Sudan, Indonesia, Azerbaijan and Kazakhstan. In 2003 Angola was China's main supplier of crude oil, followed by Saudi Arabia and Oman. China was becoming a key player in Sudan's oil industry and had troops stationed in the region. Further east, China has developed close relations with Iran, which holds the world's fifth-largest oil reserves, and wants access to Iran's untapped oil fields. In the coming years China will rely more on imports from Russia and Central Asia which can move oil in pipelines instead of relying on seaboard shipments. Reliance on land pipelines to move oil and gas from Russia will increase after a 2004 agreement to build a 2,400 km pipeline from Siberia. Michael Klare claims that within ten years 'China is expected to be totally dependent on the Persian Gulf and the Caspian Sea area for the oil it will need to sustain economic growth' (Klare 2003).

The US, China and Russia are competing for influence in Central Asia, and access to its oil and other resources. People in the region are poor and controlled by authoritarian regimes, and the newly independent countries are politically unstable. With the arrival of the US as a major player, Central Asian power politics will become a defining factor in regional affairs. China by necessity will get more involved in the regional politics for energy security and because of the sensitive nature of its western borders. Regions that are of particular importance range from Russia's far east, where more than 2 million Chinese live, and Kazakhstan in the north, to Kashmir, Nepal and Burma in the south. Demands for independence in Xianging and Tibet will reinforce China's concern about neighbourhood states such as Kirghizstan and other Central Asian republics. Klare argues that the area centred on the Persian Gulf and the Caspian Sea is the only region in the world where the interests of the great powers collide. Because of its oil resources the US 'is determined to dominate this area and to subordinate these two potential challengers [Russia, China] and prevent them from forming a common front against the United States' (Klare 2001, 2003:6). The region is potentially a major zone of confrontation in a US–China Cold War as both sides enmesh themselves in local conflicts and play power politics through proxies.

US HEGEMONY

The relationship between China and the US has deteriorated in the past decade and the mistrust between the two powers could lead to military confrontations in the coming years. Much of the problem has to do with differentials in economic development and living standards, and the incompatibility of their political regimes. Underlying the issue is their mutual perception as enemies in building up their military forces. The CIA has named China as the main adversary of the US and calls for the dismantling of the Communist Party. The Pentagon's *Defense Planning Guidance* documents in the 1990s called for 'proactive US military intervention to deter and prevent the rise of a contending peer (or equal) competitor, and asserts that the US must use any and all means necessary to prevent that from happening' (Klare 2003:3). A more recent Pentagon's *Nuclear Posture Review* lists China as a target for nuclear strikes.

The National Missile Defense (NMD) system which began under President Ronald Reagan's Star War project is aimed at China. The programme has evolved under the pressure of neoconservative forces in the Congress and Pentagon particularly under both Bush presidencies. George Bush officially opted out of the 1972 Anti-Ballistic Missile agreement signed with the USSR during the Cold War. New funds have been allocated to declare the missile defence programme operational and emplace missiles in various locations beginning with launchers in Alaska in 2004. Under the US scheme, Japan, South Korea and Australia would locate missiles in their country as part of the missile shield-interceptor programme. Some US$65 billion have been spent on the programme to date and another US$200 billion will be required to complete the project. While the missile system is aimed at China some experts believe that it is likely to be tested against other countries such as North Korea (SBS 2004).

China's leadership believes that the US 'has never abandoned its ambitions to rule the world, and its military interventionism is becoming more open' (Roy 1994:16). In 1993, the CCP's general secretary Jiang Zemin adopted a policy stating that China 'does not want confrontation with the US; China will not provoke confrontation with the US; China will not avoid confrontation with the US if the latter wants it; and China does not fear confrontation with the US' (Chanda 1993). China's military preparations include the development of a strategic nuclear force equipped with intercontinental ballistic missiles (ICBM) and short-range ballistic missiles (SRBM) in mobile launchers and hardened silos. China has about 20 ICBMs with a range of 13,000 km, many targeted at the US; and about 150 intermediate ballistic missiles (IRBM) with a range of up to 3,500 km (IISS 2002). According to the CIA, by 2015 China

will have deployed tens or several tens of missiles with nuclear warheads targeted against the US, mostly more survivable land-and sea-based mobile missiles. It also will have hundreds of shorter-range ballistic cruise missiles for use in regional conflicts. Some of these shorter-range missiles will have nuclear warheads; most will be armed with conventional warheads. (CIA 2004)

China is investing significant resources to develop its space strategic capability because it perceives space as the war zone of the future.

Both the US and China have played a major role in the proliferation of weapons of mass destruction. While China has made important financial gains in selling missile and nuclear technology the motivation behind its policy is power projection to counteract

US alliances and power projection in Asia. China has sold missile technology to Argentina, Syria, North Korea, Pakistan, Brazil, Libya, Iraq, Iran and Saudi Arabia. China is a major proliferator of weapons of mass destruction since the missiles it exports are designed to carry biological, chemical or nuclear bombs. China has sold nuclear weapon designs for missile programmes to North Korea, Pakistan, Saudi Arabia and Iran. China has exported short-range M11 tactical missiles to Pakistan as well as nuclear weapon blueprints, and is alleged to have shipped to Iran the main chemical ingredients used to make mustard and nerve gas. China's relationship with Saudi Arabia is intriguing given the latter country's close ties with the US. Some years ago China sold a number of intermediate range ballistic missiles (IRBM) to Saudi Arabia (Chanda 1988). The CSS2s have a range of more than 3,000 km and carry conventional or nuclear warheads. It is alleged that China provided Saudi Arabia with some nuclear warheads after Iraq's invasion of Kuwait in 1990 (MDN 1990). Moreover it can be assumed that since Saudi Arabia funded Pakistan's nuclear programme it has obtained some nuclear warheads for its missiles. Another possibility is that Saudi Arabia's missiles are under the control of Pakistan's military establishment.

US policy is to build security alliances and a proactive military presence in the region to prevent the rise of another power which would threaten its economic and political interests. China on the other hand wants the US out of Asia and has been described as 'an unsatisfied and ambitious power whose goal is to dominate Asia, not by invading and occupying neighbouring nations, but by being so much more powerful than they are that nothing will be allowed to happen in East Asia without China's at least tacit consent' (Bernstein and Munro 1998:4). The US–China clash is shaping a number of conflict geographies where the two powers confront each other directly or indirectly. One unstable zone is around the Taiwan issue. The US has been arming Taiwan and has made a formal commitment to defend the island-state under the Taiwan Relations Act and the Taiwan Security Enhancement Act (TSEA). If attacked by China the US would intervene and possibly carry the war to the mainland. China has said that there would be a state of war if Taiwan announced its independence. According to defence analysts China is building up its naval power 'with a view of being able to deter or destroy US aircraft carriers and rapidly subdue Taiwan by force' (Monk 2002a). A major test will come when Taiwan's President Chen introduces constitutional reforms in 2006 to move the island towards full sovereignty. There could be an element of surprise in the Taiwan issue with China invading a number of nearby islands such as Quemoy and Matsu to force some compromise with Taiwan.

There are other troublesome areas around China's core such as Hong Kong (HK). How would the US react to China's gradual abandonment of the two-system arrangement and the incorporation of HK into mainland China? What would the US do in the event of a ban on HK's democratic movement, a quick end to residents' autonomy, and a retraction on the freedoms granted under the 1984 treaty with Britain? The US–HK Policy Act of 1992 signed by former president Bush provides for some US protection to safeguard residents' human rights. US promises under the act have been denounced by China as interference in China's sovereignty. Confrontation between China and the US could take place elsewhere on the periphery as a result of their involvement in third-party conflicts. Such a scenario is possible in the South China Sea if China pursues its sovereign claims to the Spratly Islands.

On the mainland there are a number of tension areas particularly along China's southern and western borders where both the US and China are manipulating Asia's regional politics to promote their economic and strategic interests through proxies. Such situations can trigger nasty reactions exemplified in the deliberate US bombing in May 1999 of Belgrade's Chinese embassy, which was being used by the Yugoslav military to transmit military communication. Beyond that are even bigger issues such as what happens in space. China's major effort to develop its space capabilities reflects the critical strategic value it places on space in future military development. China is developing an extensive intelligence capacity by setting up communication networks in many parts of the world including Cuba, where it has operated two signals intelligence stations since early 1999 to intercept satellite-based US military communication and engage in electronic warfare.

What pathway the US eventually follows on China depends to a large extent on which faction controls the US national security establishment. According to Henry Kissinger, under president Clinton the debate was controlled by those who supported 'engagement and strategic partnership. Multiplying contacts on trade, environment, science and technology to strengthen international co-operation and internal pluralism' (Kissinger 2001). Since 2001 however, the neoconservatives have gained power, and they perceive China 'as a morally flawed, inevitable adversary – at the moment with respect to Taiwan, eventually the Western Pacific and, in time, the global equilibrium'. US neoconservatives, also dubbed hardliners and Sinophobes, want to deal with China 'not as a partner but as a rival reducing trade to non-strategic items, creating an alliance of Asian states to help share the burden of defending Asia and to contain China. This view would treat Taiwan as independent and scrap the one China policy' (Kissinger 2001).

The US is moving ahead with the national missile defence system and escalating the security stakes by subsidising an armaments race in the region. At the same time US policy is putting into place a regional balance of power which would pit an alliance of Japan, South Korea, Australia and some of the ASEAN countries against China. The US role in this arrangement is to retain global hegemony and, as Eurasia's balancer, manage Asia's balance of power to advantage. Hardliner academic John Mearsheimer argues that 'China is the most dangerous potential threat to the US in the early twenty-first century'; China is a potential hegemon and wants to dominate the affairs of Japan and Korea (Mearsheimer 2001). The US, he says, should confront China and slow down its economic growth. Another academic, Samuel Huntington, has played a role in baiting the dragon by writing his bestseller on a clash of civilisations between the West and a Sino-Islamic allegiance. However, he argues that the US should stay out of any conflict over Taiwan because to do so would lead to the intervention 'by the core state of one civilisation (the United States) in a dispute between the core state of another civilisation (China) and a member of that civilisation' (Huntington 1997:316). Such action which the US may find difficult to avoid could trigger a major war between the two and destroy the United States as we know it.

Both the US and China are moving on similarly constructed paths towards confrontation. China's economy is growing rapidly and the promise and pressure of modernity given the size of its population is unlikely to shift the country away from the formation of a one-party state with fascist characteristics. A military culture is developing in China which feeds on nationalism and the symbols of its powerful civilisation, mixed with resentment against the West for a long history of humiliation against its people. Militarism is also a dominant feature of US society. The size of the US war machine and the mindset that goes with it threatens the foundation of the country's democratic process. Capitalism in the US is a dynamic feature of the economy based on unsustainable mass consumption and continued growth to maintain the myth of an egalitarian society where the poor can always become achievers and wealthy. In an anarchic world without a world government the US and China are building a momentum in competing with each other for resources and wealth. Both encourage a culture of greed among their people while hardliners are gaining political control in an atmosphere of mutual suspicion and fear.

AUSTRALIA WALTZING WITH THE US

Australia's military establishment has become an extension of the US war machine and the militarisation of the Australian continent part of a US constructed balance of power to control political and economic development in Asia. The US has a number of bases in the country including vital intelligence gathering facilities. Existing and planned US training bases in northern Australia are likely to become permanent facilities for the storage of war material and its deployment in war operations in Asia. These and other developments will enhance Australia's role as a main staging area for the military encirclement of China.

Australia supported the US cancellation of the 1972 Anti-ballistic Missile (ABM) Treaty to enable the US to develop and deploy its national missile defence system early in the twenty-first century. Australia is an integral part of the US missile defence system. It has been involved in the research and development of the programme and has built testing facilities on the west coast. Soon Australia will have missile interceptors and radar units on the Australian continent and at sea on ships working with the US navy to protect and attack strategic areas. The US missile defence shield is an element of a balance of power scheme to tie up Australia with some members of ASEAN, Japan and South Korea to keep pressure on Taiwan and deter China from attacking the island-state.

Under Prime Minister John Howard the Australian defence budget has increased considerably to well above A$18 billion in 2003 with major increments projected for the coming decade. Australia's military is gaining greater capability to intervene in the region with the acquisition of new equipment such as three new air-warfare destroyers equipped with anti-ballistic missiles to provide cover for deployed forces, and a defence capability integrated with the US missile system. Integration into US warfare include US made F-35 fighter and expanded airborne surveillance and control systems, as well as a rapid-deployment strike force. Australia has been building an extensive spying capability mostly against China and its allies, including covert operations in the region by Australian intelligence agencies.

Australia's commitment to the US alliance and missile defence system puts it on a collision course with China. In the event that China attacks Taiwan or adjacent islands and the US retaliates Australia would necessarily get involved. Richard Armitage, a former US deputy secretary of state and Bush confidante, reminded Australians during his frequent appearances on Australian TV that it 'must stand ready to give military support if the US goes to war with China'. The US Sinophobe lobby wants to commit Australia 'to participate in any conflict that might occur however provoked and share in any consequent loss of life' (Harris 2000). In the event of a crisis over Taiwan, Australia is expected to play an active role in support of US forces and in particular deploy its Collins-class submarines in the Formosa Straits.

China has called Australia a 'lackey of the US' and warned of 'very serious' consequences if it sides with the US in the event of a clash over Taiwan. China has attacked Australia's participation in a Brisbane-based eleven-nation operation to intercept ships from North Korea and other flags suspected of carrying weapons of mass destruction or their components. China told Australia that the scheme was 'useless and antagonistic'. During Hu Jintao's address to Australia's parliament in 2003 he warned Australia that China expected it to play a 'constructive' role in the reunification of Taiwan with China and learn to accept the fact that China had different values.

9
The Americanisation of Australia

Everyone is entitled to a social and international order in which the rights and freedoms set forth in this Declaration can be realised.

UN Universal Declaration of Human Rights (1948, Article 28)

There is a long tradition in Australian studies about cultural imperialism and the Americanisation of Australia which may well have begun with the publication of Dunmore Lang's pamphlet on *The Moral and Religious Aspect of the Future America of the Southern Hemisphere* (Lang 1840). The question about US influence in shaping the country's future has become more pressing with time as US imperial ambitions are becoming more obvious and destructive. A source of concern is that Australia's political culture is increasingly a reflection of a US template in governance and social relations, and that its foreign policy is embedded in US hegemony as one of its two trusted sheriffs. An aspect of this problem is the dominance in present-day Australia of the new right in the political and economic life of the country. The ideology which structures society and legitimises the power of an oligarchy came mainly from the US because of the push–pull power of its culture and institutions, and longstanding ties between both countries which together with the UK are part of a triad which anchors Anglo-Saxon capitalism in the world system (Dore 2000a; Wallerstein 2003a).

Australia's political economy has been reshaped in recent years by the dogmas of neoliberalism. Much has been written on the subject under the heading of neoliberalism, economic rationalism, Anglo-American capitalism or the Washington consensus (Carroll and Manne 1992; Pussey 1991; Connell 2002). These economic tools have been politicised and used to expand the role and power of capitalism into new social terrains. Market forces free of social justice and political equality considerations have quickly expanded to further commodify life, culture and social relations. Neoliberalism's agenda focuses on the minimisation of the state in economic life and the privatisation of public assets, a transfer of power to market forces, the deregulation of labour and financial markets and the adoption of a free trade agenda in international relations. It is broadly complemented by an ideology of managerialism, or more simply the formation of managers and technocrats to implement neoliberal policies in the corporate world, government and other public institutions, and in other spheres of cultural and private life.

Neoliberal doctrine claims a scientific pedigree because it is anchored in the profession of economics and management and its use of complex mathematical models. But it is essentially an ideology with religious overtones which provides the neoconservative movement with the intellectual tools and strategy to capture power and the control of the state. Rooted in its discourse is a belief in social Darwinism and a vision for a socio-political order which legitimises inequality and the right of those who have achieved powerful positions and accumulated great wealth to control the affairs of the state. Social Darwinism is essentially an anti-democratic creed which preaches the natural right of an oligarchy to rule on behalf of citizens and the role of market forces to sort out the winners from the losers. A so-called free market becomes a new triage mechanism to engage individuals in a never-ending competition to gain access to wealth and power under the rule of law. Social Darwinism is a new form of feudalism and an attempt of the right to legitimise their activities and exploit others. It is old wine in a new postmodern bottle.

The new right movement is religious in character and contains a heavy dose of Christian fundamentalism to further validate its claim to hubris and provide a counterweight to the destructive process of capitalism on social relations and society generally. Christian fundamentalism brings God as a master entrepreneur and a keen dispenser of wealth to those who have the faith and give generously. Equally important is the role of the religious right in the construction of foreign policy, particularly in regard to social and international relations. Christian fundamentalism provides a worldview with a grand narrative of a Star-Wars type contest between the forces of good and evil. Satanic forces are personified by non-believers, particularly Muslims and Hindus. The religious right no longer holds the promise of paradise after death but brings the universal contest back to earth in a narrative which predicts the Second Coming of Christ when Israel is eventually restored to its old territorial sovereignty. In this scenario the Christian right plays an active role in support of Israel's right to occupy and dispossess Palestinians of their land and culture. In the final analysis the new right is about power, gaining power and using it to benefit corporations, while the world is riven by inequality, oppression and exploitation. It has little to do with social justice and implementing the United Nations Universal Declaration of Human Rights.

In recent decades the US has played a major role in the diffusion of new right ideology and strategy in Australia. It has been part of a battle of ideas, a war of the right on the left, which intensified during the Cold War and moved into a new expansionary phase following the fall of the Berlin wall in 1989. NGOs have played a major role in the new right strategy to diffuse its ideology and techniques to capture power. The role of think-tanks in Australia has been widely studied and highlighted in the work of Alex Carey (1995) and Ted Wheelwright (1995). More recently Philip Mendes and Damien Cahill have analysed the role of the Centre for Independent Studies (CIS) in the construction of hegemony in Australia (Mendes 2003; Cahill 2004). Generous funding by the corporate sector has advanced the neoconservative war against welfare bodies and environmental groups. The mining industry and Hugh Morgan, former CEO of Western Mining, have been major supporters in the funding and expansion of the CIS. Other major centres for the propagation of neoliberal ideology funded by corporations and wealthy individuals include the Global Foundation, the Institute of Public Affairs, and the Sydney Institute.

Higher education plays a critical role in the propagation of neoliberalism. University faculties of economics, commerce and management have trained and indoctrinated several generations of Australians in the science and vision of economic rationalism. Business schools have been active in elite formation using the Harvard model for their Master of Business Administration (MBA) programmes and have formed armies of managers and symbolic technocrats to implement neoliberal policies in the economy, government and society (Rees and Rodley 1995). Michael Pussey, of the University of New South Wales, described how senior economists steeped in US econometrics gained control of key ministries in the 1980s and played a major role in pushing for privatisation and the deregulation of the labour and financial markets (Pussey 1991). Their role has destroyed 'the capacity of a once excellent and highly professional public service, to deliver independent advice and policy in the public interest and without fear or favour' (Pussey 2003:10) Pussey further notes that at the time the Business Council of Australia (BCA), which brings together CEOs of some one hundred major corporations, was 'with senior Treasury and central agency officials writing national budgets sometimes almost line by line' (Pussey 2003:11).

Christian fundamentalism imported mainly from the United States has been a key to the rise to power of the new right. Much of that modern discourse originated in the 1920s among US Southern Baptists calling for America to return to *The Fundamentals* based on the literal interpretation of the bible. The importation of the religious right discourse has taken place by a process of osmosis and by what can be called the franchising of Christian evangelical churches by their controlling organisations in the US, or by setting up and funding new colonies. More recent arrivals have been the LaRouchite Citizens Electoral Council, the World Church of the Creator and the growing influence of US-based groups such as the Christian Identity organisations and militia groups. The religious right has been promoted by well-known entertainers and personalities such as long-term Australian resident Mel Gibson, who went from the *Mad Max* movies to *The Patriot* and onwards to *The Passion of the Christ*. Gibson's film discourse builds on society's disintegration and chaos, to the liberation by patriotic forces and the eventual coming of an avenging God to bring a final end to the human mess.

The US model of merging Christian fundamentalism with the expansion of capitalism is becoming more evident in Australia. There is a marriage between the market and Christian fundamentalism where religion becomes a business, a social service and a provider of employment and welfare services. The Pentecostalist churches, also known as Assemblies of God, Christian City Church, Hillsong, Catch the Fire, and others, while dispensing morality to cope with the pressures and destructive impact of market forces on society and family life, have become part of a vast tax-free economy involved in a whole range of activities from development to housing, financial and personnel services, to manufacturing activities in farming, furniture, foodstuff, and the provision of health care and education.

Brian Houston, the New Zealand migrant senior pastor of the Hillsong Church in Sydney's urban sprawl of Baulkham Hills, is the author of *You Need More Money: Discovering God's Amazing Financial Plan for your Life* (Maddox 2005). Houston and his group head a booming enterprise generating enormous amounts of wealth and power, and work closely with developers expanding Sydney's urban sprawl as well as their financial empire. Pentecostalists have close relations with politicians and business leaders. Public figures such as Peter Costello, Tony Abbott and John Anderson, Bronwyn Bishop and Peter Garett, and Kevin Judd openly profess their evangelical faith. The formation of Christian business groups follows the US pathway which links fundamentalist organisations to universities and corporations such as Macquarie University, Fairfax, Woolworths and KPMG financial services.

Another mechanism is the direct transfer of US domestic policies towards restructuring society. Part of the US template in Australia's governance is to privatise social security and transfer welfare's role to church-based agencies and empower them to deliver welfare and health services. To minimise the state's role in the delivery of public services there has been a concerted effort to conceptualise the individual's role in a risk society. The basic message is that every person has obligations and must make decisions for which he or she is held responsible, not society or the state. While you can and should insure for a better life outcome it is not the responsibility of the state to guarantee one's welfare, security and happiness. In a market economy the individual is trained not only to buy insurance against all-risks but also to undertake a course of study and personal development to successfully negotiate market forces and accumulate wealth. A risk society warns that if you want to negotiate old age you need to pay for the privilege.

Another convergence with the US is the enterprise culture being pushed by the ruling coalition. Prime Minister John Howard, who has a close relationship with President George Bush, has been inspired by the business vitality of US society and often tells Australians to be more like Americans and more entrepreneurial and competitive in their aspirations. The ownership society and enterprise culture concept, which features heavily in Howard's fourth-term agenda, is a marketing device to prepare the public for the continued efforts of the government to privatise health, education, social security and the country's infrastructure. In the same mode Australia has been replicating the US approach to resolving the country's indigenous problem by privatising communal land and forging business alliances with corporate interests to develop tourist and gambling attractions.

Manufacturing consent for US imperial policy is conducted mainly by centres and institutes which propagate strategic studies and policy statements. These rationalise the use of military force and the need for military intervention in various parts of the world to bring freedom and democracy to the rest of the world. In Australia, centres such as the Lowy Institute, the Australian Strategic Policy Institute and the Australian National University (ANU) Strategic and Defence Studies Centre play an important role to imprimatur Australia's military intervention overseas and the need for a bigger military budget. Strategic studies are often linked to media campaigns to explain threats to Western civilisation. As part of the politics of fear, past generations have lived through the yellow peril and the evil of communism, and the threat of Red China bent on invading freedom-loving states. President Johnson and Nixon's domino theory caught the imagination of the Australian public and played an important role in shaping public opinion in support of Australia's military intervention in Vietnam.

Changes in recent decades show Australia developing a form of governance and society closely resembling that of the United States, and that Australia is becoming more like US society in its politics, social pathologies and symptoms of overdevelopment. Australia's capitalism is increasingly taking on the predatory characteristics which typify its US counterpart. Privatisation, Latin for 'to deprive', has delivered a great deal of the commonwealth to corporations and wealthy individuals. The process continues unabated with a new phase featuring Public–Private Partnerships (PPP) to further transfer essential services and the country's infrastructure into exclusive property rights. These assets with their substantial debts are bundled into expensive portfolios and sold to pension funds by financiers who make fortunes in the process.

Corporate power is changing the nature of social relations and political power through its ownership of space and control of land-use. This is particularly visible in major cities where business control of urban space affects the way people live, work and interact. Urban configuration is changing rapidly because of control in the use of land and a development model which brings together major elements of the corporate sector and government institutions. Australian cities are looking more like US cities with their urban sprawl and dependence on the car for transport. Inequality is increasingly visible in the spatial segregation of the rich living in gated communities, with access to private clubs, schools and health services while the poor and superfluous population to the economy are contained in outer suburbia slums and regional towns. The haves and the elites have removed themselves from society and democratic life to set up their own national and international enclaves.

As with the United States, Australian democracy is moving away from political equality and fair elections for its citizens to a political regime controlled by an oligarchy funding political parties to further expand the reaches of capitalism and property rights. Cities are being carved out into feudal empires run by large corporations which control shopping malls, entertainment districts, marinas, sport and health facilities, housing and the transport corridors which articulate urban space. What is left of public space such as parks and museums is being slowly privatised through corporate sponsorship and space rental. Much of rural Australia has been incorporated into vast agribusiness and mining fiefdoms. Corporate control of social space symbolises a major shift in political power away from a citizen-based nation-state to authoritarian corporations. Democracy is being transformed into a regime more akin to a modern form of corporatism converging on the US model.

The control of dissent is becoming more oppressive. Since the turn of the century the politics of paranoia have gained strength with Australia's policy to wage war on terrorism. Australia's 'all the way' policy with the US invasion of Afghanistan and Iraq has further added weight to the politics of fear and allowed government to detain large numbers of refugees including many women and children in concentration camp conditions. Reactionary politics are promoting more attacks against welfare, social security, public health and education. Political and civil rights have been restricted in recent years with US Patriot Act-like federal legislation which gives intelligence agencies and police wide powers to spy on and detain citizens alleged to have information about terrorists. In such cases courtrooms are closed to the public and to the press. Attacks on dissent are part of a process on the part of the state to capture civil society through the destruction of the union movement, restrictions on the diffusion of information, a culture of secrecy, and the depoliticisation of NGOs.

Changes in recent decades raise the question about Australia's rapid adoption and conversion to US imports of a new right culture. Aspects of the equation have been discussed earlier in the genesis of a colonial society and the formation of the nation-state. The establishment of a colonial society was largely dependent on imported ideas and values. One critical element has been the ideological ingredient of legitimising the ruling elite. Part of the history of Australia can be interpreted as the replacement of a power structure based on British imperial tradition with the hegemony of an oligarchy based on the rise of corporate power and the appropriation of newly created wealth.

Philip and Roger Bell make the point that 'culture is never simply imposed from above, but is negotiated through existing patterns and traditions' (Bell and Bell 1993:9). Although the falsity of this claim can be argued in regard to the invasion of the continent and the destruction of Aboriginal culture, there is an element of truth in the context of external influence on a British colonial society and settler state. Transfer of cultural material readily takes place when appropriate conditions exist, when the cultural terrain is like soil ready to be seeded and the plant grows well because the conditions are right and all the ingredients are in place for its nurturing and growth. But the seeds are imported and the rapid conversion of Australia to economic neoliberalism and US-style political neoconservatism suggests that conditions in Australia were conducive for their rapid adoption and diffusion. The existence of an Anglo-Irish modern society has been an important factor in addition to a conservative political culture imported in recent times by several generations of migrants. Equally important has been the domination of the mass media by powerful corporate interests to produce what Alex Carrey and Noam Chomsky suggest is 'a non-critical, non-dissenting information culture congenial to US interests' (Bell and Bell 1993:5).

More critical has been the failure of the left to respond to the challenge of neoconservatives and to what David McKnight describes as the 'radical visionaries who want to overturn the established order by putting market mechanisms in almost every aspect of life' (McKnight 2004). The left began losing its way during the Hawke–Keating years of Labor in power when it made deals with the corporate world to expand their power in society and politics. It was the 1983 Hawke government which set up the Office of Asset Sales in 1987 to transfer the country's public wealth accumulated over generations to a minority of shareholders. Mark Latham, who led the Labor Party at the 2004 Federal election, became the victim of a factionalised party which had lost a sense of purpose and was under attack by powerful US lobbies. What has happened according to Roberto Michels' analysis of the transformation of political parties in a modern democracy is that progressive parties like the Australian Labor Party have been co-opted by the ruling class, its leaders becoming members of the aristocracy (Michels 1962).

Labor has lost its sense of purpose and no longer stands for social justice embedded in a process for greater political equality for all its citizens. The party has moved to the centre right and in many critical areas is indistinguishable in its policies from the conservative coalition's agenda. Labor Party leader Kim Beazley is the candidate preferred by the US because of his commitment to the US alliance and role of Australia in the US empire, and to the right of the US to detain Australians at Guantánamo Bay. Beazley supports mandatory detention for refugees and keeping children and women in detention camps, and backs the US war in Iraq and elsewhere. Soon after his election as party leader he declared that 'Labor must make Australians feel secure in their new wealth as a fundamental prerequisite for everything the party does' and indicated that 'given the choice between economic rationalism, which represents the financial interest, and social democracy, which represents democratic control of the economy in the interests of ordinary people, he is prepared to back the interests of high finance' (Davidson 2005:2).

Historians and others have written on the transition of Australia from a British colony to an American dependency. Much was said some three decades ago about Australia's role as satellite in a US empire (Wheelwright 1982) and that relations with the US were compromising Australia's national identity, interests and sovereignty (Camilleri 1980). At the beginning of the twenty-first century US imperial ambitions were more overt with the invasion of Afghanistan and Iraq and US plans to reshape the politics of the Middle East. The US is now the world's dominant military power and its policy statements clearly spell out its intentions to intervene militarily to reshape the world political map and to respond to any challenge to its hegemony. Australia is now more embedded in the US empire and has clearly demonstrated in deeds and words that the country is moving all the way with US plans to bring democracy and free trade to the rest of the world.

Dunmore Lang, a member of the New South Wales legislative council in the 1850s, had a vision for Australia as a republican federation free from British rule, and in his mind Australia would, like America, flourish as a republic. Americanisation for many republicans of that century contained the promises for Australia of the American declaration of Independence and France's revolutionary call for 'Liberty, Fraternity, and Equality'. The American dream was for many generations the dream of the possibility of constructing a better society for all people. It was the discovery of the New World, Hannah Arendt suggests, that made possible the conviction that society could eliminate poverty. She writes that the idea 'that life on earth might be blessed with abundance instead of being cursed by scarcity ... was American in origin; it grew directly out of the

American colonial experience' (Arendt 1970:15). Australian society has found an abundance of wealth but has yet to construct a sustainable social order based on social justice for all. This would require independence from British rule and the establishment of a republic based on political equality for its citizens. Australia and America's potential as a federation cannot be realised unless it can expand and become more inclusive and shared with less fortunate countries. This will not be possible while insane consumption and waste is embodied in the dream of the good life, and while the accumulation of more wealth continues to dominate the economic and political life of both countries.

Bibliography

Abbott, T. (2004) 'Menzies and the wider world. Menzies Lecture', *Australian*, 19 May.

ABC (2002) *Four Corners*. Australian Broadcasting Corporation TV, 1 July.

Abramovici, P. (2004) 'Activisme militaire de Washington en Afrique', *Le Monde Diplomatique*, Juillet.

ABS (Australian Bureau of Statistics. www.abs.gov.au/publications).

—— (1999) *1999 Yearbook of Australia*. Mental Health of Australian Adults table 9.11. (Canberra: ABS).

—— (2002) *Salinity of Australian Farms* (Canberra: Australian Bureau of Statistics).

ADB (2003) *Millennium Development Goals in the Pacific* (Manila: Asian Development Bank).

AI (1994) *Power and Impunity: Human Rights Under the New Order* (London: Amnesty International).

—— (1997) *Bougainville: The Forgotten Human Rights Tragedy* (London: Amnesty International).

AidWatch (1999) *EFIC for Beginners* (Sydney: AidWatch).

AIHW (2002) *2001 National Drug Strategy Household Survey* (Canberra: Australian Institute of Health and Welfare).

Allard, T. (2003) 'PM's grim terrorism warning to Australia', *Sydney Morning Herald*, 9 August.

—— (2004) 'Defence chiefs finally come clean', *Sydney Morning Herald*, 1 June.

ANAO (2001) *Performance Information for Commonwealth Financial Assistance Under the Natural Heritage Trust*. Department of the Environment and Heritage, Audit Report No. 43–2000–01. Australian National Audit Office (Canberra: Commonwealth of Australia).

Anderson, B. (ed. 2001) *Violence and the State in Suharto's Indonesia* (Ithaca: Cornell University Southeast Asian Program).

Anon (1994) *Can China's Armed Forces Win the Next War?* (Beijing).

Arendt, H. (1970) *On Revolution* (New York: Viking).

Argy, F. (2002) *Egalitarianism*. 2002 ISAA Annual Conference Proceedings. Independent Scholars Association of Australia, 10 October (Canberra: ISAA).

Arrighi, G. and Silver, B. (eds 1999) *Chaos and Governance in the Modern World System* (Minneapolis: University of Minnesota Press).

Arrow, K. et al. (1995) 'Economic Growth, Carrying Capacity, and the Environment', *Science*, 28 April.

ASPI (2002) *Beyond Bali: ASPI's Strategic Assessment 2002* (Canberra: Australian Strategic Policy Institute).

Austrade (2003a) *Australian Trade Commission Annual Report 2003*. Department of Foreign Affairs and Trade (Canberra: Austrade).

—— (2003b) *Austrade's Service*. Australian Trade Commission, Canberra. www.austrade.gov.au.

Bacevich, A. (2001) *American Empire: The Realities and Consequences of US Diplomacy* (Harvard: Harvard University Press).

—— (ed. 2003) *The Imperial Tense: Prospects and Problems of American Empire* (New York: Ivan R. Dee).

—— (2004) *The New American Militarism: How Americans are Seduced By War.* (Oxford: Oxford University Press).

Ball, D. (1980) *A Suitable Piece Real Estate* (Sydney: Hale & Ironmonger).

—— (2001) 'The Strategic Essence', *Australian Journal of International Affairs*, Vol. 55, No. 2.

—— (2003) 'Pine Gap had role in first strike', *Sydney Morning Herald*, 22 March.

Ball, D. and McDonald, H. (2000) *Death in Balibo, Lies in Canberra* (Sydney: Allen & Unwin).

Balmain, A. (1999) 'Irian Jaya: how Canberra helped crush freedom quest', *Sydney Morning Herald*, 26 August.

Bannister, B. and Mason, L. (2004) *How high will oil prices climb?* http://sf.indymedia.org/news/2004/10/1704048.

Bao Tong (2002) 'Fierce attack on China's ruling elite'. BBC News Radio, 29 August.

Baragwanath, C. and Howe, J. (2002) *Corporate Welfare*. Australia Institute, Discussion Paper no. 34 (Canberra: AI).

Barker, G. (2002) 'Pre-emptive defence strikes a recipe for anarchy', *Australian Financial Review*, 3 December.

Batch, J. and Baur, L. (2005) 'Management and Prevention of Obesity and its complications in Children and Adolescents', *Medical Journal of Australia*, Vol. 182, No. 3.

Bell, P. and Bell, R. (1993) *Implicated: The United States in Australia* (Sydney: Oxford University Press).

—— (eds 1998) *Americanization and Australia* (Sydney: University of New South Wales Press).

Bello, W. (2004) *Deglobalisation: Ideas for a New World Economy* (London: Zed Books).

Bernstein, R. and Munro, R. (1998) *The Coming Conflict with China* (New York: Knopf).

Bhagwati, J. (2004) *In Defense of Globalization* (New York: Oxford University Press).

Birmingham, J. (2001) 'Appeasing Jakarta: Australia's Complicity in the East Timor Tragedy', *Quarterly Essay*, Issue 2.

BLM (1995) *Bougainville.* (Sydney: Bougainville Freedom Movement).

Blumenthal, S. (2004) 'This is the new gulag', *Guardian*, 6 May.

Bohman, J. and Lutz-Bachmann, M. (eds 1997) *Perpetual Peace: Essays on Kant's Cosmopolitan Ideal* (Cambridge: MIT Press).

Booker, M. (1988) 'Someone else's country, right or wrong', *Sydney Morning Herald*, 27 January.

Borger, J. (2004) 'Faithful to George's gospel', *Guardian Weekly*, 9 July.

Bourdieu, P. (1998) 'The essence of neoliberalism', *Le Monde Diplomatique*, December.

Brain, P. (2001) *The Australian Federation 2001.* Alfred Deakin Lectures, Melbourne International Festival of the Arts, 15 May.

Brett, J. (2003) 'John Howard and the Australian Legend', *Arena Magazine*, July.

Brown, G. (1989) *Breaking the American Alliance*. Strategic and Defence Studies Centre (Canberra: Australian National University).

Brown, G. and Rayner, L. (2001) *Upside, Downside: ANZUS After Fifty Years*. Current Issues Brief No.3 (Canberra: Department of the Parliamentary Library).

Brown, P. (2005) 'Melting ice could submerge London (and New York)', *Guardian Weekly*, 23 July.

Brown, T. (2003) 'Building a strategy for the Solomons', *Australian Financial Review*, 18 July.

Brundtland, G. et al. (1988) *Our Common Future* (Oxford: Oxford University Press).

Brzezinski, Z. (1997) *The Grand Chessboard: American Primacy and Its Geostrategic Imperatives* (New York: Basic Books).

Burchill, S. (1995) 'Perspectives on Australian Foreign Policy', *Australian Journal of International Affairs*, Vol. 49, No.1.

Buruma, I. (2002) *Bad Elements* (London: Weidenfeld & Nicolson).

Bush, G. (2002) *The National Security Strategy of the United States of America*. The White House. www. whitehouse.gov/nsc/nssall.html.

Butterworth, L. and Shakespeare, R. (2002) 'Return of the chief', *Weekend Australian Magazine*, 16 February.

Cahill, D. (2004) 'Contesting Hegemony: The Radical Neo-Liberal Movement and the Ruling Class in Australia', in Hollier, D. (ed.) *Ruling Australia: The Power, Privilege and Politics of the New Ruling Class* (Melbourne: Australian Scholarly Publishing).

Calacouras, N. and Bacon, W. (2005) 'A profit powerhouse', *Sydney Morning Herald*, 1 March.

Caldicott, H. (2002a) *The New Nuclear Danger* (Melbourne: Scribe).

—— (2002b) 'Australia, the US and the Missile Shield', *Arena Magazine*, 59, June.

Calleo, D. (1987) *Beyond American Hegemony: The Future of the Western Alliance* (New York: Basic Books).

Callick, R. (2000a) 'PNG at the edge of an abyss', *Australian Financial Review*, 9 March.

—— (2000b) 'Solomons down the mine', *Australian Financial Review*, 10 June.

—— (2003) 'Taiwanese exodus to the motherland', *Australian Financial Review*, 17 January.

Cameron, G. et al. (2003) 'Overweight and Obesity in Australia', *Medical Journal of Australia*, Vol. 178, No. 9.

Camilleri, J. (1980) *Australian–American Relations: The Web of Dependence* (Sydney: Macmillan).

Carey, A. (1995) *Taking the Risk out of Democracy: Propaganda in the US and Australia* (Sydney: UNSW Press).

Carr, E. (1956) *The Twenty Years' Crisis, 1919–1939* (London: Macmillan).

Carroll, J. (2000) 'Corporate Carnivores', *AQ*, August–September.

Carroll, J. and Robert Manne, R. (eds 1992) *Shutdown: The Failure of Economic Rationalism and How to Rescue Australia* (Melbourne: Text Publishing).

Castoriadis, C. (1997) *World in Fragments* (Stanford: Stanford University Press).

Célérier, P. (2004) 'Shangaï sans toits ni lois', *Le Monde Diplomatique*, Mars.

Chanda, N. (1988) 'The third world race for ballistic missiles', *Far Eastern Economic Review*, 2 June.

—— (1993) 'Circling hawks', *Far Eastern Economic Review*, 7 October.

—— (1995) 'The new nationalism', *Far Eastern Economic Review*, 9 November.

Chang, G. (2001) *The Coming Collapse of China* (New York: Random House).

Chang, H-J. (2003a) *Kicking Away the Ladder: Development Strategy in Historical Perspective* (London: Anthem Press).

—— (2003b) 'Kicking Away the Ladder: Infant Industry Promotion in Historical Perspective', *Oxford Development Studies*, Vol. 31, No.1.

Chang, M. (2004) *Falun Gong: The End of Days* (Yale University Press).

Chase-Dunn, C. and Reifer, T. (2002) *US hegemony and biotechnology: the geopolitics of new lead technology*. The Institute for Research on World-Systems. Research paper ironws9, University of California, Riverside.

Cheeseman, G. and Kettle, J. (eds 1990) *The New Australian Militarism: Undermining Our Future Security* (Sydney: Pluto Press).

Chen Guidi and Wu Chuntao (2004) *Zhongguo nongmin diaocha (Survey of Chinese Peasants)* (Beijing: People's Literature Publication Company).

Chesterman, M. (2001) *Freedom of Speech in Australia* (London: Ashgate).

Cheung, Tai Ming (1993) 'Serve the people', *Far Eastern Economic Review*, 14 October.

CIA (2004) *Global Trends 2015*. www.cia.gov/cia/reports/globaltrends2015.

Clarke, F. et al. (2003) *Corporate Collapse: Accounting, Regulatory and Ethical Failure* (Sydney: Cambridge University Press).

CLW (2001) *Council for a Livable World*. www.clw.org.

Cohen, D. (2001) 'Pacific hates', *Guardian Weekly*, 15 February.

Comfort, A. (1950) *Authority and Delinquency in the Modern State* (London: Routledge & Kegan Paul).

Connell, B. (2002) 'Rage against the dying of the light', *The Australian*, 23 October.

Coombs, D. (1980) 'Towards an end of 200 years of aggression and injustice', *National Times*, 8 June.

Cooper, R. (2003) 'God's general set on terrorists', *Sydney Morning Herald*, 17 October.

Cornell, A. (2003) 'RBA endorses the bubble word', *Australian Financial Review*, 14 November.

Cost (2005) www.costofwar.com.

Cox, H. (1999) 'The Market as God: Living in the New Dispensation', *The Atlantic Monthly*, Vol. 283, No. 3.

Dallaire, R. (2004) *Shake Hands with the Devil: The Failure of Humanity in Rwanda* (Montreal: Carroll & Graf).

Daly, H. (1996) *Beyond Growth* (Boston: Beacon Press).

Danforth, J. (2005) 'In the name of politics', *New York Times*, 30 March.

Davidson, K. (2005) 'The Tin Man', *Dissent*, Autumn/Winter.

Davis, M. (2002) 'Howard embraces America's values', *Sydney Morning Herald*, 13 June.

—— (2003a) 'Free trade deals pose danger to growth', *Sydney Morning Herald*, 6 June.

—— (2003b) 'What price free trade?', *Australian Financial Review*, 21 July.

—— (2004) 'Latham acts to placate US', *Australian Financial Review*, 13 July.

Day, D. (2001) *Claiming a Continent: A New History of Australia* (Sydney: Harper Collins).

Denoon, D. (2003) *Perspective*. ABC Radio National, 5 February.

DFAT (2001) *Composition of Trade, Australia 2001*. Department of Foreign Affairs and Trade. (Canberra: DFAT).

—— (2004) *Transnational Terrorism: The Threat to Australia*. Department of Foreign Affairs and Trade (Canberra: Government of Australia). www.dfat.gov.au/publications.

Diamond, S. (1992) *Compromised Campus: The Collaboration of Universities with the Intelligence Communities* (New York: Oxford University Press).

Dickson, B. (1997) *Democratization in China and Taiwan* (London: Clarendon Press).

—— (2003) *Red Capitalists in China* (Cambridge: Cambridge University Press).

Divecha, S. (2002) 'Explanation demanded on Lihir sea dumping', *Mining Monitor*, Vol. 7, No. 4.

Dixon, N. (1994) *On the Psychology of Military Incompetence* (London: Pimlico).

Dobell, G. (2003a) *PM*. ABC, Radio National, 20 October.

—— (2003b) *The South Pacific: Policy Taboos, Popular Amnesia and Political Failures*. Lecture at the Menzies Research Centre Lecture Series on Australian Security, Canberra, February.

DOD (2002) *Nuclear Posture Review* (Washington DC: US Department of Defense).

Dore, R. (2000a) 'Worldwide Anglo-Saxon Capitalism?', *New Left Review*, 6, November.

—— (2000b) *Stockmarket Capitalism, Welfare Capitalism: Japan, Germany versus the Anglo-Saxons* (Oxford: Oxford University Press).

Doyle, M. (1983) 'Kant, Liberal Legacies and Foreign Affairs', *Philosophy and Public Affairs*, Vol. 12, Nos. 3–4.

—— (1986) *Empires* (Ithaca: Cornell University Press).

Duncan, R. et al. (2004) *Demographic Change and Demand for Food in Australia*. Paper presented at the ABARE Outlook Conference 2004 (Canberra: Australian Bureau of Agriculture and Resource Economics).

EA (2002) *State of the Environment 2001: Australian State of the Environment*. Commonwealth Scientific and Industrial Research Organisation (Melbourne: CSIRO).

Eccleston, R. (2004) 'World Bank warns on Asian migrant influx', *The Australian*, 4 February.

Edwards, P. (2001) 'Curtin: MacArthur and the Surrender of Sovereignty: A Historiographical Assessment', *Australian Journal of International Affairs*, Vol. 55, No. 2.

Einstein, A. (1949) 'Why Socialism?', *Monthly Review*, May.

Elias, R. (2002) 'Terrorism and American Foreign Policy', *Pacific Ecologist*, Summer.

Ellsberg, D. (1972) *Papers on the War* (New York: Simon & Schuster).

Ellul, J. (1964) *The Technological Society* (New York: Vintage).

ERC (2002) 'The changing face of poverty in Australia', *Just Comment*, Vol. 5, No. 4. (Homebush NSW: Edmund Rice Centre).

Erikson, E. (1966) 'Ontogeny of Ritualization', *Philosophical Transactions of the Royal Society of London. Series B*, Vol. 251.

Falk, R. (2002) *Predatory Globalisation* (London: Polity Press).

Ferguson, N. (2003) *Empire* (London: Allen Lane).

—— (2004) *Colussus: The Rise and Fall of the American Empire* (London: Penguin).

Fesl, E. (1993) *Conned!* (Brisbane: University of Queensland Press).

Field, M. (2002) 'Solomons losing another war', *Australian Financial Review*, 10 May.

Fisher, F. (1990) *Technocracy and the Politics of Expertise* (London: Sage Publications).

FitzGerald, S. (1997) *Is Australia an Asian Country?* (Sydney: Allen & Unwin).

Flannery, T. (1994) *The Future Eaters* (Melbourne: Reed Books).

Foran, B. and Poldy, F. (2002) *Future Dilemmas: Options to 2050 for Australia's Population, Technology, Resources and Environment* (Sydney: CSIRO).

Forbes, M. (2004) 'Iraq claims hardened after Bush call', *Sydney Morning Herald*, 3 March.

Frankel, B. (2004) *Zombies, Lilliputians and Sadists: The Power of the Living Dead and the Future of Australia* (Perth: Curtin University Press).

Fraser, M. (1999) *Australia seen as fueling arms race in Northeast Asia*, October 4. www.fas.org/news/australia.

—— (2001) 'An Australian Critique', *Australian Journal of International Affairs*, Vol. 55, No. 2.

Freney, D. (1977) *The CIA's Australian Connection* (Sydney: Freney).

Friedman, T. (1999) *The Lexus and the Olive Tree* (New York: Farrar, Strauss & Giroux).

Fromm, E. (1965) *Escape from Freedom* (New York: Discus Books).

—— (1982) *To Have or To Be?* (New York: Bantam Books).

Fukuyama, F. (1989) 'The End of History?', *The National Interest*, Summer.

Galbraith, J. (1992) *The Culture of Contentment* (Boston: Houghton Mifflin).

Galbraith, P. (2004) 'How to get out of Iraq', *New York Review of Books*, 13 May.

Garnaut, R. (1989) *Australian and the Northeast Asia Ascendancy*. Australian Commonwealth (Canberra: Australian Government Publishing Service).

—— (2004) 'FTA worsens our woeful trade outlook', *The Australian*, 10 February.

Garran, R. (2000) 'Papers reveal Timor truth', *The Australian*, 13 September.

George, S. (2003) 'Globalizing Rights?', in Matthew Gibney (ed.) *Globalizing Rights* (Oxford: Oxford University Press).

Girard, R. (1977) *Violence and the Sacred* (Baltimore: John Hopkins University Press).

Goldstein, R. (2002) 'Foundations are in place for martial law in the US', *Sydney Morning Herald*, 27 July.

Goldworthy, D. (ed. 2003) *Facing North* (Melbourne: Melbourne University Press).

Gowan, P. (1999) *The Global Gamble: Washington's Faustian Bid for World Dominance* (London: Verso).

Gray, J. (1999) *False Dawn: The Delusions of Global Capitalism* (New York: Granta).

—— (2003) *Al Qaeda and What it Means to be Modern* (London: Faber & Faber).

Greenhill, R. (2003) 'Globalisation and its Consequences', in Pettifor, A. (ed. 2003) *Real Economic Outlook – The Legacy of Globalisation: Debt and Deflation* (London: Palgrave).

Greenlees, D. and Garran, R. (2002) *The Inside Story of East Timor's Fight for Freedom* (Sydney: Allen & Unwin).

Grimmett, R. (1999) *Instances of Use of US Armed Forces Abroad, 1798–1999*. Congressional Research Service Report, 17 May, Washington DC.

Gurtov, M. (1991) *Global Politics in the Human Interest* (London: Lynne Rienner).

Hamilton, C. (1997) *The Genuine Progress Indicator*. Discussion paper No. 14. Australia Institute (Canberra: Australia Institute).

—— (2002) *Overconsumption in Australia: The Rise of the Middle-Class Battler*. Australia Institute Discussion Paper No. 49 (Canberra: Australia Institute).

—— (2003a) *Sacrificing Democracy for Growth*. The Reid Oration. Australia Institute Newsletter, September.

—— (2003b) *Comfortable, Relaxed and Drugged to the Eye-balls*. Australia Institute Occasional Paper, June (Canberra: Australia Institute).

Harcourt, T. (2003) 'A downturn, that's so not fashionable', *Australian Financial Review*, 26 September.

Harries, O. (1993) 'Clash of civilizations', *The Australian*, 3 April.

—— (2004) *Benign or Imperial?* (Sydney: Allen & Unwin).

Harris, S. (2000) 'Don't misread China's intentions', *Australian Financial Review*, 16 March.

Hartcher, O. (2000) 'Poor politics is no defense', *Australian Financial Review*, 1 December.

Hartcher, P. (2002a) '$US180bn farm aid trade threat', *Australian Financial Review*, 10 May.

—— (2002b) 'Fertile fields for welfare farmers', *Weekend Australian Financial Review*, 8 June.

Harvey, D. (2003) *The New Imperialism* (Oxford: Oxford University Press).

Heilbroner, R. (1988) *Behind the Veils of Economics* (New York: W.W. Norton).

—— (1988b) 'The Coming Meltdown of Traditional Capitalism', *Ethics and International Affairs*, 2.

Herold, M. (2002) *A Dossier on Civilian Victims of United States Aerial Bombing of Afghanistan*. www.unknownews.net/casualties.htm. See also www.cursor. org/stories/civilian_deaths.

Hersch, S. (2004) 'The Gray Zone', *The New Yorker*, 5 May.

—— (2005) 'The Coming Wars', *The New Yorker*, 17 January.

HIC (2002) *Health Statistics* (Canberra: Health Insurance Commission).

Hickie (2001) 'A National Depression Project', *Medical Journal of Australia*, Vol. 175, No. S1–S56.

Hippel, Von K. (2000) *Democracy by Force: US Military Intervention in the Post-Cold War World* (Cambridge: Cambridge University Press).

Hobsbawn, E. (2003) 'Où va l'empire américain?', *Le Monde Diplomatique*, Juin.

Hobson, J. (1938) *Imperialism* (London: Allen & Unwin).

Hoegh-Guldberg, O. et al. (2000) *Pacific in Peril*. Greenpeace Report on Climate Change (Sydney: Greenpeace).

Hofstadter, R. (1992) *Social Darwinism in American Thought* (Boston: Beacon Press).

Hollier, N. (ed. 2004) *Ruling Australia: The Power, Privilege and Politics of the New Ruling Class* (Melbourne: Australian Scholarly Publishing).

Hope, D. (2000) 'Beneath the bottom line', *The Australian Magazine*, 6 May.

Hopkins, T. and Wallerstein, I. et al. (1996) *The Age of Transition* (Sydney: Pluto Press).

Horta, J. (1998) 'Time to break East Timor chains', *Sydney Morning Herald*, 10 September.

—— (1999) 'To history's dustbin, Mr. Keating', *Sydney Morning Herald*, 9 October.

Howard, M. (1991) *Fiji: Race and Politics in an Island State* (Vancouver: UBC Press).

Hughes, H. (2004) 'Jobs for men real answer in Solomons', *The New Zealand Herald*, 13 February.

Huntington, S. (1997) *The Clash of Civilizations and the Remaking of the World Order* (New York: Touchstone Books).

IISS (2002) *Military Balance 2002–2003*. International Institute for Strategic Studies (London: Oxford University Press).

Indermaur, D. et al. (2003) *Penal Populism and Public Opinion* (Sydney: Oxford University Press).

Iraq (2004) www.iraqbodycount.net/bodycount.htm.

Jacobs, J. (2004) *Dark Age Ahead* (New York: Random House).

Johnson, C. (1998) 'Economic Crisis in East Asia: The Clash of Capitalisms', *Cambridge Journal of Economics*, 22.

—— (1999) 'How America's crony capitalists ruined their rivals', *Sydney Morning Herald*, 5 July.

—— (2000) *Blowback: The Costs and Consequences of American Empire* (New York: Metropolitan Books).

—— (2004a) *The Sorrows of Empire: Militarism, Secrecy and the End of the Republic* (New York: Henry Holt).

—— (2004b) *America's Empire of Bases*. www.TomDisptach.com.

Jolliffe, J. (2001) 'Australia covered up Indonesia atrocities in Timor, says army officer', *Sydney Morning Herald*, 9 May.

Judt, T. (2005) 'The New World Order', *New York Review of Books*, 14 July.

Kant, I. (1983) *Perpetual Peace and other Essays*. Translated by Ted Humphrey (Indianapolis: Hackett Publishing).

Kaplan, R. (1997) 'Was Democracy Just a Moment?', *The Atlantic Monthly*, December.

Kasper, W. (2001) 'Smaller government the answer for this small nation', *Sydney Morning Herald*, 6 March.

Kaye, L. (1994) 'Labour pains', *Far East Economic Review*, 16 June.

Kayrooz, C. et al. (2001) *Academic Freedom and the Commercialisation of Australian Universities*. Australia Institute Discussion Paper No. 37 (Canberra: AI).

Keating, P. (2003) 'Beware Mad Max world of US', *Sydney Morning Herald*, 16 October.

—— (2004) 'Keating to US: Labor won't be bullied', *Sydney Morning Herald*, 8 July.

Kelly, S. (2001) *Wealth on Retirement*. 9th Annual Colloquium of Superannuation Researchers, University of New South Wales.

Kelly, S. et al. (2003) *Income and Wealth Report: Income and Wealth of Generation X*. National Center for Social and Economic Modelling (Canberra University: NATSEM).

Kennedy, P. (1989) *The Rise and Fall of the Great Powers* (New York:Vintage Books).

Kerr, N. (2002) 'NZ pays price for letting mateship die', *Australian Financial Review*, 13 June.

Khosrokhavar, F. (2004) 'L'Afghanistan abandonné aux seigneurs de la guerre', *Le Monde Diplomatique*, Octobre.

Kiernan, V. (2005) *America: The New Imperialism* (London: Verso).

Kinnear, P. (ed. 2001) *The Idea of a University: Enterprise or Academy?* Australia Institute Discussion Paper No. 39 (Canberra: AI).

Kissinger, H. (1994) *Diplomacy* (New York: Simon & Schuster).

—— (2001) 'Keeping the Middle Kingdom away from the edge', *Sydney Morning Herald*, 11 April.

Klare, M. (2001) *Resource Wars* (New York: Metropolitan Books).

—— (2003) 'The New Geopolitics', *Monthly Review*, Vol. 55, No. 3.

Klein, N. (2001) 'Time to fight free-trade laws that benefit multinationals', *Guardian Weekly*, 15 March.

Kornhauser, W. (1959) *The Politics of Mass Society* (New York: Free Press).

Krugman, P. (2003) *The Great Unraveling* (New York: Norton).

Kwong, J. (1997) *The Political Economy of Corruption in China* (New York: M.E. Sharpe).

Lal, V. (1990) *Fiji Coups in Paradise: Race, Politics and Military Intervention* (London: Zed Books).

Lamont, L. (2003) 'How Eddie Ye's federal court gamble went wrong', *Sydney Morning Herald*, 9 June.

Lang, Dunmore (1840) *The Moral and Religious Aspect of the Future America of the Southern Hemisphere* (New York: James Van Norden Press).

Langton, M. (2002) *Treaties and agreements as instruments of order in and between civil societies*. Paper presented to the National Treaty Conference, Canberra, 27–29 August.

Lansbury, R. (2005) Tough times ahead as proposed workplace reforms miss the boat. *Sydney Morning Herald*, 27 June.

Lapham, L. (2002) 'Who's really winning in America's jihad?', *Australian Financial Review*, 4 January.

Lapido, D. (2001) 'The Rise of America's Prison-Industrial Complex', *New Left Review*, 7.

Lasch, C. (1971) 'The Making of the War Class', *Columbia Forum*, Winter.

Laurence, C. (2001) 'Media suppress the news that Bush lost election to Gore', *Sydney Morning Herald*, 22 October.

Lokuge, K. and Denniss, R. (2003) *Trading in Our Health System*. Australia Institute Discussion Paper No. 55 (Canberra: AI).

Lowe, I. (2005) *A Big Fix: Radical Solutions for Australia's Environmental Crisis* (Melbourne: Black Inc).

Lunn, H. (1999) *Act of Free Choice*. SBS TV Dateline, 25 August.

Maccoby, M. (1984) *The Gamesmen: The New Corporate Leaders* (New York: Simon & Schuster).

Macfarlane, D. (2002) 'PM lashes union for US dock support', *Sydney Morning Herald*, 9 October.

Macintyre, S. (1999) *A Concise History of Australia* (Cambridge: Cambridge University Press).

Macken, J. (2005) 'The new gospel of prosperity', *Australian Financial Review*, 7 February.

Mackie, J. (1998) *An Asia-Pacific Prognosis to 2020*. Department of the Parliamentary Library, Information and Research Services, Background Paper No. 13, Commonwealth of Australia.

Maddox, M. (2003) *God under Howard: The Rise of the Religious Right in Australian Politics* (Sydney: Allen & Unwin).

Mailer, N. (2003a) 'Only in America', *New York Review of Books*, 27 March.

—— (2003b) 'There's one way to protect democracy – send in the fascists', *Sydney Morning Herald*, 28 February.

Manning, M. and Windybank, S. (2003) *Papua New Guinea on the Brink*. Issue Analysis No. 30, Center for Independent Studies (Sydney: CIS).

Marcos, Subcommandante (1997) 'The Fourth World War has Begun', *Le Monde Diplomatique*, Septembre.

Martin, J. (2000) 'Recent Developments in the Solomon Islands Economy', *Pacific Economic Bulletin*, Vol. 15, No. 1.

McCoy, A. (1991) *The Politics of Heroin: CIA Complicity in the Global Drug Trade* (New York: Lawrence Hill).

McDaniel, C. and Gowdy, J. (2000) *Paradise for Sale* (Berkeley: University of California Press).

McDonald, H. (2000) 'Sounding the gap', *Sydney Morning Herald*, 21 October.

—— (2001) 'Polishing the rusty shield', *Sydney Morning Herald*, 11 September.

—— (2002) 'Australia's bloody East Timor secret', *Sydney Morning Herald*, 14 March.

McKnight, D. (2004) 'Rethinking Right and Left: ideas for a renewal', *Australian Fabian News*, Vol. 44, No. 3.

McQueen, H. (1991) *Japan to the Rescue* (Sydney: William Heinemann).

—— (1998) *Temper Democratic* (Kent Town: Wakefield Press).

MDN (1990) 'Did Chinese ship Saudis nuclear warheads?', *Mainichi Daily News*, December.

Meaney, N. (1996) *Fears and Phobias: E. L. Piesse and the Problems of Japan, 1909–39* (Canberra: Australian National Library).

—— (1999) *Towards a New Vision: Australia and Japan Through 100 Years.* (Sydney: Kangaroo Press).

Mearsheimer, J. (2001) *The Tragedy of Great Power Politics* (New York: Norton).

Mendes, P. (2003) 'The Discompassion Industry: The Campaign against Welfare Bodies', *Overland*, 170.

Michaelson, C. (2004) 'The Price of Freedom', *The Diplomat*, August.

Michels, R. (1962) *Political Parties: A Sociological Study of the Oligarchical Tendencies of Modern Democracy* (New York: Free Press).

Mining Monitor (2000) 'Troops considered by cabinet before mine built', *Mining Monitor*, March. www.mpi.org.au.

Mirsky, J. (1997) 'China: the Defining Moment', *New York Review of Books*, 9 January.

—— (2001) 'Inside the Whale', *New York Review of Books*, 20 December.

—— (2003) 'Secrecy and the spread of SARS', *Australian Financial Review*, 16 May.

Mitchell, P. and Schoeffel, J. (eds 2002) *Understanding Power: The Indispensable Chomsky* (New York: The New Press).

Monk, P. (2001a) 'Whitlam knew', *Inside Indonesia*, October.

—— (2001b) 'Secret Intelligence and Escape Clauses: Australia and the Indonesian Annexation of East Timor, 1963–1975', *Critical Asian Studies*, Vol. 33, No. 2.

—— (2002a) *Coming to the party: transparency in the political and economic life of China.* Address to Transparency International, Melbourne 25 July.

—— (2002b) 'Maritime power and the augmented Indies', *Australian Financial Review*, 2 August.

Moore, B. (1984) *Social Origins of Dictatorship and Democracy* (London: Penguin).

Moyers, B. (2005) 'Welcome to Doomsday', *New York Review of Books*, March.

Murdoch, L. (1993) 'The peacemaker', *Sydney Morning Herald*, 2 October.

—— (2000) 'Diggers had covert role in Timor: Jakarta', *Sydney Morning Herald*, 21 February.

Muzaffar, C. (1992) *The New World Order: Gold or God?* ABC Radio National, Indian Pacific Program, January–February. Australian Broadcasting Corporation.

Nathan, A. (1997) *China's Transition* (New York: Simon & Schuster).

NewMatilda (2005) *Human Rights Act for Australia Campaign Launch.* Introduction to the campaign launch, Sydney Town Hall, 5 October. www.newmatilda.com.

Nicolas, S. and Samartino, A. (2003) *Do Multinationals Enterprises Benefit Australia?* Committee for Economic Development of Australia (Canberra: CEDA).

NLWR (2002) *Australian Terrestrial Biodiversity Assessment 2002.* Part 6: Mammals. National Land and Water Resources Audit (Canberra: Commonwealth of Australia).

O'Callaghan, M. (1999) *Enemies Within* (Sydney: Doubleday).

—— (2000) 'How we dropped the coconut', *The Australian*, 27 May.

—— (2002) 'Dollar crisis shocks MPs in Solomons', *Sydney Morning Herald*, 27 March.

—— (2003) '1200 troops for the Solomons', *The Australian*, 26 June.

O'Dea, J. (2003) 'Differences in Overweight and Obesity among Australian School Children', *Medical Journal of Australia*, Vol. 179, No. 1.

Orr, G. et al. (2003) *Realising Democracy: Electoral Law in Australia* (Sydney: Federation Press).

Oxfam (2002) *Cultivating Poverty: The Impact of US Cotton Subsidies on Africa*. Oxfam Briefing Paper 30 (Oxford: Oxfam International).

Paul, E. (2001) *Australia: Too Many People?* (Aldershot: Ashgate).

PC (2001) *Report on Government Services 2001*. Volume 1, Part C: Health. Productivity Commission (Canberra: Productivity Commission).

PD (2001) 'Over half of China's cars owned by individuals', *People's Daily*, 10 May.

Pelletiere, S. (2004) *The Iran–Iraq War* (London: Praeger).

Perkins, J. (2004) *Confessions of an Economic Hit Man* (San Francisco: Berrett-Koehler).

Pheasant, B. (2002) 'Life after Ok Tedi', *Australian Financial Review Magazine*.

Pettifor, A. (ed. 2003) *Real World Economic Outlook* (London: Palgrave).

Phillips, D. (1983) *Cold War Two and Australia* (Sydney: Allen & Unwin).

Pilger, J. (1992) *A Secret Country* (London: Vintage).

—— (2002) *The New Rulers of the World* (London: Verso).

Pope, J. (2003) 'Access to information: whose right and whose information?', in *Global Corruption Report 2003*. Transparency International (London: Profile Books).

Power, S. (2001) 'Bystanders to Genocide', *Atlantic Monthly*, September.

Powers, T. (2003) 'War and Its Consequences', *New York Review of Books*, 27 March.

Poynting, S. et al. (2004) *Bin Laden in the Suburbs* (Sydney: Institute of Criminology).

Priest, D. (2003) *The Mission: Waging War and Keeping Peace with America's Military* (New York: Norton).

Pussey, M. (1991) *Economic Rationalism in Canberra: A Nation-Building State Changes its Mind* (Cambridge: Cambridge University Press).

—— (2003) *The Experience of Middle Australia: The Dark Side of Economic Reform* (Cambridge: Cambridge University Press).

Putnam, R. (1977) 'Elite Transformation in Advanced Industrial Societies: An Empirical Assessment of the Theory of Technocracy', *Comparative Political Studies*, Vol. 10, No. 3.

Qinglian, H. (1998) *China's Pitfall* (Hong Kong: Mingjing Chubanshe).

Rashid, A. (2004) 'The mess in Afghanistan', *Australian Financial Review*, 6 February.

Rees, J. (1989) 'Innocents abroad', *Far Eastern Economic Review*, 23 November.

Rees, M. (2003) 'The Final Countdown', *New Scientist*, No.178, May.

Rees, S. and Rodley, G. (eds 1995) *The Human Costs of Managerialism* (Sydney: Pluto Press).

Reus-Smit, C. (2002) 'It will be a dangerous game when all nations can strike first', *Sydney Morning Herald*, 2 December.

Reuters (2001) 'Bush blocks book on US in Indonesia', *Australian Financial Review*, 30 July.

Reynolds, H. (2003) *North of Capricorn: The Untold Story of Australia's North* (Sydney: Allen & Unwin).

Richardson, G. (1994) *Whatever it Takes* (Sydney: Bantam).

Riley, M. (2003a) 'Howard push to hose down sheriff furore', *Sydney Morning Herald*, 17 October.

—— (2003b) 'It's war or terror blitz, says PM', *Sydney Morning Herald*, 14 March.

Roberts, G. (2002) 'A$1.3bn mine sinks islanders golden days of fish in a cyanide sea', *Sydney Morning Herald*, 9 April.

Roberts, L. et al. (2004) 'Mortality before and after the 2003 invasion of Iraq', *The Lancet*, Vol. 364, 30 October.

Robotham, J. (2002) 'Anti-depressants have little more effect than placebos, claims study', *Sydney Morning Herald*, 21 October.

Rohland, K. (2003) *Papua New Guinea and the Pacific*. Radio Australia, Asia-Pacific Lecture Series. 14 January.

Romei, S. (1999) 'Peter Singer', *Weekend Australian*, 18 December.

Roughan, J. and Hite, S. (2002) 'Mobilising Domestic Resources for the Better Life in Solomon Islands', *Development Bulletin* 58, July.

Roy, A. (2004) *Peace and the New Corporate Liberation Theology*. The City of Sydney Peace Prize Lecture by Arundhati Roy. Centre for Peace and Conflict Studies Occasional Paper No. 2. University of Sydney.

Roy, D. (1994) 'Hegemon on the Horizon', *International Security*, Vol. 19, No. 1.

Ruthven, M. (2002) *A Fury for God: The Islamist Attack on America* (London: Granta).

Ryn, C. (2003) 'The Ideology of American Empire', *Orbis*, Summer.

Sagan, E. (1991) *The Honey and the Hemlock* (New York: Basic Books).

Said, E. (1994) *Culture and Imperialism* (London: Vintage).

Sala, I. (2002) 'Assimilation forcée dans le Xinjiang Chinois', *Le Monde Diplomatique*, Février.

Saul, J. (2004) 'The end of globalism', *Australian Financial Review*, 20 February.

SBS (2002) *Terror, Trade and Protection*. SBS TV Sydney, Dateline, 28 October.

—— (2004a) *Dateline*. SBS TV Sydney, 3 November.

—— (2004b) *Missile Defence*. SBS TV Sydney, 22 July.

Scott, P. (1985) 'The United States and the Overthrow of Sukarno, 1965–1967', *Pacific Affairs*, Vol. 58, Summer.

Seccombe, M. (2003) 'No2 friend seeks a hand, and not just for clapping', *Sydney Morning Herald*, 25 October.

Sexton, M. (1981) *Australia's Vietnam Secret* (Ringwood: Penguin).

—— (2000) *Uncertain Justice: Inside Australia's Legal System* (Sydney: New Holland).

Sham-Ho, H. (2002) *Hansard*. New South Wales Legislative Council, 12 November.

Shoebridge, N. (2003) 'Higher the price, better the feeling', *Australian Financial Review*, 13 October.

Shoup, D. (1969) 'The New American Militarism', *Atlantic Monthly*, April, Vol. 223.

Singer, P. (1972) 'Famine, Affluence and Morality', *Philosophy and Public Affairs*, 1.

Skehan, C. (2000) 'US secretly criticised PM's East Timor plea, says Lee', *Sydney Morning Herald*, 18 September.

—— (2001) 'Rebels demand Australian ties be cut', *Sydney Morning Herald*, 23 March.

Small, M. (2002) 'The Happy Fat', *New Scientist*, 24 August.

Smith, D. (2001) 'Shock and Disbelief', *The Atlantic Monthly*, February.

Smith, N. (2004) *American Empire: Roosevelt's Geographer and the Prelude to Globalisation* (Berkeley: University of California Press).

Soros, G. (2004) *The Bubble of American Supremacy* (Sydney: Allen & Unwin).

Stephens, T. (1999) 'For Australian eyes only', *Sydney Morning Herald*, 7 December.

Stewart, C. (2002) 'Buying paper planes', *Weekend Australian Magazine*, 26 October.

Stiglitz, J. (2002) *Globalisation and its Discontents* (New York: W.W. Norton).

—— (2004) 'Bush has blown his opportunity to keep US strong', *Australian Financial Review*, 29 October.

Strutt, S. (2000) 'Singapore top foreign Queensland investor', *Australian Financial Review*, 29 September.

Suettinger, R. (2003) *Beyond Tiananmen: The Politics of US–China Relations 1989–2000* (Washington: Brookings Institution).

Sutherland, W. and Robertson, R. (2001) *Government by the Gun* (Sydney: Pluto Press).

Suvin, D. (2005) 'Displaced Persons', *New Left Review*, January.

Tawney, R. (1961) *The Acquisitive Society* (London: Collins).

Therborn, G. (2003) 'The Twilight Zone of Capitalism', *New Left Review*, July.

Thorne, P. (2002) 'Keep on taking the beads and mirrors', *Dissent*, Summer.

Thurow, L. (1996) *The Future of Capitalism* (New York: William Morrow).

TI (2003) www.transparency.org. Transparency International, Update 45, 5 February.

—— (2004) *National Provident Fund* www.transparencypng.org.pg.

Tingle, L. (2003) 'PM: intelligence has crucial role', *Australian Financial Review*, 21 March.

Toohey, B. (1983) 'How Asia betrayed Australia to the American', *National Times*, 6 May.

Toohey, B. and Pinwill, W. (1989) *Oyster: The Story of the Australian Secret Intelligence Service* (Sydney: Heinemann).

Townsend, M. and Harris, P. (2004) 'Now the Pentagon tells Bush: climate change will destroy us', *Observer*, 22 February.

Turton, H. (2002) *The Aluminium Smelting Industry*. Australia Institute Paper No. 44 (Canberra: AI).

Turton, H. and Hamilton, C. (1999) *Population Growth and Greenhouse Gas Emissions*. Australia Institute Paper No. 26 (Canberra: AI).

UN (2005) *Investing in Development*. United Nations Millennium Project (New York: UN).

UN-Habitat (2003) *The Challenge of the Slums: Global Report on Human Settlements 2003*. London: Earthscan Publications.

UNICEF (2005) *Childhood under Threat: The State of the World's Children* (New York: Unicef).

Unity (2003) www.australianunity.com.au/au/info/wellbeingindex.

US (2003) *Empty Promises: The IMF, the World Bank, and the Planned Failures of Global Capitalism*. US Network for Global Economic Justice (Washington DC: 50years Network). www.50years.org.

UTS (1991) http://austlii.law.uts.edu.au/au/other/media.OLD/798.html.

—— (2002) *Points of friction*. University of Technology, Sydney. http://journalism.uts.edu.au/archive/vilification/media/htm.

Vallely, P. (1987) 'Praise the lord – and the bomb', *Sydney Morning Herald*, 23 April.

Verrender, I. (1996) 'Rip-off yarns', *Sydney Morning Herald*, 28 December.

Victoria, B. (2002) 'Time to recognise a forgotten ally', *Australian Financial Review*, 19 April.

Vidal, G. (1987) *Armageddon?* (London: Andre Deutsch).

—— (2003) *Interview with Gore Vidal*. Dateline, SBS TV Sydney, 12 March.

Vulliamy, E. (1999) 'US trained butchers of East Timor', *Guardian Weekly*, 23 September.

Wahlquist, A. (2000) 'Land forecast rubs salt in the wounds of farmers', *The Australian*, 17 May.

Wainwright, E. (2003) *Our Failing Neighbour: Australia and the Future of the Solomon Islands*. Policy Report of the Australian Strategic Policy Institute (Canberra: ASPI).

Walker, D. (1999) *Anxious Nation: Australia and the Rise of Asia, 1850–1939* (Brisbane: Queensland University Press).

Wallerstein, I. (1995) *After Liberalism* (New York: Free Press).

—— (1999) *The End of the World as We Know It: Social Science for the Twenty-First Century* (Minneapolis: University of Minnesota Press).

—— (2002a) 'The Eagle Has Crash Landed', *Foreign Policy*, Vol. 131, July.

—— (2002b) 'Revolts against the System', *New Left Review*, November.

—— (2003a) *The Decline of American Power* (New York: The New Press).

—— (2003b) 'US Weakness and the Struggle for Hegemony', *Monthly Review*, Vol. 55, No. 3.

Wang, Hui (2002) 'Aux origines du néolibéralisme en Chine', *Le Monde Diplomatique*, Avril.

Watson, R. (ed. 2005) *Millennium Ecosystem Assessment 2005*. Millennium Assessment, Washington DC.

Westing, A. and Pfeiffer, E. (1972) 'The Cratering of Indochina', *Scientific American*, Vol. 226, No. 5.

Wheelwright, T. (1982) *Australia: A Client State* (Ringwood: Penguin).

—— (1995) 'The Complicity of Think-Tanks', in Rees, S. and Rodley, G. (eds 1998) *The Human Costs of Managerialism* (Sydney: Pluto Press).

White, H. (2004) 'In for the long haul with PNG', *Sydney Morning Herald*, 14 January.

Whyte, J. (2000) 'Report warns of Pacific peril', *Australian Financial Review*, 27 October.

Wilkie, A. (2004) *Axis of Deceit* (Sydney: SCB Distributors).

Windschuttle, K. (2001) *The Fabrication of Aboriginal History* (Sydney: Macleay Press).

Wise, R. (2001) 'The navigator of the political reefs', *Sydney Morning Herald*, 19 November.

Woodley, B. (1999) 'Passport to secret trip of shame', *Weekend Australian*, 16 October.

Woodward, B. (2001) *Bush at War* (New York: Simon & Schuster).

—— (2004) *Plan of Attack* (New York: Simon & Schuster).

WWF (1998) *Living Planet Report 1998* (Gand, Switzerland: World Wildlife Fund).

—— (2004) *Living Planet Report 2004*. www.panda.org.

Yang, D. (1998) *Beyond Beijing* (London: Routledge).

Yarwood, A. (1964) *Asian Migration to Australia: The Background to Exclusion, 1896–1923* (Cassell: Melbourne).

Zifcak, S. (2003a) 'Discarding the UN', *Australia Institute Newsletter*, No. 35, June.

—— (2003b) *The New Anti-Internationalism: Australia and the United Nations Human Rights Treaty System*. Paper No. 54, Australia Institute (Canberra: Australia Institute).

Zolo, D. (1997) *Cosmopolis* (London: Polity Press).

Index

Compiled by Sue Carlton